The Big Ninja Foodi XL Pro Air Oven Cookbook

1000 Days Easy and Affordable Bake, Air Fry, Toast the Best Meals for Beginners and Advanced Users

Robin Brickner

TABLE OF CONTENTS

Introduction

Hello and welcome!

Everyone is busy nowadays, and it can be difficult for home cooks or moms to feed their families with freshly- prepared, healthy, and tasty meals. We all know that there is no replacement for eating together around the dining table and enjoy delicious and healthy meals. You need an appliance that will let you cook nutritious, healthy, and freshly-prepared meals with a minimum of fuss and muss. It would help if you had an oven that could cook more than one dish at a time. The Ninja Foodi XL Pro Air Oven is perfect for your family. This oven has a large capacity and many useful functions. Now, you don't need to cook in batches because you can use different levels in the oven without rotating the pan or flipping the food.

The Ninja Foodi XL Pro Air Oven has true surround convection with a heating element in the back, top, and bottom, along with a powerful fan that ensures no cold spots, so the food cooks perfectly. This oven needs very little oil to cook the food. You get crispy, tender, and delicious food.

The Ninja Foodi XL Pro Air Oven comes with an air fry basket, a Ninja roast tray, two removable wire racks, a crumb tray, and two Ninja sheet pans. It has many different functions such as whole roast, air roast, air fry, toast, bake, broil, bagel, dehydrate, reheat, and pizza. You can cook your favorite recipes using Ninja Foodi XL Pro Air Oven. The Ninja Foodi XL Pro Air Oven has come up with its XL Pro Air Fry Oven to meet the needs of those who want to cook large-serving sizes, such as whole turkey, chicken, and whole fish, etc.

If you are a foodie and love to cook various meals for your family and beloved ones, the Ninja Foodi XL Pro air oven is a perfect choice.

What is the Ninja Foodi XL Pro Air Oven?

The Ninja Foodi XL Pro Air Oven is a powerful convection oven with a rear-positioned fan that blows hot air around the food as it cooks. With its fantastic speed, it's fuss-free to create delicious and healthy food, beautifully caramelized food, and perfect food texture. One of the best features of the Ninja Foodi XL Pro Air Oven is its immense capacity, including two cooking racks. You can prepare the whole turkey in this oven along with vegetables.

The parts included are following:

- Main Unit
- Roast Tray
- Air Fry Basket
- Sheet Pan
- Removable Crumb Tray
- Two Wire Racks

Functions of Ninja Foodi XL Pro Air Oven

There are ten different functions in Ninja Foodi XL Pro Air Oven. You can select your favorite (or according to recipe instruction) function and start cooking.

The functions of Ninja Foodi XL Pro Air Oven are following:

Whole Roast

Using this function, you can cook whole turkey breast, chicken, pork tenderloin, leg of lamb, ham along with a pan of vegetables at the same time. You will get your food brown and crispy on the outside and juicy and tender on the inside. This oven has a large capacity, and you can make a meal for 2, 4, 6, or oven 12 people simultaneously. Two racks are used for cooking food at the same time.

Air Roast

This function lets you cook sheet pan meals such as sheet pan fajita, meatballs, chicken breast, vegetables, yielding the same results as the whole roast. You will get your food brown and crispy on the outside and juicy and tender on the inside with this function. You can roast a lot of vegetables using this function.

Air Fry

If you want deep or shallow frying food, you can use the "AIR FRY" function. You can use this function for "French fries", "Chicken wings", and "Chicken nuggets", etc. You can prepare this with very little oil. Place food into the AIR FRY BASKET. The best thing about this oven is that you don't need to shake the basket.

Bake

The bake function needs no fan and even heat from the top and the bottom elements. You can bake cookies, cakes, and bread using this function. You can bake family-sized meals at once using this oven.

Dehydrate

Dehydration is a wonderful way to preserve food. You can dehydrate vegetables, fruits, and snacks. If you want to dry food, you can use this function without cooking. This function needs a lot of time with low temperatures.

Toast

The toast function uses no fan and even heat from the top and the bottom of the elements. You can toast nine slices of bread using Ninja Foodi XL Pro Air Oven at once. The time is set automatically by the number of slices. You can set the oven according to how light or dark you want to toast the bread.

Bagel

This function will toast up to nine bagel halves perfectly. On this function, you don't need to adjust the temperature. Time is automatically set up according to the number of slices. The bagel function uses no fan, but slightly low heat from the top and bottom elements.

Broil

The broil function uses medium convection fan speed and high heat from the top and bottom elements. You can use this function for fish fillets, steaks, and chops.

Reheat

If you are worrying about leftover food and want to reheat it, then the reheat option in Ninja Foodi XL Pro Air Oven solves that problem. Reheat uses high heat from the top and bottom and makes your food crispy and tender.

Pizza

If you are a pizza-lover, Ninja Foodi XL Pro Air Oven has your favorite option. You can cook your pizza at home easily.

Ninja Foodi XL Pro Air Oven Users' Guide

The control panel is where you choose how to cook the food, set the temperature and time, and specify the darkness of bagels and toast. There are 13 buttons present on the Ninja Foodi XL Pro Air Oven. Let's learn how to use it.

Power Button

This button is used to turn the unit on or off.

Time Display

When you are cooking the food, the time display shows your cook time. The time will start to count down as soon as your unit finishes preheating.

Preheat

It flashes on the display when the unit is preheating.

Slices

Flashes when using bagel or toast function to a selected number of slices.

Temperature Display

It shows you the cooking temperature.

Rack Level

It depends on the function you choose; the illuminated rack level will show where the accessory should be placed in the unit.

2 Level

When you press the button to select 2-level cooking and rack levels will update.

Function +/- Buttons

If you want to select the cooking function, then press this function.

Start/Stop Button

Press this button to stop or start the cooking.

Light Button

Press to turn the oven's interior light on or off.

Shade

Flashes when using bagel or toast function to selected desired shade.

Temp/Shade +/- Buttons

If you want to adjust the temperature, press the temp +/- buttons. But, if you are using bagel or toast functions, default temperature will be set by the shade level you have chosen.

Time/Slices +/- Buttons

If you want to adjust the cooking time, press the time buttons. But, if you are using the bagel or toast function, time will be changed by the number of bagel/slices halves you have chosen.

Cleaning and Maintenance of Ninja Foodi XL Pro Air Oven

It is simple to maintain and clean up the Ninja Foodi XL Pro Air Oven. Follow these simple steps:

Everyday cleaning:

- Firstly, unplug the appliance before start cleaning. Let it cool if it is hot. Then, start the cleaning process.
- Empty the crumb tray frequently, hand-wash when necessary.
- If the food is stuck onto the walls and glass door, clean it with a soft and damp sponge.
- Clean the main unit and control panel with a damp cloth.

Deep cleaning:

- Remove all accessories from the Ninja Foodi XL Pro Air Oven, including crumb tray. Wash the air fry basket with a non-abrasive cleaning brush.
- Wash the oven glass door and oven base with a soft cloth and soapy water but do not use an abrasive or chemical cleaner; otherwise, it will damage the oven's surface.
- Soak the sheet pan and roast the tray in soapy water to remove the tough grease or stuck food. Then, wash with a brush. When dry all parts of the unit, place them back in the unit. Now, you can use it again.

Note: Never put the main unit in the dishwasher or soak in water.

Ham and Cheese Scones

Prep Time: 15 minutes.
Cook Time: 25 minutes.
Serves: 6
Ingredients:
- 2 cups all-purpose flour
- 1 tablespoon baking powder
- 2 teaspoons sugar
- 1 teaspoon kosher salt
- 2 tablespoons butter, cubed
- 1 cup ham, diced, cooked
- ¼ cup scallion, chopped
- 4 ounces cheddar cheese, shredded
- ¼ cup milk
- ¾ cup heavy cream

Preparation:
1. Whisk baking powder with flour, sugar, salt, and butter in a mixing bowl.
2. Beat milk, cream, and all other ingredients in another bowl.
3. Stir in the flour-butter mixture and mix well until it forms a smooth dough.
4. Place this scones dough on a floured surface and spread it into a 7-inch round sheet.
5. Cut this dough sheet into 6 wedges of equal size.
6. Place these wedges in the cooking pan, lined with parchment paper.
7. Transfer the pan to the 2nd rack position of Ninja Foodi XL Pro Air Oven and close the door.
8. Select the "Bake" Mode using FUNCTION +/- buttons and select Rack Level 2.
9. Set its cooking time to 25 minutes and temperature to 400 degrees F, then press "START/STOP" to initiate cooking.
10. When baked, serve the scones with morning eggs.

Serving Suggestion: Serve the scones with the cream cheese dip.
Variation Tip: Add chopped parsley to the scones.
Nutritional Information Per Serving:
Calories 387 | Fat 6g |Sodium 154mg | Carbs 37.4g | Fiber 2.9g | Sugar 15g | Protein 15g

Cheddar & Cream Omelet

Prep Time: 10 minutes
Cook Time: 8 minutes
Serves: 2
Ingredients:
- 4 eggs
- ¼ cup cream
- 1 teaspoon fresh parsley, minced
- Salt and ground black pepper, as required
- ¼ cup Cheddar cheese, grated

Preparation:
1. In a bowl, add the eggs, cream, parsley, salt, and black pepper and beat well.
2. Place the egg mixture into Ninja sheet pan.
3. Press "Power" button of Ninja Foodi XL Pro Air Oven and select "Air Fry" function.
4. Press TEMP/SHADE +/- buttons to set the temperature at 350 degrees F.
5. Now press TIME/SLICES +/- buttons to set the cooking time to 8 minutes.
6. Press "Start/Stop" button to start.
7. When the unit beeps to show that it is preheated, open the oven door.
8. Arrange pan over the wire rack into the rails of Level 4.
9. After 4 minutes, sprinkle the omelet with cheese evenly.
10. When cooking time is completed, open the oven door, and remove the baking pan.
11. Cut the omelet into 2 portions and serve hot.

Serving Suggestions: Serve alongside the toasted bread slices.
Variation Tip: You can add the seasoning of your choice.
Nutritional Information per Serving:
Calories: 202 | Fat: 15.1g|Sat Fat: 6.8g|Carbohydrates: 1.8g|Fiber: 0g|Sugar: 1.4g|Protein: 14.8g

Mushrooms Frittata

Prep Time: 15 minutes.
Cook Time: 15 minutes.
Serves: 2
Ingredients:
- 1 cup egg whites
- 2 tablespoons skim milk
- ¼ cup tomato, sliced
- ¼ cup mushrooms, sliced
- 2 tablespoons fresh chives, chopped
- Black pepper, to taste

Preparation:
1. Beat egg whites with mushrooms and the rest of the ingredients in a bowl.
2. Spread this egg white mixture in a suitable casserole dish.
3. Transfer the dish to the 2nd rack position of Ninja Foodi XL Pro Air Oven and close the door.
4. Select the "Air Fry" Mode using FUNCTION +/- buttons and select Rack Level 2.
5. Set its cooking time to 15 minutes and temperature to 320 degrees F, then press "START/STOP" to initiate cooking.
6. Slice and serve warm.

Serving Suggestion: Serve the mushrooms frittata with crispy bacon on the side.
Variation Tip: Add chopped bell pepper to the frittata.
Nutritional Information Per Serving:
Calories 354 | Fat 7.9g |Sodium 704mg | Carbs 6g | Fiber 3.6g | Sugar 6g | Protein 18g

Sweet Potato Rosti

Prep Time: 15 minutes
Cook Time: 15 minutes
Serves: 2
Ingredients:
- ½ pound sweet potatoes, peeled, grated and squeezed
- 1 tablespoon fresh parsley, chopped finely
- Salt and ground black pepper, as required

Preparation:
1. In a large bowl, mix the grated sweet potato, parsley, salt, and black pepper together.
2. Arrange the sweet potato mixture into the lightly greased the sheet pan and shape it into an even circle.
3. Press "Power" button of Ninja Foodi XL Pro Air Oven and select "Air Fry" function.
4. Press TEMP/SHADE +/- buttons to set the temperature at 355 degrees F.
5. Now press TIME/SLICES +/- buttons to set the cooking time to 15 minutes.
6. Press "Start/Stop" button to start.
7. When the unit beeps to show that it is preheated, open the oven door and insert the pan on wire rack on Level 3.
8. When cooking time is completed, open the oven door.
9. Cut the potato rosti into wedges and serve immediately.

Serving Suggestions: Serve alongside the yogurt dip.
Variation Tip: Potato can also be used Instead of sweet potato.
Nutritional Information per Serving:
Calories: 160 | Fat: 2.1g|Sat Fat: 1.4g|Carbohydrates: 30.3g|Fiber: 4.7g|Sugar: 0.6g|Protein: 2.2g

Cloud Eggs

Prep Time: 10 minutes
Cook Time: 7 minutes
Serves: 2
Ingredients:
- 2 eggs, whites and yolks separated
- Pinch of salt
- Pinch of freshly ground black pepper

Preparation:
1. In a bowl, add the egg white, salt and black pepper and beat until stiff peaks form.
2. Line a baking pan with parchment paper.
3. Carefully, make a pocket in the center of each egg white circle.
4. Now press TIME/SLICES +/- buttons to set the cooking time to 7 minutes.
5. Press "Power" button of Ninja Foodi XL Pro Air Oven and select "Broil" function.
6. Press the TEMP/SHADE +/- buttons to select LO.

7. Press "START/STOP" button to start.
8. When the unit beeps to show that it is pre-heated, open the lid and insert the baking pan in the oven.
9. Place 1 egg yolk into each egg white pocket after 5 minutes of cooking.
10. When cooking time is completed, open the lid and serve.
Serving Suggestions: Serve alongside toasted bread slices.
Variation Tip: Add some seasoning of your choice.
Nutritional Information per Serving:
Calories: 63 | Fat: 4.4g|Sat Fat: 1.4g|Carbohydrates: 0.3g|Fiber: 0g|Sugar: 0.3g|Protein: 5.5g

Ham & Egg Cups

Prep Time: 10 minutes
Cook Time: 18 minutes
Serves: 6
Ingredients:
- 6 ham slices
- 6 eggs
- 6 tablespoons cream
- 3 tablespoon mozzarella cheese, shredded
- ¼ teaspoon dried basil, crushed

Preparation:
1. Lightly grease 6 cups of a silicone muffin tin.
2. Line each prepared muffin cup with 1 ham slice.
3. Crack 1 egg into each muffin cup and top with cream.
4. Sprinkle with cheese and basil.
5. Press "Power" button of Ninja Foodi XL Pro Air Oven and select "Air Fry" function.
6. Press TEMP/SHADE +/- buttons to set the temperature at 350 degrees F.
7. Now press TIME/SLICES +/- buttons to set the cooking time to 18 minutes.
8. Press "Start/Stop" button to start.
9. When the unit beeps to show that it is pre-heated, open the oven door.
10. Arrange the muffin tin over the wire rack and insert on Level 3.
11. When cooking time is completed, open the oven door, and place the muffin tin onto another wire rack to cool for about 5 minutes.
12. Carefully invert the muffins onto the platter and serve warm.

Serving Suggestions: Serve alongside the buttered bread slices.
Variation Tip: Use room temperature eggs.
Nutritional Information per Serving:
Calories: 156 | Fat: 10g|Sat Fat: 4.1g|Carbohydrates: 2.3g|Fiber: 0.4g|Sugar: 0.6g|Protein: 14.3g

Ricotta Toasts with Salmon

Prep Time: 10 minutes
Cook Time: 4 minutes
Serves: 2
Ingredients:
- 4 bread slices
- 1 garlic clove, minced
- 8 ounces ricotta cheese
- 1 teaspoon lemon zest
- Freshly ground black pepper, to taste
- 4 ounces smoked salmon

Preparation:
1. In a food processor, add the garlic, ricotta, lemon zest and black pepper and pulse until smooth.
2. Spread ricotta mixture over each bread slices evenly. Evenly arrange the bread slices in the air fry basket.
3. Press "Power" button of Ninja Foodi XL Pro Air Oven and select "Air Fry" function.
4. Press TEMP/SHADE +/- buttons to set the temperature at 355 degrees F.
5. Now press TIME/SLICES +/- buttons to set the cooking time to 4 minutes.
6. Press "Start/Stop" button to start.
7. When the unit beeps to show that it is pre-heated, open the oven door and slide basket into rails of Level 3.
8. When cooking time is completed, open the oven door and transfer the slices onto serving plates.
9. Top with salmon and serve.

Serving Suggestions: Serve with the garnishing of fresh herbs.
Variation Tip: Ricotta cheese can be replaced with feta.
Nutritional Information per Serving:
Calories: 274 | Fat: 12g|Sat Fat: 6.3g|Carbohydrates: 15.7g|Fiber: 0.5g|Sugar: 1.2g|Protein: 24.8g

Bacon, Spinach & Egg Cups

Prep Time: 15 minutes
Cook Time: 16 minutes
Serves: 3

Ingredients:

- 3 eggs
- 6 cooked bacon slices, chopped
- 2 cups fresh baby spinach
- ⅓ cup heavy cream
- 3 tablespoons Parmesan cheese, grated
- Salt and ground black pepper, as required

Preparation:

1. Heat a nonstick skillet over medium-high heat and cook the bacon for about 5 minutes.
2. Add the spinach and cook for about 2-3 minutes.
3. Stir in the heavy cream and Parmesan cheese and cook for about 2-3 minutes.
4. Remove from the heat and set aside to cool slightly.
5. Grease 3 (3-inch) ramekins.
6. Crack 1 egg in each prepared ramekin and top with bacon mixture.
7. Press "Power" button of Ninja Foodi XL Pro Air Oven and select "Air Fry" function.
8. Press TEMP/SHADE +/- buttons to set the temperature at 350 degrees F.
9. Now press TIME/SLICES +/- buttons to set the cooking time to 5 minutes.
10. Press "START/STOP" button to start.
11. When the unit beeps to show that it is preheated, open the lid and grease the air fry basket.
12. Arrange the ramekins into the air fry basket and insert in the oven.
13. When cooking time is completed, open the lid and sprinkle each ramekin with salt and black pepper.
14. Serve hot.

Serving Suggestions: Serve alongside the English muffins.
Variation Tip: Use freshly grated cheese.
Nutritional Information per Serving:
Calories: 442 | Fat: 34.5g|Sat Fat: 12.9g|Carbohydrates: 2.3g|Fiber: 0.5g|Sugar: 0.4g|Protein: 29.6g

Date Bread

Prep Time: 15 minutes
Cook Time: 22 minutes
Serves: 10

Ingredients:

- 2½ cups dates, pitted and chopped
- ¼ cup butter
- 1 cup hot water
- 1½ cups flour
- ½ cup brown sugar
- 1 teaspoon baking powder
- 1 teaspoon baking soda
- ½ teaspoon salt
- 1 egg

Preparation:

1. In a large bowl, add the dates, butter and top with the hot water. Set aside for about 5 minutes.
2. In a separate bowl, mix together the flour, brown sugar, baking powder, baking soda, and salt.
3. In the same bowl of dates, add the flour mixture and egg and mix well.
4. Grease a non-stick loaf pan.
5. Place the mixture into the prepared pan.
6. Press "Power" button of Ninja Foodi XL Pro Air Oven and select "Air Fry" function.
7. Press TEMP/SHADE +/- buttons to set the temperature at 340 degrees F.
8. Now press TIME/SLICES +/- buttons to set the cooking time to 22 minutes.
9. Press "START/STOP" button to start.
10. When the unit beeps to show that it is preheated, open the lid.
11. Place the pan into the air fry basket and insert in the oven.
12. When cooking time is completed, open the lid and place the pan onto a wire rack for about 10-15 minutes.
13. Carefully, invert the bread onto the wire rack to cool completely cool before slicing.
14. Cut the bread into desired sized slices and serve.

Serving Suggestions: Serve these bread slices with butter.
Variation Tip: Use soft dates.
Nutritional Information per Serving:
Calories: 129 | Fat: 5.4g|Sat Fat: 3.1g|Carbohydrates: 55.1g|Fiber: 4.1g|Sugar: 35.3g|Protein: 3.6g

Eggs, Tofu & Mushroom Omelet

Prep Time: 15 minutes
Cook Time: 35 minutes
Serves: 2

Ingredients:

- 2 teaspoons canola oil
- ¼ of onion, chopped
- 1 garlic clove, minced
- 3½ ounces fresh mushrooms, sliced
- 8 ounces silken tofu, pressed, drained and crumbled
- Salt and ground black pepper, as needed
- 3 eggs, beaten

Preparation:

1. In a skillet, heat the oil over medium heat and sauté the onion, and garlic for about 4-5 minutes.
2. Add the mushrooms and cook for about 4-5 minutes.
3. Remove from the heat and stir in the tofu, salt, and black pepper.
4. Place the tofu mixture into sheet pan and top with the beaten eggs.
5. Press "Power" button of Ninja Foodi XL Pro Air Oven and select "Air Fry" function.
6. Press TEMP/SHADE +/- buttons to set the temperature at 355 degrees F.
7. Now press TIME/SLICES +/- buttons to set the cooking time to 25 minutes.
8. Press "Start/Stop" button to start.
9. When the unit beeps to show that it is preheated, open the oven door.
10. Arrange pan over the wire rack on the Level 3.
11. When cooking time is completed, open the oven door, and remove the pan.
12. Cut into equal-sized wedges and serve hot.

Serving Suggestions: Serve alongside the greens.

Variation Tip: Make sure to drain the tofu completely.

Nutritional Information per Serving:
Calories: 224 | Fat: 14.5g|Sat Fat: 2.9g|Carbohydrates: 6.6g|Fiber: 0.9g|Sugar: 3.4g|Protein: 17.9g

Savory Parsley Soufflé

Prep Time: 10 minutes
Cook Time: 8 minutes
Serves: 2

Ingredients:

- 2 tablespoons light cream
- 2 eggs
- 1 tablespoon fresh parsley, chopped
- 1 fresh red chili pepper, chopped
- Salt, as required

Preparation:

1. Grease 2 soufflé dishes.
2. In a bowl, add all the ingredients and beat until well combined.
3. Divide the mixture into prepared soufflé dishes.
4. Press "Power" button of Ninja Foodi XL Pro Air Oven and select "Air Fry" function.
5. Now press TIME/SLICES +/- buttons to set the cooking time to 8 minutes.
6. Press TEMP/SHADE +/- buttons to set the temperature at 390 degrees F.
7. Press "START/STOP" button to start.
8. When the unit beeps to show that it is preheated, open the lid and grease the air fry basket.
9. Arrange the soufflé dishes into the air fry basket and insert in the oven.
10. When cooking time is completed, open the lid and serve hot.

Serving Suggestions: Serve alongside a piece of crusty bread.

Variation Tip: You can replace chives with parsley.

Nutritional Information per Serving:
Calories: 108 | Fat: 9g|Sat Fat: 4.3g|Carbohydrates: 1.1g|Fiber: 0.22g|Sugar: 0.5g|Protein: 6g

Breakfast Bake

Prep Time: 15 minutes.
Cook Time: 50 minutes.
Serves: 6

Ingredients:

- 24 ounces bulk pork sausage
- 1 medium bell pepper, chopped
- 1 medium onion, chopped
- 3 cups frozen hash brown potatoes
- 2 cups shredded Cheddar cheese
- 1 cup Bisquick mix
- 2 cups milk
- ¼ teaspoon pepper
- 4 eggs

Preparation:

1. Whisk Bisquick with milk, eggs, and pepper in a mixer.
2. Sauté pork sausage, onion, and bell pepper in a 10-inch skillet over medium heat.
3. Stir cook until the sausage turns brown in color, then transfer to a casserole dish.
4. Toss in potatoes, 1 ½ cups of cheese, and the Bisquick mixture.
5. Transfer the casserole dish to the 2nd rack position of Ninja Foodi XL Pro Air Oven and close the door.
6. Select the "Bake" Mode using FUNCTION +/- buttons and select Rack Level 2.
7. Set its cooking time to 45 minutes and temperature to 350 degrees F, then press "START/STOP" to initiate cooking.
8. Drizzle the remaining cheese over the casserole and bake for 5 minutes.
9. Serve.

Serving Suggestion: Serve the bake with crispy bacon and bread.
Variation Tip: Top egg with fresh herbs or chopped bell pepper.
Nutritional Information Per Serving:
Calories 297 | Fat 15g |Sodium 202mg | Carbs 58.5g | Fiber 4g | Sugar 1g | Protein 33g

Puffed Egg Tarts

Prep Time: 15 minutes.
Cook Time: 21 minutes.
Serves: 4

Ingredients:

- ½ (17.3-ounce package) frozen puff pastry, thawed
- ¾ cup Cheddar cheese, shredded
- 4 large eggs
- 1 tablespoon fresh parsley, minced

Preparation:

1. Spread the pastry sheet on a floured surface and cut it into 4 squares of equal size.
2. Place the four squares in the air fry basket and roast tray with sheet pan.
3. Transfer the sheet to the 3rd rack position of Ninja Foodi XL Pro Air Oven and close the door.
4. Select the "Air Fry" Mode using FUNCTION +/- buttons and select Rack Level 3.
5. Set its cooking time to 10 minutes and temperature to 300 degrees F, then press "START/STOP" to initiate cooking.
6. Press the center of each pastry square using the back of a metal spoon,
7. Divide cheese into these indentations and crack one egg into each pastry.
8. Return to the Ninja Foodi XL Pro Air Oven and close its lid.
9. Select the "Air Fry" mode and cook for 11 minutes at 350 degrees F.
10. Garnish the squares with parsley.
11. Serve warm.

Serving Suggestion: Serve these tarts with crispy bacon on the side.
Variation Tip: Add crumbled bacon on top before baking.
Nutritional Information Per Serving:
Calories 305 | Fat 15g |Sodium 548mg | Carbs 26g | Fiber 2g | Sugar 1g | Protein 19g

Parmesan Eggs in Avocado Cups

Prep Time: 10 minutes
Cook Time: 22 minutes
Serves: 2

Ingredients:

- 1 large ripe but firm avocado, halved and pitted
- 2 eggs
- Salt and ground black pepper, as required
- 2 tablespoons Parmesan cheese, grated
- Pinch of cayenne pepper
- 1 teaspoon fresh chives, minced

Preparation:

1. With a spoon, scoop out some of the flesh from the avocado halves to make a hole.
2. Arrange the avocado halves onto a baking pan.
3. Crack 1 egg into each avocado half and sprinkle with salt and black pepper.
4. Press "Power" button of Ninja Foodi XL Pro Air Oven and select "Air Fry" function.
5. Press TEMP/SHADE +/- buttons to set the temperature at 350 degrees F.
6. Now press TIME/SLICES +/- buttons to set the cooking time to 22 minutes.
7. Press "START/STOP" button to start.
8. When the unit beeps to show that it is preheated, open the lid and grease the air fry basket.
9. Arrange the avocado halves into the air fry basket and insert in the oven.
10. After 12 minutes of cooking, sprinkle the top of avocado halves with Parmesan cheese.
11. When cooking time is completed, open the lid and transfer the avocado halves onto a platter.
12. Sprinkle with cayenne pepper and serve hot with the garnishing of chives.

Serving Suggestions: Serve alongside baby greens.

Variation Tip: Add some seasoning as you like.

Nutritional Information per Serving:
Calories: 286 | Fat: 25.2g|Sat Fat: 6.1g|Carbohydrates: 9g|Fiber: 0.9g|Sugar: 0.9g|Protein: 9.5g

Sweet & Spiced Toasts

Prep Time: 10 minutes
Cook Time: 4 minutes
Serves: 3

Ingredients:

- ¼ cup sugar
- ½ teaspoon ground cinnamon
- ⅛ teaspoon ground cloves
- ⅛ teaspoon ground ginger
- ½ teaspoons vanilla extract
- ¼ cup salted butter, softened
- 6 bread slices

Preparation:

1. In a bowl, add the sugar, vanilla, cinnamon, pepper, and butter. Mix until smooth.
2. Spread the butter mixture evenly over each bread slice.
3. Press "Power" button of Ninja Foodi XL Pro Air Oven and select "Air Fry" function.
4. Press TEMP/SHADE +/- buttons to set the temperature at 400 degrees F.
5. Now press TIME/SLICES +/- buttons to set the cooking time to 4 minutes.
6. Press "START/STOP" button to start.
7. When the unit beeps to show that it is preheated, open the lid and grease the air fry basket.
8. Place the bread slices into the prepared air fry basket, buttered-side up and insert in the oven.
9. Flip the slices once halfway through.
10. When cooking time is completed, open the lid and transfer the French toasts onto a platter.
11. Serve warm.

Serving Suggestions: Serve with the drizzling of maple syrup.

Variation Tip: Adjust the ratio of spices according to your taste.

Nutritional Information per Serving:
Calories: 261 | Fat: 12g|Sat Fat: 3.6g|Carbohydrates: 30.6g|Fiber: 0.3g|Sugar: 22.3g|Protein: 9.1g

Raisin Bran Muffins

Prep Time: 15 minutes.
Cook Time: 18 minutes.
Serves: 6

Ingredients:

- 1 cup wheat bran
- 1 cup boiling water
- 4 ounces plain, non-fat Greek yogurt
- 2 large eggs
- 1 ½ cup whole wheat flour
- 5 ½ ounces all-purpose flour
- ¾ cup sugar
- ½ ounce ground cinnamon
- 2 teaspoons baking powder
- ¾ teaspoon kosher salt
- ¼ teaspoon baking soda
- ⅛ teaspoon grated nutmeg
- 6 ounces butter
- 1 cup golden raisins
- ¾-ounce flaxseed

Preparation:

1. Mix wheat bran with boiling water in a bowl and leave it for 5 minutes.
2. Add eggs, wheat flour, sugar, Greek yogurt, cinnamon, salt, baking soda, baking powder, butter, and nutmeg into the wheat bran, then mix well in a mixer.
3. Stir in raisins and mix the batter gently.
4. Divide this bran muffin batter into 12 greased muffin cups.
5. Transfer the muffin cups to the 2nd rack position of Ninja Foodi XL Pro Air Oven and close the door.
6. Select the "Bake" Mode using FUNCTION +/- buttons and select Rack Level 2.
7. Set its cooking time to 18 minutes and temperature to 400 degrees F, then press "START/STOP" to initiate cooking.
8. Serve fresh.

Serving Suggestion: Serve these muffins with caramel sauce.

Variation Tip: Inject apple sauce into the muffins.

Nutritional Information Per Serving:
Calories 204 | Fat 32g |Sodium 890mg | Carbs 4.3g | Fiber 4g | Sugar 8g | Protein 5g

Blueberry-Lemon Scones

Prep Time: 15 minutes.
Cook Time: 25 minutes.
Serves: 6

Ingredients:

- 2 cups all-purpose flour
- 1 tablespoon baking powder
- 2 teaspoons sugar
- 1 teaspoon kosher salt
- 2 ounces refined coconut oil
- 1 cup fresh blueberries
- ¼ ounce lemon zest
- 8 ounces coconut milk

Preparation:

1. Blend coconut oil with salt, sugar, baking powder, and flour in a food processor.
2. Transfer this flour mixture to a mixing bowl.
3. Now add coconut milk and lemon zest to the flour mixture, then mix well.
4. Fold in blueberries and mix the prepared dough well until smooth.
5. Spread this blueberry dough into a 7-inch round and place it in a pan.
6. Refrigerate the blueberry dough for 15 minutes, then slice it into 6 wedges.
7. Layer the sheet pan with a parchment sheet.
8. Place the blueberry wedges in the lined cooking pan.
9. Transfer the scones to the 2nd rack position of Ninja Foodi XL Pro Air Oven and close the door.
10. Select the "Bake" Mode using FUNCTION +/- buttons and select Rack Level 2.
11. Set its cooking time to 25 minutes and temperature to 400 degrees F, then press "START/STOP" to initiate cooking.
12. Serve fresh.

Serving Suggestion: Serve the scones with blueberry jam.

Variation Tip: Stuff the scones with blueberry jam.

Nutritional Information Per Serving:
Calories 312 | Fat 25g |Sodium 132mg | Carbs 44g | Fiber 3.9g | Sugar 3g | Protein 1.9g

Banana Bread

Prep Time: 15 minutes.
Cook Time: 25 minutes.
Serves: 6

Ingredients:

- 4 medium bananas, peeled and sliced
- ¼ cup plain Greek yogurt
- 2 large eggs
- ½-ounce vanilla extract
- 10 ounces all-purpose flour
- ¾ cup sugar
- 3 ounces oat flour
- 1 teaspoon baking powder
- 1 teaspoon baking soda
- ¾ teaspoon kosher salt
- ¾ teaspoon ground cinnamon
- ½ teaspoon ground cloves
- ¼ teaspoon ground nutmeg
- ¾ cup coconut oil
- 1 cup toasted pecan

Preparation:

1. Layer a 10.5-by-5.5-inch loaf pan with a parchment sheet and keep it aside.
2. Mash the banana in a suitable bowl and add eggs, vanilla, and Greek yogurt, then mix well.
3. Cover this banana yogurt mixture and leave it for 30 minutes.
4. Meanwhile, mix cinnamon, flour, sugar, baking powder, oat flour, salt, baking soda, coconut oil, cloves, and nutmeg in a mixer.
5. Now slowly add banana mash mixture to the flour and continue mixing until smooth.
6. Fold in nuts and mix gently until evenly incorporated.
7. Spread this banana-nut batter in the prepared loaf pan.
8. Transfer the loaf pan to the 2nd rack position of Ninja Foodi XL Pro Air Oven and close the door.
9. Select the "Bake" Mode using FUNCTION +/- buttons and select Rack Level 2.
10. Set its cooking time to 25 minutes and temperature to 350 degrees F, then press "START/STOP" to initiate cooking.
11. Slice and serve.

Serving Suggestion: Serve the bread with fried eggs and crispy bacon.

Variation Tip: Add some crushed oats for a different texture.

Nutritional Information Per Serving:
Calories 331 | Fat 2.5g |Sodium 595mg | Carbs 69g | Fiber 12g | Sugar 12g | Protein 7g

Pumpkin Muffins

Prep Time: 15 minutes.
Cook Time: 15 minutes.
Serves: 6

Ingredients:

- 1 cup pumpkin puree
- 2 cups oats
- ½ cup honey
- 2 medium eggs beaten
- 1 teaspoon coconut butter
- 1 tablespoon cocoa nibs
- 1 tablespoon vanilla essence
- 1 teaspoon nutmeg

Preparation:

1. Whisk pumpkin puree with remaining ingredients in a mixer until smooth.
2. Divide this pumpkin oat batter into 12 muffin cups of a muffin tray.
3. Transfer the tray to the 2nd rack position of Ninja Foodi XL Pro Air Oven and close the door.
4. Select the "Air Fry" Mode using FUNCTION +/- buttons and select Rack Level 2.
5. Set its cooking time to 15 minutes and temperature to 360 degrees F, then press "START/STOP" to initiate cooking.
6. Serve fresh.

Serving Suggestion: Serve the pumpkin muffins with morning pudding.

Variation Tip: Add shredded pumpkin flesh for good texture.

Nutritional Information Per Serving:
Calories 234 | Fat 5.1g |Sodium 231mg | Carbs 46g | Fiber 5g | Sugar 2.1g | Protein 7g

Simple Bread

Prep Time: 15 minutes
Cook Time: 18 minutes
Serves: 4

Ingredients:

- ⅞ cup whole-wheat flour
- ⅞ cup plain flour
- 1¾ ounces pumpkin seeds
- 1 teaspoon salt
- ½ of sachet instant yeast
- ½-1 cup lukewarm water

Preparation:

1. In a bowl, mix the flours, pumpkin seeds, salt and yeast and mix well together.
2. Slowly, add the desired amount of water and mix until a soft dough ball forms.
3. With your hands, knead the dough until smooth and elastic.
4. Place the dough ball into a bowl.
5. With a plastic wrap, cover the bowl and set aside in a warm place for 30 minutes or until doubled in size.
6. Press "Power" button of Ninja Foodi XL Pro Air Oven and select "Air Fry" function.
7. Press TEMP/SHADE +/- buttons to set the temperature at 350 degrees F.
8. Now press TIME/SLICES +/- buttons to set the cooking time to 18 minutes.
9. Press "START/STOP" button to start.
10. Place the dough ball in a greased cake pan and brush the top of the dough with water.
11. When the unit beeps to show that it is preheated, open the lid.
12. Place the cake pan into the air fry basket and insert in the oven.
13. When cooking time is completed, open the lid and place the pan onto a wire rack for about 10-15 minutes.
14. Carefully, invert the bread onto the wire rack to cool completely before slicing.
15. Cut the bread into desired sized slices and serve.

Serving Suggestions: Serve with your favorite jam.
Variation Tip: Add some nuts for a crispy taste.
Nutritional Information per Serving:
Calories: 268 | Fat: 6g|Sat Fat: 1.1g|Carbohydrates: 43.9g|Fiber: 2.5g|Sugar: 1.1g|Protein: 9.2g

Mushroom Frittata

Prep Time: 15 minutes
Cook Time: 36 minutes
Serves: 4

Ingredients:

- 2 tablespoons olive oil
- 1 shallot, sliced thinly
- 2 garlic cloves, minced
- 4 cups white mushrooms, chopped
- 6 large eggs
- ¼ teaspoon red pepper flakes, crushed
- Salt and ground black pepper, as required
- ½ teaspoon fresh dill, minced
- ½ cup cream cheese, softened

Preparation:

1. In a skillet, heat the oil over medium heat and cook the shallot, mushrooms and garlic for about 5-6 minutes, stirring frequently.
2. Remove from the heat and transfer the mushroom mixture into a bowl.
3. In another bowl, add the eggs, red pepper flakes, salt and black peppers and beat well.
4. Add the mushroom mixture and stir to combine.
5. Place the egg mixture into a greased baking pan and sprinkle with the dill.
6. Spread cream cheese over egg mixture evenly.
7. Press "Power" button of Ninja Foodi XL Pro Air Oven and select "Air Fry" function.
8. Press TEMP/SHADE +/- buttons to set the temperature at 330 degrees F.
9. Now press TIME/SLICES +/- buttons to set the cooking time to 30 minutes.
10. Press "START/STOP" button to start.
11. When the unit beeps to show that it is preheated, open the lid.
12. Arrange pan over the wire rack and insert in the oven.
13. When cooking time is completed, open the lid and place the baking pan onto a wire rack for about 5 minutes.
14. For better taste, let the frittata sit at room temperature for a few minutes to set before cutting.
15. Cut into equal-sized wedges and serve.

Serving Suggestions: Serve with green salad.
Variation Tip: Feel free to add some seasoning as you like.
Nutritional Information per Serving:
Calories: 290 | Fat: 24.8g|Sat Fat: 9.7g|Carbohydrates: 5g|Fiber: 0.8g|Sugar: 1.9g|Protein: 14.1g

Potato & Corned Beef Casserole

Prep Time: 15 minutes
Cook Time: 1 hour 20 minutes
Serves: 3

Ingredients:

- 3 Yukon Gold potatoes
- 2 tablespoons unsalted butter
- ½ of onion, chopped
- 2 garlic cloves, minced
- 2 tablespoons vegetable oil
- ½ teaspoon salt
- 12 ounces corned beef
- 3 eggs

Preparation:

1. Press "Power" button of Ninja Foodi XL Pro Air Oven and select "Bake" function.
2. Press TEMP/SHADE +/- buttons to set the temperature at 350 degrees F.
3. Now press TIME/SLICES +/- buttons to set the cooking time to 30 minutes.
4. Press "START/STOP" button to start.
5. When the unit beeps to show that it is preheated, open the lid and grease the air fry basket.
6. Place the potatoes into the prepared air fry basket and insert in the oven.
7. When cooking time is completed, open the lid and transfer the potatoes onto a tray.
8. Set aside to cool for about 15 minutes.
9. After cooling, cut the potatoes into ½-inch-thick slices.
10. In a skillet, melt the butter over medium heat and cook the onion and garlic for about 10 minutes.
11. Remove from the heat and place the onion mixture into a casserole dish.
12. Add the potato slices, oil salt and corned beef and mix well.
13. Press "Power" button of Ninja Foodi XL Pro Air Oven and select "Bake" function.
14. Now press TIME/SLICES +/- buttons to set the cooking time to 40 minutes.
15. Press TEMP/SHADE +/- buttons to set the temperature at 350 degrees F.
16. Press "START/STOP" button to start.
17. When the unit beeps to show that it is preheated, open the lid.
18. Arrange the casserole dish over the wire rack and insert in the oven.
19. After 30 minutes of cooking, remove the casserole dish and crack 3 eggs on top.
20. When cooking time is completed, open the lid and serve immediately.

Serving Suggestions: Serve with fresh baby kale.

Variation Tip: Cut the potatoes in equal-sized slices.

Nutritional Information per Serving:
Calories: 542 | Fat: 35.6g|Sat Fat: 14.1g|Carbohydrates: 33.1g|Fiber: 2.8g|Sugar: 2.3g|Protein: 24.7g

Savory Sausage & Beans Muffins

Prep Time: 15 minutes
Cook Time: 20 minutes
Serves: 6

Ingredients:

- 4 eggs
- ½ cup cheddar cheese, shredded
- 3 tablespoons heavy cream
- 1 tablespoon tomato paste
- ¼ teaspoon salt
- Pinch of freshly ground black pepper
- Cooking spray
- 4 cooked breakfast sausage links, chopped
- 3 tablespoons baked beans

Preparation:

1. Grease a 6 cups muffin pan.

2. In a bowl, add the eggs, cheddar cheese, heavy cream, tomato paste, salt and black pepper and beat until well combined.
3. Stir in the sausage pieces and beans.
4. Divide the mixture into prepared muffin cups evenly.
5. Press "Power" button of Ninja Foodi XL Pro Air Oven and select "Bake" function.
6. Press TEMP/SHADE +/- buttons to set the temperature at 350 degrees F.
7. Now press TIME/SLICES +/- buttons to set the cooking time to 20 minutes.
8. Press "START/STOP" button to start.
9. When the unit beeps to show that it is preheated, open the lid.
10. Arrange the muffin pan over the wire rack and insert in the oven.
11. When cooking time is completed, open the lid and place the muffin pan onto a wire rack to cool for 5 minutes before serving.

Serving Suggestions: Serve with drizzling of melted butter.

Variation Tip: You can use cooked beans of your choice.

Nutritional Information per Serving:
Calories: 258 | Fat: 20.4g|Sat Fat: 9.3g|Carbohydrates: 4.2g|Fiber: 0.8g|Sugar: 0.9g|Protein: 14.6g

Savory French Toast

Prep Time: 10 minutes
Cook Time: 5 minutes
Serves: 2

Ingredients:
- ¼ cup chickpea flour
- 3 tablespoons onion, finely chopped
- 2 teaspoons green chili, seeded and finely chopped
- ½ teaspoon red chili powder
- ¼ teaspoon ground turmeric
- ¼ teaspoon ground cumin
- Salt, to taste
- Water, as needed
- 4 bread slices

Preparation:
1. Add all the ingredients except bread slices in a large bowl and mix until a thick mixture forms.
2. With a spoon, spread the mixture over both sides of each bread slice.
3. Arrange the bread slices into the lightly greased air fry basket.
4. Press "Power" button of Ninja Foodi XL Pro Air Oven and select "Air Fry" function.
5. Now press TIME/SLICES +/- buttons to set the cooking time to 5 minutes.
6. Press TEMP/SHADE +/- buttons to set the temperature at 390 degrees F.
7. Press "Start/Stop" button to start.
8. When the unit beeps to show that it is preheated, open the oven door and insert the air fry basket on the rails of Level 3 in oven.
9. Flip the bread slices once halfway through.
10. When cooking time is completed, open the oven door and serve warm.

Serving Suggestions: Serve with the topping of butter.

Variation Tip: You can add herbs of your choice in flour batter.

Nutritional Information per Serving:
Calories: 151 | Fat: 2.3g|Sat Fat: 0.3g|Carbohydrates: 26.7g|Fiber: 5.4g|Sugar: 4.3g|Protein: 6.5g

Pancetta & Spinach Frittata

Prep Time: 15 minutes
Cook Time: 16 minutes
Serves: 2

Ingredients:
- ¼ cup pancetta
- ½ of tomato, cubed
- ¼ cup fresh baby spinach
- 3 eggs
- Salt and ground black pepper, as required
- ¼ cup Parmesan cheese, grated

Preparation:
1. Heat a nonstick skillet over medium heat and cook the pancetta for about 5 minutes.
2. Add the tomato and spinach cook for about 2-3 minutes.
3. Remove from the heat and drain the grease from skillet.
4. Set aside to cool slightly.
5. Meanwhile, in a small bowl, add the eggs, salt and black pepper and beat well.
6. In the bottom of a greased sheet pan, place the pancetta mixture and top with the eggs, followed by the cheese.
7. Press "Power" button of Ninja Foodi XL Pro Air Oven and select "Air Fry" function.

8. Press TEMP/SHADE +/- buttons to set the temperature at 355 degrees F.
9. Now press TIME/SLICES +/- buttons to set the cooking time to 8 minutes.
10. Press "Start/Stop" button to start.
11. When the unit beeps to show that it is preheated, open the oven door.
12. Arrange pan over the wire rack on Level 3.
13. When cooking time is completed, open the oven door, and remove the pan.
14. Cut into equal-sized wedges and serve.

Serving Suggestions: Serve alongside the green salad.
Variation Tip: You can use bacon instead of pancetta.
Nutritional Information per Serving:
Calories: 287 | Fat: 20.8g|Sat Fat: 7.2g|Carbohydrates: 1.7g|Fiber: 0.3g|Sugar: 0.9g|Protein: 23.1g

Carrot & Raisin Bread

Prep Time: 15 minutes
Cook Time: 35 minutes
Serves: 8

Ingredients:
- 2 cups all-purpose flour
- 1½ teaspoons ground cinnamon
- 2 teaspoons baking soda
- ½ teaspoon salt
- 3 eggs
- ½ cup sunflower oil
- ½ cup applesauce
- ¼ cup honey
- ¼ cup plain yogurt
- 2 teaspoons vanilla essence
- 2½ cups carrots, peeled and shredded
- ½ cup raisins
- ½ cup walnuts

Preparation:
1. Line the bottom of a greased sheet pan with parchment paper.
2. In a medium bowl, sift together the flour, baking soda, cinnamon, and salt.
3. In a large bowl, add the eggs, oil, applesauce, honey, and yogurt and with a hand-held mixer, mix on medium speed until well combined.
4. Add the eggs, one at a time and whisk well.
5. Add the vanilla and mix well.
6. Add the flour mixture and mix until just combined.
7. Fold in the carrots, raisins, and walnuts.
8. Place the mixture into the greased sheet pan.
9. With a piece of foil, cover the pan loosely.
10. Press "Power" button of Ninja Foodi XL Pro Air Oven and press FUNCTION +/- buttons to select "Air Fry" function.
11. Press TEMP/SHADE +/- buttons to set the temperature at 350 degrees F.
12. Now press TIME/SLICES +/- buttons to set the cooking time to 30 minutes.
13. Press "Start/Stop" button to start.
14. When the unit beeps to show that it is preheated, open the oven door.
15. Arrange the pan over wire rack on Level 3.
16. After 25 minutes of cooking, remove the foil.
17. When cooking time is completed, open the oven door and place the pan onto a wire rack to cool for about 10 minutes.
18. Carefully invert the bread onto the wire rack to cool completely before slicing.
19. Cut the bread into desired-sized slices and serve.

Serving Suggestions: Serve with butter.
Variation Tip: Dried cranberries can also be used instead of raisins.
Nutritional Information per Serving:
Calories: 441 | Fat: 20.3g|Sat Fat: 2.2g|Carbohydrates: 57.6g|Fiber: 5.7g|Sugar: 23.7g|Protein: 9.2g

Banana & Walnut Bread

Prep Time: 15 minutes
Cook Time: 25 minutes
Serves: 10

Ingredients:
- 1½ cups self-rising flour
- ¼ teaspoon bicarbonate of soda
- 5 tablespoons plus 1 teaspoon butter
- ⅔ cup plus ½ tablespoon caster sugar
- 2 medium eggs
- 3½ ounces walnuts, chopped
- 2 cups bananas, peeled and mashed

Preparation:
1. In a bowl, mix together the flour and bicarbonate of soda.
2. In another bowl, add the butter and sugar and beat until pale and fluffy.
3. Add the eggs, one at a time, along with a little flour and mix well.
4. Stir in the remaining flour and walnuts.

5. Add the bananas and mix until well combined.
6. Grease sheet pan.
7. Place the mixture into the prepared pan.
8. Press "Power" button of Ninja Foodi XL Pro Air Oven and select "Air Fry" function.
9. Press TEMP/SHADE +/- buttons to set the temperature at 355 degrees F.
10. Now press TIME/SLICES +/- buttons to set the cooking time to 10 minutes.
11. Press "Start/Stop" button to start.
12. When the unit beeps to show that it is preheated, open the oven door.
13. Arrange the pan over wire rack on Level 3.
14. After 10 minutes of cooking, set the temperature at 340 degrees F for 15 minutes.
15. When cooking time is completed, open the oven door and place the pan onto a wire rack to cool for about 10 minutes.
16. Carefully invert the bread onto the wire rack to cool completely before slicing.
17. Cut the bread into desired sized slices and serve.

Serving Suggestions: Serve with strawberry jam.

Variation Tip: Walnuts can be replaced with pecans.

Nutritional Information per Serving:
Calories: 270 | Fat: 12.8g|Sat Fat: 4.3g|Carbohydrates: 35.5g|Fiber: 2g|Sugar: 17.2g|Protein: 5.8g

Breakfast Potatoes

Prep Time: 10 minutes
Cook Time: 25 minutes
Serves: 7

Ingredients:

- 3 pounds red potatoes, diced
- ½ cup sweet onion, diced
- 2 green bell peppers, sliced
- 2 red bell peppers, sliced
- ½ teaspoon garlic powder
- ½ teaspoon seasoned salt
- ½ teaspoon fennel seed
- Cooking spray

Preparation:

1. Begin by prepping the veggies and, if necessary, chopping them.
2. Apply a light application of cooking oil spray to the air fry basket.
3. Fill the air fry basket with all of the vegetables.
4. Top evenly with seasonings.
5. Apply a generous application of cooking oil spray.
6. Turn on your Ninja Foodi XL Pro Air Oven and select "Air Fry".
7. Select the timer for 20 minutes and the temperature for 360 degrees F.
8. When the unit beeps to show that it has preheated, open the oven and insert the air fry basket on the rail of Level 3 in oven.
9. It's a good idea to check on the basket after around 10-15 minutes to mix or toss it up.
10. Serve once everything is ready.

Serving Suggestions: Top with sesame seeds before serving.

Variation Tip: You can also add olives.

Nutritional Information per Serving:
Calories: 187| Fat: 2g|Sat Fat: 0g|Carbohydrates: 38g|Fiber: 4g|Sugar: 8g|Protein: 5g

Breakfast Casserole

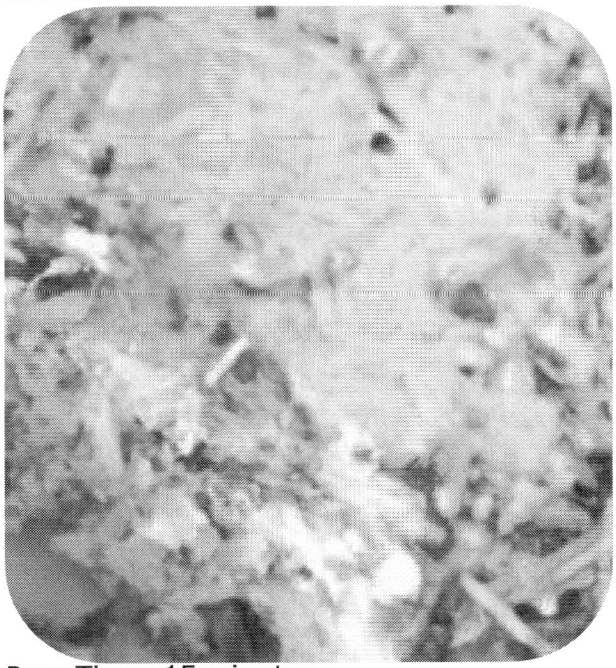

Prep Time: 15 minutes
Cook Time: 30 minutes
Serves: 8

Ingredients:

- 8 eggs
- 1 pound pork sausage
- 1½ cups whole milk
- 850g frozen hash browns, shredded
- 2 cups cheddar cheese
- 1½ teaspoons salt
- ¼ teaspoon garlic powder

Preparation:

1. Toss the uncooked ground sausage into the pan.
2. Sauté and cook for 6-8 minutes, or until sausage is browned.
3. Mix in the frozen hash browns thoroughly.
4. Mix in 1 cup of cheese.
5. Whisk together the eggs, Cheddar cheese, and spices in a separate basin. Fill the pot with the egg mixture.
6. Place the mixture into the roast tray.
7. Install a sheet pan on Level 3 in oven. Turn on your Ninja Foodi XL Pro Air Oven and select "Air Fry".

8. Select the timer for 30 minutes and the temperature for 350 degrees F.
9. When the unit beeps to show that it has preheated, open the oven and insert the roast tray on the sheet pan in oven.
10. Serve while hot.
Serving Suggestions: You can also add olives.
Variation Tip: You can use cream cheese instead of milk.
Nutritional Information per Serving:
Calories: 350| Fat: 29g|Sat Fat: 12g|Carbohydrates: 1g|Fiber: 1g|Sugar: 1g|Protein: 21g

French Toast

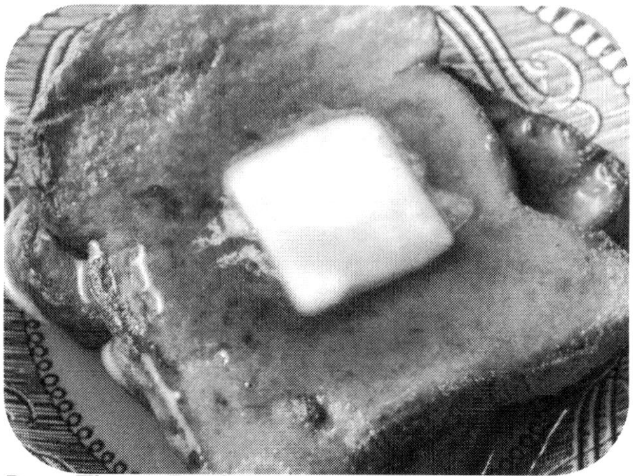

Prep Time: 5 minutes
Cook Time: 6 minutes
Serves: 4
Ingredients:
- 1 cup heavy cream
- 1 egg, beaten
- ¼ powdered sugar
- 1 teaspoon cinnamon
- 8 slices of bread

Preparation:
1. Place your bread on the wire rack.
2. Turn on your Ninja Foodi XL Pro Air Oven and select "Air Roast".
3. Select the timer for 4 minutes and the temperature for 390 degrees F.
4. While the bread is toasting, combine the remaining ingredients in a mixing bowl.
5. Dip bread in batches into the mixture, making sure both sides are covered.
6. Separate them on the air fry basket and wire rack evenly.
7. Now again, turn on your Ninja Foodi XL Pro Air Oven and select "Air Fry".
8. Select the timer for 4 minutes and the temperature for 390 degrees F.
9. When the unit beeps to show that it has preheated, open the oven. Insert the air fry basket on the rail of Level 3 in oven and the wire rack on Level 1.
10. Serve with butter.

Serving Suggestions: Top with maple syrup.
Variation Tip: You can also use low-carb bread.
Nutritional Information per Serving:
Calories: 342| Fat: 29g|Sat Fat: 15g|Carbohydrates: 16g|Fiber: 8g|Sugar: 2g|Protein: 13g

Breakfast Pizzas with Muffins

Prep Time: 5 minutes
Cook Time: 6 minutes
Serves: 3
Ingredients:
- 6 eggs, cooked and scrambled
- 1 pound ground sausage
- ½ cup Colby jack cheese, shredded
- 3 egg muffins, sliced in half
- Olive oil spray

Preparation:
1. Using olive oil cooking spray, spray the air fry basket.
2. Place each half in the basket.
3. Using a light layer of olive oil spray, lightly coat the English muffins and top with scrambled eggs and fried sausages.
4. Add cheese on top of each one.
5. Insert a wire rack on Level 3. Turn on your Ninja Foodi XL Pro Air Oven and select "Bake".
6. Select the timer for 5 minutes and the temperature for 355 degrees F.
7. When the unit beeps to show that it has preheated, open the oven and insert the air fry basket on the wire rack of Level 3 in oven.
8. Serve hot.

Serving Suggestions: Top with fresh parsley.
Variation Tip: You can also add fennel seeds.
Nutritional Information per Serving:
Calories: 429 | Fat: 32g|Sat Fat: 11g|Carbohydrates: 15g|Fiber: 1g|Sugar: 1g|Protein: 20g

Sausage Patties

Prep Time: 5 minutes
Cook Time: 6 minutes
Serves: 6
Ingredients:
- 1 pound pork sausage patties
- Fennel seeds

Preparation:
2. Prepare the sausage by slicing it into patties or using new patties, then flavor it with fennel seed or your favorite seasoning.
3. Insert a wire rack on Level 3.
4. Turn on your Ninja Foodi XL Pro Air Oven and select "Broil".
5. Select the timer for 8 minutes and temperature to LO.
6. When the unit beeps to show that it has preheated, open the oven and insert the air fry basket on the wire rack.
7. Cook for another 4 minutes after carefully flipping the patties.
8. Serve.

Serving Suggestions: Serve with garlic sauce.
Variation Tip: You can use any seasoning.
Nutritional Information per Serving:
Calories: 123 | Fat: 10g|Sat Fat: 3g|Carbohydrates: 1g|Fiber: 0g|Sugar: 0g|Protein: 7g

Hash Browns

Prep Time: 5 minutes
Cook Time: 5 minutes
Serves: 2
Ingredients:
- 4 hash brown patties
- Cooking oil spray

Preparation:
1. Coat the air fry basket with your preferred cooking oil spray.
2. Place the hash brown patties in the oven in an even layer on Level 3.
3. Spray them with your favorite cooking oil spray.
4. Turn on your Ninja Foodi XL Pro Air Oven and select "Air Fry".
5. Select the timer for 5 minutes and the temperature for 390 degrees F.
6. Dish out and serve immediately.

Serving Suggestions: Serve with maple syrup.
Variation Tip: Sprinkle sugar on top.
Nutritional Information per Serving:
Calories: 64 | Fat: 19.1g|Sat Fat: 2.9g|Carbohydrates: 8g|Fiber: 1g|Sugar: 0g|Protein: 1g

Hard Boiled Eggs

Prep Time: 5 minutes
Cook Time: 12 minutes
Serves: 6
Ingredients:
- 6 eggs

Preparation:
1. Add the eggs in the air fry basket.
2. Turn on your Ninja Foodi XL Pro Air Oven and select "Air Fry".
3. Select the timer for 12 minutes and the temperature for 300 degrees F.
4. When the unit beeps to show that it has preheated, open the oven and insert the air fry basket on the rail of Level 3 in oven. Close the oven door and let it cook.
5. After the cooking time has been completed, immerse for 5 minutes in a bowl of icy water.
6. After that, peel and serve.

Serving Suggestions: Serve with bread.
Variation Tip: Sprinkle salt and pepper on top.
Nutritional Information per Serving:
Calories: 72 | Fat: 5g|Sat Fat: 2g|Carbohydrates: 80|Fiber: 0g|Sugar: 0g|Protein: 6g

Cinnamon Sugar Donuts

Prep Time: 10 minutes
Cook Time: 5 minutes
Serves: 8

Ingredients:

- 450g refrigerated flaky jumbo biscuits
- ½ cup granulated white sugar
- 2 teaspoons ground cinnamon
- 4 tablespoons butter, melted
- Olive oil spray

Preparation:

1. Combine the sugar and cinnamon in a bowl; leave aside.
2. Take the biscuits out of the can, divide them, and lay them out on a flat surface. Make holes in each biscuit with a 1-inch-round biscuit cutter.
3. Using an olive or coconut oil spray, lightly coat the roast tray.
4. In the roast tray, arrange 4 doughnuts in a single layer. Make certain they aren't in contact.
5. Turn on your Ninja Foodi XL Pro Air Oven and select "Bake".
6. Select the timer for 5 minutes and the temperature for 360 degrees F.
7. When the unit beeps to show that it has preheated, open the oven and insert the roast tray on sheet pan into the rail of Level 3 in oven.
8. Serve and enjoy!

Serving Suggestions: Serve with chocolate sauce.

Variation Tip: Sprinkle sugar on top.

Nutritional Information per Serving:
Calories: 316 | Fat: 15g|Sat Fat: 5g|Carbohydrates: 42g|Fiber: 1g|Sugar: 16g|Protein: 3g

Zucchini Fritters

Prep Time: 15 minutes
Cook Time: 7 minutes
Serves: 4

Ingredients:

- 10½ ounces zucchini, grated and squeezed
- 7 ounces Halloumi cheese
- ¼ cup all-purpose flour
- 2 eggs
- 1 teaspoon fresh dill, minced
- Salt and ground black pepper, as required

Preparation:

1. In a large bowl and mix all the ingredients together.
2. Make small-sized fritters from the mixture.
3. Press "Power" button of Ninja Foodi XL Pro Air Oven and select "Air Fry" function.
4. Press TEMP/SHADE +/- buttons to set the temperature at 355 degrees F.
5. Now press TIME/SLICES +/- buttons to set the cooking time to 7 minutes.
6. Press "Start/Stop" button to start.
7. When the unit beeps to show that it is preheated, open the oven door.
8. Arrange fritters into the air fry basket and insert into the rails of Level 3.
9. When cooking time is completed, open the oven door and serve warm.

Serving Suggestions: Serve with the topping of sour cream.

Variation Tip: Make sure to squeeze the zucchini completely.

Nutritional Information per Serving:
Calories: 253 | Fat: 17.2g|Sat Fat: 1.4g|Carbohydrates: 10g|Fiber: 1.1g|Sugar: 2.7g|Protein: 15.2g

Broiled Bacon

Prep Time: 10 minutes
Cook Time: 10 minutes
Serves: 6

Ingredients:

- 1 pound bacon

Preparation:

1. Evenly distribute the bacon in the air fry basket.
2. Turn on your Ninja Foodi XL Pro Air Oven and select "Broil".
3. Select the unit for 5 minutes at LO.
4. When the unit beeps to show that it has preheated, open the oven and insert the air fry basket on the rail of Level 3 in oven.
5. With tongs, remove the bacon and place it on a paper towel-lined dish.
6. Allow cooling before serving.

Serving Suggestions: Serve with steamed rice.
Variation Tip: Sprinkle salt and pepper on top.
Nutritional Information per Serving:
Calories: 177 | Fat: 13g|Sat Fat: 5g|Carbohydrates: 1g|Fiber: 0g|Sugar: 0g|Protein: 13g

Egg in Hole

Prep Time: 5 minutes
Cook Time: 10 minutes
Serves: 1

Ingredients:

- 1 piece toast
- 1 egg
- Salt and pepper, to taste

Preparation:

1. Use nonstick cooking spray to spray your roast tray
2. Place a piece of bread on the roast tray.
3. Remove the bread by poking a hole in it with a cup or a cookie cutter.
4. Into the hole, crack the egg.
5. Turn on your Ninja Foodi XL Pro Air Oven and select "Air Fry".
6. Select the timer for 6 minutes and the temperature for 330 degrees F.
7. When the unit beeps to show that it has preheated, open the oven and insert the roast tray on sheet pan into the rail of Level 3 in oven.
8. Dish out and sprinkle with salt and pepper to serve.

Serving Suggestions: Serve with toasted bacon.
Variation Tip: You can also add cheese on top.
Nutritional Information per Serving:
Calories: 136 | Fat: 6g|Sat Fat: 2g|Carbohydrates: 13g|Fiber: 1g|Sugar: 2g|Protein: 8g

Snacks and Appetizer Recipes

Carrot Chips

Prep Time: 15 minutes.
Cook Time: 15 minutes.
Serves: 8

Ingredients:

- 2 pounds carrots, sliced
- ¼ cup olive oil
- 1 tablespoon of sea salt
- 1 teaspoon ground cumin
- 1 teaspoon ground cinnamon

Preparation:

1. Toss the carrot slices with oil, cumin, and cinnamon in a large bowl.
2. Grease the sheet pan and spread the carrot slices in it.
3. Transfer the sheet pan to the 2nd rack position of Ninja Foodi XL Pro Air Oven and close the door.
4. Select the "Bake" Mode using FUNCTION +/- buttons and select Rack Level 2.
5. Set its cooking time to 15 minutes and temperature to 450 degrees F, then press "START/STOP" to initiate cooking.
6. Flip the chips after 7-8 minutes of cooking and resume baking.
7. Serve fresh.

Serving Suggestion: Serve the chips with tomato ketchup or cheese dip.
Variation Tip: Toss the carrot chips with maple-honey syrup to coat.
Nutritional Information Per Serving:
Calories 182 | Fat 2g |Sodium 350mg | Carbs 12.2g | Fiber 0.7g | Sugar 1g | Protein 4.3g

Cod Nuggets

Prep Time: 15 minutes
Cook Time: 18 minutes
Serves: 5

Ingredients:

- 1 cup all-purpose flour
- 2 eggs
- ¾ cup breadcrumbs
- Pinch of salt
- 2 tablespoons olive oil
- 1 pound cod, cut into 1x2½-inch strips

Preparation:

1. In a shallow dish, place the flour.
2. Crack the eggs in a second dish and beat well.
3. In a third dish, mix together the breadcrumbs, salt and oil.
4. Coat the nuggets with flour, then dip into beaten eggs and finally, coat with the breadcrumbs.
5. Press "Power" button of Ninja Foodi XL Pro Air Oven and select "Air Fry" function.
6. Press TEMP/SHADE +/- buttons to set the temperature at 390 degrees F.
7. Now press TIME/SLICES +/- buttons to set the cooking time to 8 minutes.
8. Press "START/STOP" button to start.
9. When the unit beeps to show that it is preheated, open the lid.
10. Arrange the nuggets in air fry basket and insert in the oven.
11. When cooking time is completed, open the lid and transfer the nuggets onto a platter.
12. Serve warm.

Serving Suggestions: Enjoy with tartar sauce.
Variation Tip: Use fresh fish.
Nutritional Information per Serving:
Calories: 323 | Fat: 9.2g|Sat Fat: 1.7g|Carbohydrates: 30.9g|Fiber: 1.4g|Sugar: 1.2g|Protein: 27.7g

Crispy Avocado Fries

Prep Time: 15 minutes
Cook Time: 7 minutes
Serves: 2

Ingredients:

- ¼ cup all-purpose flour
- Salt and ground black pepper, as required
- 1 egg
- 1 teaspoon water
- ½ cup panko breadcrumbs
- 1 avocado, peeled, pitted, and sliced into 8 pieces
- Non-stick cooking spray

Preparation:

1. In a shallow bowl, mix together the flour, salt, and black pepper.
2. In a second bowl, mix well egg and water.
3. In a third bowl, put the breadcrumbs.
4. Coat the avocado slices with flour mixture, then dip into egg mixture and finally, coat evenly with the breadcrumbs.
5. Now, spray the avocado slices evenly with cooking spray.
6. Press "Power" button of Ninja Foodi XL Pro Air Oven and select "Air Fry" function.
7. Press TEMP/SHADE +/- buttons to set the temperature at 400 degrees F.
8. Now press TIME/SLICES +/- buttons to set the cooking time to 7 minutes.
9. Press "Start/Stop" button to start.
10. When the unit beeps to show that it is pre-heated, open the oven door.
11. Arrange the avocado fries into the air fry basket on Ninja sheet pan on Level 3.
12. When cooking time is completed, open the oven door, and transfer the avocado fries onto a platter.
13. Serve warm.

Serving Suggestions: Serve with ketchup.
Variation Tip: Make sure to use firm avocados that are not too ripe.
Nutritional Information per Serving:
Calories: 391 | Fat: 23.8g|Sat Fat: 5.6g|Carbohydrates: 24.8g|Fiber: 7.3g|Sugar: 0.8g|Protein: 7g

Fiesta Chicken Fingers

Prep Time: 15 minutes.
Cook Time: 12 minutes.
Serves: 4

Ingredients:

- ¾-pound boneless chicken breasts, cut into strips
- ½ cup buttermilk
- ¼ teaspoon pepper
- 1 cup all-purpose flour
- 3 cups corn chips, crushed
- 1 envelope taco seasoning
- Sour cream ranch dip or salsa

Preparation:

1. Coat the chicken with pepper and flour.
2. Mix corn chips with taco seasoning.
3. Dip the chicken fingers in the buttermilk, then coat with the corn chips.
4. Place the chicken fingers in the air fry basket and spray with cooking oil.
5. Transfer the basket to the 4th rack position of Ninja Foodi XL Pro Air Oven and close the door.
6. Select the "Air Fry" Mode using FUNCTION +/- buttons and select Rack Level 4.
7. Set its cooking time to 12 minutes and temperature to 325 degrees F, then press "START/STOP" to initiate cooking.
8. Flip the chicken fingers once cooked halfway through, then resume cooking.
9. Serve warm with sour cream ranch dip or fresh salsa.

Serving Suggestion: Serve the chicken fingers with chili garlic sauce.
Variation Tip: Use mayonnaise to coat the fingers for a rich taste.
Nutritional Information Per Serving:
Calories 218 | Fat 12g |Sodium 710mg | Carbs 44g | Fiber 5g | Sugar 3g | Protein 24g

Pumpkin Fries

Prep Time: 15 minutes.
Cook Time: 12 minutes.
Serves: 6

Ingredients:

- ½ cup plain Greek yogurt
- 2 tablespoons maple syrup
- 3 teaspoons chipotle peppers in adobo sauce
- ⅛ teaspoon salt
- 1 medium pie pumpkin
- ¼ teaspoon garlic powder
- ¼ teaspoon ground cumin
- ¼ teaspoon chili powder
- ¼ teaspoon pepper

Preparation:

1. Peel and cut the pumpkin into sticks.
2. Mix garlic powder, cumin, chili powder, salt, and black pepper.
3. Coat the pumpkin sticks with the spice mixture.
4. Spread the pumpkin fries in the air fry basket and spray them with cooking spray.
5. Transfer the basket to the 3rd rack position of Ninja Foodi XL Pro Air Oven and close the door.
6. Select the "Air Fry" Mode using FUNCTION +/- buttons and select Rack Level 3.
7. Set its cooking time to 12 minutes and temperature to 400 degrees F, then press "START/STOP" to initiate cooking.
8. Toss the fries once cooked halfway through, then resume cooking.
9. Mix yogurt with maple syrup and adobo sauce in a bowl.
10. Serve fries with its sauce.

Serving Suggestion: Serve the pumpkin chips with tomato ketchup.

Variation Tip: Coat the pumpkin fries with breadcrumbs before cooking.

Nutritional Information Per Serving:
Calories 215 | Fat 16g |Sodium 255mg | Carbs 31g | Fiber 1.2g | Sugar 5g | Protein 4.1g

Beef Taquitos

Prep Time: 15 minutes
Cook Time: 8 minutes
Serves: 6

Ingredients:

- 6 corn tortillas
- 2 cups cooked beef, shredded
- ½ cup onion, chopped
- 1 cup pepper jack cheese, shredded
- Olive oil cooking spray

Preparation:

1. Arrange the tortillas onto a smooth surface.
2. Place the shredded meat over one corner of each tortilla, followed by onion and cheese.
3. Roll each tortilla to secure the filling and secure with toothpicks.
4. Spray each taquito with cooking spray evenly.
5. Arrange the taquitos onto the greased sheet pan.
6. Place the tofu mixture in the greased sheet pan.
7. Press "Power" button of Ninja Foodi XL Pro Air Oven and select "Air Fry" function.
8. Press TEMP/SHADE +/- buttons to set the temperature at 400 degrees F.
9. Now press TIME/SLICES +/- buttons to set the cooking time to 8 minutes.
10. Press "START/STOP" button to start.
11. When the unit beeps to show that it is preheated, open the lid and insert the sheet pan in oven.
12. When cooking time is completed, open the lid and transfer the taquitos onto a platter.
13. Serve warm.

Serving Suggestions: Serve with yogurt dip.

Variation Tip: You can use any kind of cooked meat in this recipe.

Nutritional Information per Serving:
Calories: 228| Fat: 9.6g|Sat Fat: 4.8g|Carbohydrates: 12.3g|Fiber: 1.7g|Sugar: 0.6g|Protein: 22.7g

Roasted Cashews

Prep Time: 5 minutes
Cook Time: 5 minutes
Serves: 6

Ingredients:

- 1½ cups raw cashew nuts
- 1 teaspoon butter, melted
- Salt and freshly ground black pepper, as required

Preparation:

1. In a bowl, mix all the ingredients together.
2. Press "Power" button of Ninja Foodi XL Pro Air Oven and select "Air Fry" function.
3. Press TEMP/SHADE +/- buttons to set the temperature at 355 degrees F.
4. Now press TIME/SLICES +/- buttons to set the cooking time to 5 minutes.
5. Press "Start/Stop" button to start.
6. When the unit beeps to show that it is preheated, open the oven door.
7. Arrange the cashews into the air fry basket on sheet pan on Level 3.
8. Shake the cashews once halfway through.
9. When cooking time is completed, open the oven door, and transfer the cashews into a heatproof bowl.
10. Serve warm.

Serving Suggestions: Serve with a sprinkling of little salt.

Variation Tip: Make sure to use raw walnuts.

Nutritional Information per Serving:
Calories: 202 | Fat: 16.5g|Sat Fat: 3.5g|Carbohydrates: 11.2g|Fiber: 1g|Sugar: 1.7g|Protein: 5.3g

Cheesy Broccoli Bites

Prep Time: 15 minutes
Cook Time: 12 minutes
Serves: 5

Ingredients:

- 1 cup broccoli florets
- 1 egg, beaten
- ¾ cup cheddar cheese, grated
- 2 tablespoons Parmesan cheese, grated
- ¾ cup panko breadcrumbs
- Salt and freshly ground black pepper, as needed

Preparation:

1. In a food processor, add the broccoli and pulse until finely crumbled.
2. In a large bowl, mix together the broccoli and remaining ingredients.
3. Make small equal-sized balls from the mixture.
4. Press "Power" button of Ninja Foodi XL Pro Air Oven and select "Air Fry" function.
5. Press TEMP/SHADE +/- buttons to set the temperature at 350 degrees F.
6. Now press TIME/SLICES +/- buttons to set the cooking time to 12 minutes.
7. Press "Start/Stop" button to start.
8. When the unit beeps to show that it is preheated, open the oven door.
9. Arrange the broccoli balls into the air fry basket on Level 3.
10. When cooking time is completed, open the oven door and transfer the broccoli bites onto a platter.
11. Serve warm.

Serving Suggestions: Serve with your favorite dipping sauce.

Variation Tip: You can use cheese of your choice.

Nutritional Information per Serving:
Calories: 153 | Fat: .2g|Sat Fat: 4.5g|Carbohydrates: 4g|Fiber: 0.5g|Sugar: 0.5g|Protein: 7.1g

Risotto Bites

Prep Time: 15 minutes
Cook Time: 10 minutes
Serves: 4

Ingredients:

- 1½ cups cooked risotto
- 3 tablespoons Parmesan cheese, grated
- ½ egg, beaten
- 1½ ounces mozzarella cheese, cubed
- ⅓ cup breadcrumbs

Preparation:

1. In a bowl, add the risotto, Parmesan and egg and mix until well combined.
2. Make 20 equal-sized balls from the mixture.
3. Insert a mozzarella cube in the center of each ball.
4. With your fingers smooth the risotto mixture to cover the ball.
5. In a shallow dish, place the breadcrumbs.
6. Coat the balls with the breadcrumbs evenly.
7. Press "Power" button of Ninja Foodi XL Pro Air Oven and select "Air Fry" function. Select 2 LEVEL.
8. Press TEMP/SHADE +/- buttons to set the temperature at 390 degrees F.
9. Now press TIME/SLICES +/- buttons to set the cooking time to 10 minutes.
10. Press "Start/Stop" button to start.
11. When the unit beeps to show that it is preheated, open the oven door.
12. Separate 10 balls into the air fry basket on Level 3 and 10 into Ninja sheet pan on Level 1.
13. When cooking time is completed, open the oven door, and transfer the risotto bites onto a platter.
14. Serve warm.

Serving Suggestions: Serve with blue cheese dip.

Variation Tip: Make sure to use dry breadcrumbs.

Nutritional Information per Serving:
Calories: 340 | Fat: 4.3g|Sat Fat: 2g|Carbohydrates: 62.4g|Fiber: 1.3g|Sugar: 0.7g|Protein: 11.3g

Onion Rings

Prep Time: 15 minutes.
Cook Time: 15 minutes.
Serves: 4

Ingredients:

- ½ cup all-purpose flour
- 1 teaspoon paprika
- 1 teaspoon salt, divided
- ½ cup buttermilk
- 1 egg
- 1 cup panko breadcrumbs
- 2 tablespoons olive oil
- 1 sweet onion, sliced into rings

Preparation:

1. Mix flour with paprika and salt on a plate.
2. Coat the onion rings with the flour mixture.
3. Beat egg with buttermilk in a bowl and dip all the onion rings.
4. Spread the breadcrumbs in a bowl.
5. Coat the onion rings with breadcrumbs.
6. Place the onion rings in the air fry basket and spray them with cooking oil.
7. Transfer the basket to the 3rd rack position of Ninja Foodi XL Pro Air Oven and close the door.
8. Select the "Air Fry" Mode using FUNCTION +/- buttons and select Rack Level 3.
9. Set its cooking time to 15 minutes and temperature to 400 degrees F, then press "START/STOP" to initiate cooking.
10. Serve warm.

Serving Suggestion: Serve the onion rings with chili sauce or mayo dip.

Variation Tip: Coat the onion rings with parmesan cheese.

Nutritional Information Per Serving:
Calories 106 | Fat 5g |Sodium 244mg | Carbs 16g | Fiber 1g | Sugar 1g | Protein 7g

Potato Chips

Prep Time: 15 minutes.
Cook Time: 25 minutes.
Serves: 2

Ingredients:

- 1 medium Russet potato, sliced
- 1 tablespoon canola oil
- ¼ teaspoon sea salt
- ¼ teaspoon black pepper
- 1 teaspoon chopped fresh rosemary

Preparation:

1. Fill a suitable glass bowl with cold water and add sliced potatoes.
2. Leave the potatoes for 20 minutes, then drain them. Pat dry the chips with a paper towel.
3. Toss the potatoes with salt, black pepper, and oil to coat well.
4. Spread the potato slices in the air fry basket evenly.
5. Transfer the basket to the 3rd rack position of Ninja Foodi XL Pro Air Oven and close the door.
6. Select the "Air Fry" Mode using FUNCTION +/- buttons and select Rack Level 3.
7. Set its cooking time to 25 minutes and temperature to 375 degrees F, then press "START/STOP" to initiate cooking.
8. Garnish with rosemary.
9. Serve warm.

Serving Suggestion: Serve the chips with tomato sauce.
Variation Tip: Toss the potato chips with paprika.
Nutritional Information Per Serving:
Calories 134 | Fat 3g |Sodium 216mg | Carbs 27g | Fiber 3g | Sugar 4g | Protein 1g

Avocado Fries

Prep Time: 15 minutes.
Cook Time: 20 minutes.
Serves: 4

Ingredients:

- ½ cup panko breadcrumbs
- ½ teaspoon salt
- 1 avocado, peeled, pitted, and sliced
- 1 cup egg, whisked

Preparation:

1. Toss breadcrumbs with salt in a shallow bowl.
2. First, dip the avocado strips in the egg, then coat them with panko.
3. Spread these slices in the air fry basket.
4. Transfer the sandwich to the 2nd rack position of Ninja Foodi XL Pro Air Oven and close the door.
5. Select the "Bake" Mode using FUNCTION +/- buttons and select Rack Level 2.
6. Set its cooking time to 20 minutes and temperature to 400 degrees F, then press "START/STOP" to initiate cooking.
7. Serve fresh.

Serving Suggestion: Serve the fries with chili sauce or mayonnaise dip.
Variation Tip: Coat the fries with crushed cornflakes for crisper.
Nutritional Information Per Serving:
Calories 110 | Fat 9g |Sodium 318mg | Carbs 19g | Fiber 5g | Sugar 3g | Protein 7g

Baked Potatoes

Prep Time: 15 minutes.
Cook Time: 45 minutes.
Serves: 3

Ingredients:

- 3 russet potatoes, scrubbed and rinsed
- Cooking spray
- ½ teaspoon sea salt
- ½ teaspoon garlic powder

Preparation:

1. Rub the potatoes with salt and garlic powder.
2. Place the potatoes in the air fry basket and spray with cooking spray.
3. Transfer the basket to the 2nd rack position of Ninja Foodi XL Pro Air Oven and close the door.
4. Select the "Bake" Mode using FUNCTION +/- buttons and select Rack Level 2.
5. Set its cooking time to 45 minutes and temperature to 350 degrees F, then press "START/STOP" to initiate cooking.
6. Make a slit on top of the potatoes and score the flesh inside.
7. Serve warm.

Serving Suggestion: Serve the baked potatoes with butter sauce or mayo dip.
Variation Tip: Add shredded cheese and crumbled bacon to the toppings.
Nutritional Information Per Serving:
Calories 269 | Fat 5g |Sodium 510mg | Carbs 37g | Fiber 5g | Sugar 4g | Protein 1g

Pasta Chips

Prep Time: 15 minutes.
Cook Time: 10 minutes.
Serves: 4

Ingredients:

- ½ tablespoon olive oil
- ½ tablespoon nutritional yeast
- 1 cup bow tie pasta
- ⅔ teaspoon Italian Seasoning Blend
- ¼ teaspoon salt

Preparation:

1. Cook and boil the pasta in salted water half of the time as stated on the box, then drain it.
2. Toss the boiled pasta with salt, Italian seasoning, nutritional yeast, and olive oil in a bowl.
3. Spread this pasta in the air fry basket.
4. Transfer the basket to the 3rd rack position of Ninja Foodi XL Pro Air Oven and close the door.
5. Select the "Air Fry" Mode using FUNCTION +/- buttons and select Rack Level 3.
6. Set its cooking time to 5 minutes and temperature to 390 degrees F, then press "START/STOP" to initiate cooking.
7. Toss the pasta and continue air frying for another 5 minutes.
8. Enjoy.

Serving Suggestion: Serve the chips with white cheese dip.
Variation Tip: Drizzle white peppers ground on top before baking.
Nutritional Information Per Serving:
Calories 167 | Fat 2g |Sodium 48mg | Carbs 26g | Fiber 2g | Sugar 0g | Protein 1g

Buttermilk Biscuits

Prep Time: 15 minutes
Cook Time: 8 minutes
Serves: 8

Ingredients:

- ½ cup cake flour
- 1¼ cups all-purpose flour
- ¼ teaspoon baking soda
- ½ teaspoon baking powder
- 1 teaspoon granulated sugar
- Salt, to taste
- ¼ cup cold unsalted butter, cut into cubes
- ¾ cup buttermilk
- 2 tablespoons butter, melted

Preparation:

1. In a large bowl, sift together flours, baking soda, baking powder, sugar and salt.
2. With a pastry cutter, cut cold butter and mix until coarse crumb forms.
3. Slowly, add buttermilk and mix until a smooth dough forms.
4. Place the dough onto a floured surface and with your hands, press it into ½ inch thickness.
5. With a 1¾-inch round cookie cutter, cut the biscuits.
6. Arrange the biscuits into sheet pan and coat with the butter.
7. Press "Power" button of Ninja Foodi XL Pro Air Oven and select "Air Fry" function.
8. Press TEMP/SHADE +/- buttons to set the temperature at 400 degrees F.
9. Now press TIME/SLICES +/- buttons to set the cooking time to 8 minutes.
10. Press "Start/Stop" button to start.
11. When the unit beeps to show that it is preheated, open the oven door.
12. Arrange pan over the wire rack on Level 3.
13. When cooking time is completed, open the oven door and place the sheet pan onto a wire rack for about 5 minutes.
14. Carefully invert the biscuits onto the wire rack to cool completely before serving.

Serving Suggestions: Serve with the drizzling of melted butter.
Variation Tip: Shortening can also be used instead of butter.

Nutritional Information per Serving:
Calories: 187 | Fat: 9.1g|Sat Fat: 5.6g|Carbohydrates: 22.6g|Fiber: 0.8g|Sugar: 1.7g|Protein: 3.7g

Ranch Kale Chips

Prep Time: 15 minutes.
Cook Time: 5 minutes.
Serves: 6

Ingredients:

- 2 tablespoons olive oil
- 4 cups kale leaves
- 2 teaspoons vegan ranch seasoning
- 1 tablespoon nutritional yeast flakes
- ¼ teaspoon salt

Preparation:

1. Toss the kale leaves with oil, salt, yeast, and ranch seasoning in a large bowl.
2. Spread the seasoned kale leaves in the oven.
3. Transfer the air fry basket to the 3rd rack position of Ninja Foodi XL Pro Air Oven and close the door.
4. Select the "Air Fry" Mode using FUNCTION +/- buttons and select Rack Level 3.
5. Set its cooking time to 5 minutes and temperature to 370 degrees F, then press "START/STOP" to initiate cooking.
6. Serve warm.

Serving Suggestion: Serve the chips with a cream cheese dip on the side.
Variation Tip: Drizzle shredded parmesan on top before cooking.

Nutritional Information Per Serving:
Calories 123 | Fat 8g |Sodium 146mg | Carbs 8g | Fiber 5g | Sugar 1g | Protein 7g

Potato Croquettes

Prep Time: 15 minutes
Cook Time: 8 minutes
Serves: 4

Ingredients:

- 2 medium Russet potatoes, peeled and cubed
- 2 tablespoons all-purpose flour
- ½ cup Parmesan cheese, grated
- 1 egg yolk
- 2 tablespoons fresh chives, minced
- Pinch of ground nutmeg
- Salt and freshly ground black pepper, as needed
- 2 eggs
- ½ cup breadcrumbs
- 2 tablespoons vegetable oil

Preparation:

1. In a pan of a boiling water, add the potatoes and cook for about 15 minutes.
2. Drain the potatoes well and transfer into a large bowl.
3. With a potato masher, mash the potatoes and set aside to cool completely.
4. In the bowl of mashed potatoes, add the flour, Parmesan cheese, egg yolk, chives, nutmeg, salt, and black pepper and mix until well combined.
5. Make small equal-sized balls from the mixture.
6. Now, roll each ball into a cylinder shape.
7. In a shallow dish, crack the eggs and beat well.
8. In another dish, mix the breadcrumbs and oil together.
9. Dip the croquettes in egg mixture and then coat with the breadcrumb mixture.
10. Press "Power" button of Ninja Foodi XL Pro Air Oven and select "Air Fry" function.
11. Press TEMP/SHADE +/- buttons to set the temperature at 390 degrees F.
12. Now press TIME/SLICES +/- buttons to set the cooking time to 8 minutes.
13. Press "START/STOP" button to start.
14. When the unit beeps to show that it is preheated, open the lid.
15. Arrange the croquettes in air fry basket and insert in the oven.
16. When cooking time is completed, open the lid and transfer the croquettes onto a platter.
17. Serve warm.

Serving Suggestions: Serve with mustard sauce.

Variation Tip: Make sure to use dried breadcrumbs.

Nutritional Information per Serving:
Calories: 283 | Fat: 13.4g|Sat Fat: 3.8g|Carbohydrates: 29.9g|Fiber: 3.3g|Sugar: 2.3g|Protein: 11.5g

Mini Hot Dogs

Prep Time: 15 minutes.
Cook Time: 4 minutes.
Serves: 8

Ingredients:

- 8 ounces refrigerated crescent rolls
- 24 cocktail hot dogs

Preparation:

1. Spread the crescent rolls into 8 triangles and cut each into 3 triangles.
2. Place one mini hot dog at the center of each crescent roll.
3. Wrap the rolls around the hot dog and place them in the air fry basket.
4. Transfer the basket to the 3rd rack position of Ninja Foodi XL Pro Air Oven and close the door.
5. Select the "Air Fry" Mode using FUNCTION +/- buttons and select Rack Level 3.
6. Set its cooking time to 4 minutes and temperature to 325 degrees F, then press "START/STOP" to initiate cooking.
7. Serve warm.

Serving Suggestion: Serve the hot dogs with tomato ketchup or cream cheese dip.

Variation Tip: Drizzle butter on top of the wrapped hot dogs.

Nutritional Information Per Serving:
Calories 152 | Fat 4g |Sodium 232mg | Carbs 17g | Fiber 1g | Sugar 0g | Protein 24g

Eggplant Fries

Prep Time: 15 minutes.

Cook Time: 10 minutes.

Serves: 4

Ingredients:

- 2 large eggs
- ½ cup grated Parmesan cheese
- ½ cup toasted wheat germ
- 1 teaspoon Italian seasoning
- ¾ teaspoon garlic salt
- 1 (1 ¼ pounds) eggplant, peeled
- Cooking spray
- 1 cup marinara sauce, warmed

Preparation:

1. Cut the eggplant into sticks.
2. In a bowl, whisk the eggs. Mix parmesan cheese, wheat germ, seasoning, and garlic salt in another bowl.
3. Coat the eggplant sticks first with the eggs then into the parmesan mixture.
4. Place the eggplant fries in the air fry basket and spray them with cooking spray.
5. Transfer the basket to the 3rd rack position of Ninja Foodi XL Pro Air Oven and close the door.
6. Select the "Air Fry" Mode using FUNCTION +/- buttons and select Rack Level 3.
7. Set its cooking time to 10 minutes and temperature to 375 degrees F, then press "START/STOP" to initiate cooking.
8. Serve warm with marinara sauce.

Serving Suggestion: Serve the eggplant fries with tomato sauce.

Variation Tip: Drizzle paprika on top for more spice.

Nutritional Information Per Serving:

Calories 201 | Fat 7g |Sodium 269mg | Carbs 35g | Fiber 4g | Sugar 12g | Protein 6g

Roasted Peanuts

Prep Time: 5 minutes

Cook Time: 14 minutes

Serves: 6

Ingredients:

- 1½ cups raw peanuts
- Nonstick cooking spray

Preparation:

1. Press "Power" button of Ninja Foodi XL Pro Air Oven and select "Air Fry" function.
2. Press TEMP/SHADE +/- buttons to set the temperature at 320 degrees F.
3. Now press TIME/SLICES +/- buttons to set the cooking time to 14 minutes.
4. Press "START/STOP" button to start.
5. When the unit beeps to show that it is preheated, open the lid.
6. Arrange the peanuts in air fry basket and insert in the oven.
7. While cooking, toss the peanuts twice.
8. After 9 minutes of cooking, spray the peanuts with cooking spray.
9. When cooking time is completed, open the lid and transfer the peanuts into a heatproof bowl.
10. Serve warm.

Serving Suggestions: Serve with a sprinkling of little cinnamon.

Variation Tip: Choose raw peanuts.

Nutritional Information per Serving:

Calories: 207 | Fat: 18g|Sat Fat: 2.5g|Carbohydrates: 5.9g|Fiber: 3.1g|Sugar: 1.5g|Protein: 9.4g

Glazed Chicken Wings

Prep Time: 15 minutes
Cook Time: 25 minutes
Serves: 4

Ingredients:

- 1½ pounds chicken wingettes and drumettes
- ⅓ cup tomato sauce
- 2 tablespoons balsamic vinegar
- 2 tablespoons maple syrup
- ½ teaspoon liquid smoke
- ¼ teaspoon red pepper flakes, crushed
- Salt, as required

Preparation:

1. Arrange the wings onto the greased sheet pan.
2. Press "Power" button of Ninja Foodi XL Pro Air Oven and select "Air Fry" function.
3. Press TEMP/SHADE +/- buttons to set the temperature at 380 degrees F.
4. Now press TIME/SLICES +/- buttons to set the cooking time to 25 minutes.
5. Press "START/STOP" button to start.
6. When the unit beeps to show that it is preheated, open the lid and insert the sheet pan in oven.
7. Meanwhile, in a small pan, add the remaining ingredients over medium heat and cook for about 10 minutes, stirring occasionally.
8. When cooking time is completed, open the lid and place the chicken wings into a bowl.
9. Add the sauce and toss to coat well.
10. Serve immediately.

Serving Suggestions: Serve with your favorite dip.

Variation Tip: Honey can replace the maple syrup.

Nutritional Information per Serving:

Calories: 356 | Fat: 12.7g|Sat Fat: 3.5g|Carbohydrates: 7.9g|Fiber: 0.3g|Sugar: 6.9g|Protein: 49.5g

Cauliflower Poppers

Prep Time: 10 minutes
Cook Time: 20 minutes
Serves: 6

Ingredients:

- 3 tablespoons olive oil
- 1 teaspoon paprika
- ½ teaspoon ground cumin
- ¼ teaspoon ground turmeric
- Salt and ground black pepper, as required
- 1 medium head cauliflower, cut into florets

Preparation:

1. In a bowl, place all ingredients and toss to coat well.
2. Place the cauliflower mixture in the greased sheet pan.
3. Press "Power" button of Ninja Foodi XL Pro Air Oven and select the "Bake" function.
4. Press TEMP/SHADE +/- buttons to set the temperature at 450 degrees F.
5. Now press TIME/SLICES +/- buttons to set the cooking time to 20 minutes.
6. Press "START/STOP" button to start.
7. When the unit beeps to show that it is preheated, open the lid and insert the sheet pan in oven.
8. Flip the cauliflower mixture once halfway through.
9. When cooking time is completed, open the lid and transfer the cauliflower poppers onto a platter.
10. Serve warm.

Serving Suggestions: Serve with a squeeze of lemon juice.

Variation Tip: Feel free to use spices of your choice.

Nutritional Information per Serving:

Calories: 73 | Fat: 7.1g|Sat Fat: 1g|Carbohydrates: 2.7g|Fiber: 1.3g|Sugar: 1.1g|Protein: 1g

Zucchini Fries

Prep Time: 10 minutes
Cook Time: 12 minutes
Serves: 4

Ingredients:

- 1 pound zucchini, sliced into 2½-inch sticks
- Salt, as required
- 2 tablespoons olive oil
- ¾ cup panko breadcrumbs

Preparation:

1. In a colander, add the zucchini and sprinkle with salt. Set aside for about 10 minutes.
2. Gently pat dry the zucchini sticks with the paper towels and coat with oil.
3. In a shallow dish, add the breadcrumbs.
4. Coat the zucchini sticks with breadcrumbs evenly.
5. Press "Power" button of Ninja Foodi XL Pro Air Oven and select "Air Fry" function.
6. Press TEMP/SHADE +/- buttons to set the temperature at 400 degrees F.
7. Now press TIME/SLICES +/- buttons to set the cooking time to 12 minutes.
8. Press "START/STOP" button to start.
9. When the unit beeps to show that it is preheated, open the lid.
10. Arrange the zucchini fries in air fry basket and insert in the oven.
11. When cooking time is completed, open the lid and transfer the zucchini fries onto a platter.
12. Serve warm.

Serving Suggestions: Serve with ketchup.
Variation Tip: You can use breadcrumbs of your choice.
Nutritional Information per Serving:
Calories: 151 | Fat: 8.6g|Sat Fat: 1.6g|Carbohydrates: 6.9g|Fiber: 1.3g|Sugar: 2g|Protein: 1.9g

Persimmon Chips

Prep Time: 10 minutes
Cook Time: 10 minutes
Serves: 2

Ingredients:

- 2 ripe persimmons, cut into slices horizontally
- Salt and ground black pepper, as required

Preparation:

1. Arrange the persimmons slices onto the greased sheet pan.
2. Press "Power" button of Ninja Foodi XL Pro Air Oven and select "Air Fry" function.
3. Press TEMP/SHADE +/- buttons to set the temperature at 400 degrees F.
4. Now press TIME/SLICES +/- buttons to set the cooking time to 10 minutes.
5. Press "START/STOP" button to start.
6. When the unit beeps to show that it is preheated, open the lid.
7. Insert the sheet pan in oven.
8. Flip the chips once halfway through.
9. When cooking time is completed, open the lid and transfer the chips onto a platter.
10. Serve warm.

Serving Suggestions: Serve with a sprinkling of ground cinnamon.
Variation Tip: You can use these chips in a homemade trail mix.
Nutritional Information per Serving:
Calories: 32 | Fat: 0.1g|Sat Fat: 0g|Carbohydrates: 8.4g|Fiber: 0g|Sugar: 0g|Protein: 0.2g

Tortilla Chips

Prep Time: 10 minutes
Cook Time: 3 minutes
Serves: 3

Ingredients:

- 4 corn tortillas, cut into triangles
- 1 tablespoon olive oil
- Salt, to taste

Preparation:

1. Coat the tortilla chips with oil and then sprinkle each side of the tortillas with salt.
2. Press "Power" button of Ninja Foodi XL Pro Air Oven and select "Air Fry" function.
3. Press TEMP/SHADE +/- buttons to set the temperature at 390 degrees F.
4. Now press TIME/SLICES +/- buttons to set the cooking time to 3 minutes.
5. Press "START/STOP" button to start.
6. When the unit beeps to show that it is preheated, open the lid.
7. Arrange the tortilla chips in air fry basket and insert in the oven.
8. When cooking time is completed, open the lid and transfer the tortilla chips onto a platter.
9. Serve warm.

Serving Suggestions: Serve with guacamole.
Variation Tip: Use whole grain tortillas.
Nutritional Information per Serving:
Calories: 110 | Fat: 5.6g|Sat Fat: 0.8g|Carbohydrates: 14.3g|Fiber: 2g|Sugar: 0.3g|Protein: 1.8g

Spicy Carrot Fries

Prep Time: 10 minutes
Cook Time: 12 minutes
Serves: 2

Ingredients:

- 1 large carrot, peeled and cut into sticks
- 1 tablespoon fresh rosemary, chopped finely
- 1 tablespoon olive oil
- ¼ teaspoon cayenne pepper
- Salt and ground black pepper, as required

Preparation:

1. In a bowl, add all the ingredients and mix well.
2. Press "Power" button of Ninja Foodi XL Pro Air Oven and select "Air Fry" function.
3. Press TEMP/SHADE +/- buttons to set the temperature at 390 degrees F.
4. Now press TIME/SLICES +/- buttons to set the cooking time to 12 minutes.
5. Press "Start/Stop" button to start.
6. When the unit beeps to show that it is preheated, open the oven door.
7. Arrange the carrot fries into the air fry basket on Level 3.
8. When cooking time is completed, open the oven door and transfer the carrot fries onto a platter.
9. Serve warm.

Serving Suggestions: Serve with mustard sauce.
Variation Tip: You can add the spices of your choice.
Nutritional Information per Serving:
Calories: 81 | Fat: 8.3g|Sat Fat: 1.1g|Carbohydrates: 4.7g|Fiber: 1.7g|Sugar: 1.8g|Protein: 0.4g

Beet Chips

Prep Time: 10 minutes
Cook Time: 15 minutes
Serves: 6

Ingredients:

- 4 medium beetroots, peeled and thinly sliced
- 2 tablespoons olive oil
- ¼ teaspoon smoked paprika
- Salt, to taste

Preparation:

1. In a large bowl and mix together all the ingredients.
2. Press "Power" button of Ninja Foodi XL Pro Air Oven and select "Air Fry" function. Select 2 LEVEL.
3. Press TEMP/SHADE +/- buttons to set the temperature at 325 degrees F.
4. Now press TIME/SLICES +/- buttons to set the cooking time to 15 minutes.
5. Press "Start/Stop" button to start.
6. When the unit beeps to show that it is preheated, open the oven door.
7. Separate the beetroot chips into the air fry basket on Level 4 and sheet pan on Level 2.
8. Toss the beet chips once halfway through.
9. When cooking time is completed, open the oven door and transfer the beet chips onto a platter.
10. Serve at room temperature.

Serving Suggestions: Serve with a sprinkling of cinnamon.
Variation Tip: For a beautiful presentation, use colorful beets.
Nutritional Information per Serving:
Calories: 70 | Fat: 4.8g|Sat Fat: 0.7g|Carbohydrates: 6.7g|Fiber: 1.4g|Sugar: 5.3g|Protein: 1.1g

Crispy Prawns

Prep Time: 15 minutes
Cook Time: 8 minutes
Serves: 4

Ingredients:

- 1 egg
- ½ pound nacho chips, crushed
- 12 prawns, peeled and deveined

Preparation:

1. In a shallow dish, beat the egg.
2. In another shallow dish, place the crushed nacho chips.
3. Coat the prawn into egg and then roll into nacho chips.
4. Press "Power" button of Ninja Foodi XL Pro Air Oven and select "Air Fry" function.
5. Press TEMP/SHADE +/- buttons to set the temperature at 355 degrees F.
6. Now press TIME/SLICES +/- buttons to set the cooking time to 8 minutes.
7. Press "Start/Stop" button to start.
8. When the unit beeps to show that it is preheated, open the oven door.
9. Arrange the prawns into the air fry basket on Level 3.
10. When cooking time is completed, open the oven door and serve immediately.

Serving Suggestions: Serve alongside your favorite dip.
Variation Tip: Make sure to pat dry the shrimp thoroughly before applying the coating.
Nutritional Information per Serving:
Calories: 386 | Fat: 17g|Sat Fat: 2.9g|Carbohydrates: 36.1g|Fiber: 2.6g|Sugar: 2.2g|Protein: 21g

Potato Bread Rolls

Prep Time: 20 minutes
Cook Time: 33 minutes
Serves: 8

Ingredients:

- 5 large potatoes, peeled
- 2 tablespoons vegetable oil, divided
- 2 small onions, finely chopped
- 2 green chilies, seeded and chopped
- 2 curry leaves
- ½ teaspoon ground turmeric
- Salt, as required
- 8 bread slices, trimmed

Preparation:

1. In a pan of boiling water, add the potatoes and cook for about 15-20 minutes.
2. Drain the potatoes well and with a potato masher, mash the potatoes.
3. In a skillet, heat 1 teaspoon of oil over medium heat and sauté the onion for about 4-5 minutes.
4. Add the green chilies, curry leaves, and turmeric and sauté for about 1 minute.
5. Add the mashed potatoes and salt and mix well.
6. Remove from the heat and set aside to cool completely.
7. Make 8 equal-sized oval-shaped patties from the mixture.
8. Wet the bread slices completely with water.
9. Press each bread slice between your hands to remove the excess water.
10. Place 1 bread slice in your palm and place 1 patty in the center of the bread.
11. Roll the bread slice in a spindle shape and seal the edges to secure the filling.
12. Coat the roll with some oil.
13. Repeat with the remaining slices, filling and oil.
14. Press "Power" button of Ninja Foodi XL Pro Air Oven and select "Air Fry" function. Select 2 LEVEL.
15. Press TEMP/SHADE +/- buttons to set the temperature at 390 degrees F.
16. Now press TIME/SLICES +/- buttons to set the cooking time to 13 minutes.
17. Press "Start/Stop" button to start.
18. When the unit beeps to show that it is preheated, open the oven door.
19. Separate the bread rolls into the air fry basket on Level 4 and sheet pan on wire rack on Level 2.
20. When cooking time is completed, open the oven door and transfer the rolls onto a platter.
21. Serve warm.

Serving Suggestions: Serve alongside the ketchup.
Variation Tip: Remove the moisture from bread slices completely.
Nutritional Information per Serving:
Calories: 222 | Fat: 4g|Sat Fat: 0.8g|Carbohydrates: 42.5g|Fiber: 6.2g|Sugar: 3.8g|Protein: 4.8g

Spicy Spinach Chips

Prep Time: 10 minutes
Cook Time: 10 minutes
Serves: 4

Ingredients:

- 2 cups fresh spinach leaves, torn into bite-sized pieces
- ½ tablespoon coconut oil, melted
- ⅛ teaspoon garlic powder
- Salt, as required

Preparation:

1. In a large bowl, mix all the ingredients together.
2. Arrange the spinach pieces onto the greased sheet pan.
3. Press "Power" button of Ninja Foodi XL Pro Air Oven and select "Air Fry" function.
4. Press TEMP/SHADE +/- buttons to set the temperature at 300 degrees F.
5. Now press TIME/SLICES +/- buttons to set the cooking time to 10 minutes.
6. Press "START/STOP" button to start.
7. When the unit beeps to show that it is preheated, open the lid.

8. Insert the sheet pan in oven.
9. Toss the spinach chips once halfway through.
10. When cooking time is completed, open the lid and transfer the spinach chips onto a platter.
11. Serve warm.

Serving Suggestions: Serve with a sprinkling of cayenne pepper.

Variation Tip: Make sure to pat dry the spinach leaves before using.

Nutritional Information per Serving:
Calories: 18 | Fat: 1.5g|Sat Fat: 0g|Carbohydrates: 0.5g|Fiber: 0.3g|Sugar: 0.1g|Protein: 0.5g

Bacon-Wrapped Filled Jalapeno

Prep Time: 10 minutes
Cook Time: 15 minutes
Serves: 6

Ingredients:
- 12 jalapenos
- 226g cream cheese
- ½ cup cheddar cheese, shredded
- ¼ teaspoon garlic powder
- ⅛ teaspoon onion powder
- 12 slices bacon, thinly cut
- Salt and pepper, to taste

Preparation:
1. Discard the seeds from the jalapenos by cutting them in half and removing the stems.
2. Combine cream cheese, shredded cheddar cheese, garlic powder, onion powder, salt, and pepper. To blend, stir everything together.
3. Fill each jalapeno just to the top with the cream mixture using a tiny spoon.
4. Turn on Ninja Foodi XL Pro Air Oven and select "Bake".
5. Insert a wire rack on Level 3. Select the timer for 15 minute and temperature for 350 degrees F. Press START/STOP to begin.
6. Cut each slice of bacon in half.
7. Wrap one piece of bacon around each half of a jalapeño.
8. In the sheet pan, arrange the bacon-wrapped filled jalapenos in an even layer.
9. When the unit beep to signify it has preheated, slide the sheet pan on wire rack in the oven.
10. Serve and enjoy!

Serving Suggestions: Serve with ketchup.

Variation Tip: You can also sprinkle black pepper on top.

Nutritional Information per Serving:
Calories: 188 | Fat: 17g|Sat Fat: 10g|Carbohydrates: 4g|Fiber: 1g|Sugar: 3g|Protein: 5g

Tofu Nuggets

Prep Time: 10 minutes
Cook Time: 15 minutes
Serves: 4

Ingredients:
- 400g extra firm tofu
- ⅓ cup nutritional yeast
- ¼ cup water
- 1 tablespoon garlic powder
- 1 teaspoon onion powder
- 1 teaspoon sweet paprika
- 1 teaspoon poultry spice

Preparation:
1. Press the tofu for 10 minutes.
2. Add all ingredients to a bowl and stir to combine.
3. Over the bowl, break the tofu into bite-sized chunks. Use your thumb to create rough, rounded edges as you go.
4. Fold the chunks into the paste gently, taking care not to break the tofu.
5. Place the tofu in air fry basket in a single layer.
6. Turn on Ninja Foodi XL Pro Air Oven and select "Air Fry".
7. Select the timer for 15 minutes and the temperature for 350 degrees F.
8. When the unit beeps to signified it has preheated, quickly open the oven and slide the air fry basket into the rail of Level 3. Close the oven door and let it cook.
9. Halfway through, pause and shake the basket. Serve immediately or save for later.

Serving Suggestions: Serve with any sauce.

Variation Tip: You can use black pepper instead of paprika.

Nutritional Information per Serving:
Calories: 83 | Fat: 2g|Sat Fat: 1g|Carbohydrates: 6g|Fiber: 2g|Sugar: 1g|Protein: 11g

Fried Pickles

Prep Time: 10 minutes
Cook Time: 15 minutes
Serves: 4

Ingredients:

- ½ cup Italian style bread crumbs
- ½ cup panko bread crumbs
- ¼ cup parmesan cheese
- 1 tablespoon garlic powder
- 1 teaspoon Cajun seasoning
- 2 eggs
- 1½ cups dill pickles, sliced and drained
- Cooking spray

Preparation:

1. In a mixing bowl, combine Italian-style bread crumbs, Panko bread crumbs, Parmesan cheese, garlic powder, and Cajun spice.
2. Whisk together the eggs in a separate bowl.
3. Cover the slightly dry pickle slices completely with egg using a fork.
4. Dip the pickle slices in the breadcrumb mixture and completely coat them.
5. Using nonstick cooking spray, lightly coat the air fry basket. Place the pickle slices in the air fry basket gently.
6. Turn on Ninja Foodi XL Pro Air Oven and select "Air Fry".
7. Select the timer for 10 minutes and the temperature for 360 degrees F.
8. When the unit beeps to signify it has preheated, open the oven and slide the air fry basket into the rail of Level 3 in oven.
9. When the fried pickles are done, carefully remove them with tongs from the Ninja Foodi and serve.

Serving Suggestions: Serve with your favorite ranch dressing.

Variation Tip: You can use any pickle.

Nutritional Information per Serving:
Calories: 150 | Fat: 5g|Sat Fat: 2g|Carbohydrates: 17g|Fiber: 2g|Sugar: 2g|Protein: 8g

Zucchini Chips

Prep Time: 10 minutes
Cook Time: 13 minutes
Serves: 6

Ingredients:

- 2 large zucchinis, sliced
- ¾ cup panko bread crumbs
- 1 teaspoon Old bay
- 1 teaspoon garlic salt
- 1 egg, beaten
- Olive oil spray

Preparation:

1. Combine the panko and seasoning on a dish and stir well.
2. In a separate bowl, whisk the egg.
3. Dip zucchini slices in the egg one at a time, then coat with the bread crumb mixture on all sides.
4. Using olive oil cooking spray, lightly coat the air fry basket and roast tray. Place the zucchini in the air fry basket and roast tray gently.
5. Turn on Ninja Foodi XL Pro Air Oven and select "Air Fry". Select 2 LEVEL.
6. Select the timer for 13 minutes and the temperature for 350 degrees F.
7. When the unit beeps to signify it has preheated, slide your air fry basket into rail of Level 4 and roast tray on the sheet pan into rail of Level 2.
8. Remove and enjoy immediately.

Serving Suggestions: Serve with any sauce.

Variation Tip: You can skip old bay and use pepper.

Nutritional Information per Serving:
Calories: 41 | Fat: 1g|Sat Fat: 1g|Carbohydrates: 6g|Fiber: 1g|Sugar: 1g|Protein: 2g

Baked Mozzarella Sticks

Prep Time: 5 minutes
Cook Time: 8 minutes
Serves: 6

Ingredients:

- ½ cup Italian Style bread crumbs
- ¾ cup panko break crumbs
- ¼ cup parmesan cheese
- 1 tablespoon garlic powder
- 12 mozzarella cheese sticks
- Cooking spray

Preparation:

1. Make mozzarella sticks by freezing them for an hour or two. Take the mozzarella sticks out of the fridge and cut them in half so that each one is 2-3 inches long.
2. Combine the Panko, Italian Style bread crumbs, parmesan cheese, and garlic powder on a dish and stir well.
3. Whisk together the eggs in a separate bowl.
4. Cover the mozzarella stick completely with egg with a fork, then dip and totally cover the mozzarella stick in the breadcrumb mixture.
5. On a nonstick pan, arrange mozzarella sticks in a single layer.
6. Freeze for an hour and take the mozzarella sticks out of the freezer and dip them in the egg and breadcrumb mixture once more.
7. Using cooking spray, lightly coat the roast tray. Place the cheese sticks.
8. Insert the wire rack on Level 3. Turn on Ninja Foodi XL Pro Air Oven and select "Bake".
9. Select the timer for 10 minutes and the temperature for 360 degrees F.
10. When the unit beeps to signify it has preheated, slide the roast tray onto the wire rack in the oven.
11. Remove and serve.

Serving Suggestions: Serve with marinara sauce.
Variation Tip: You can use any cheese sticks.
Nutritional Information per Serving:
Calories: 130 | Fat: 8g|Sat Fat: 4g|Carbohydrates: 7g|Fiber: 1g|Sugar: 1g|Protein: 9g

Corn on the Cob

Prep Time: 5 minutes
Cook Time: 13 minutes
Serves: 2

Ingredients:

- 2 ears corn
- 2 tablespoons butter, melted
- ½ teaspoon dried parsley
- ¼ teaspoon sea salt
- 2 tablespoons parmesan cheese, shredded

Preparation:

1. Remove any silk from both ears of corn. If desired, cut corns in half.
2. In a mixing dish, combine melted butter, parsley, and sea salt. Using a pastry brush, evenly coat the corn. If used, wrap corn with foil.
3. Place corn inside the roast tray side by side.
4. Turn on Ninja Foodi XL Pro Air Oven and select "Air Roast".
5. Select the timer for 12 minutes and the temperature for 350 degrees F.
6. When the unit beeps to signify it has preheated, slide the roast tray on the sheet pan into the rail of Level 3. Close the oven door and let it cook.
7. Remove from the Ninja Foodi XL Pro Air Oven to serve hot.

Serving Suggestions: Top with fresh parsley.
Variation Tip: You can use any cheese.
Nutritional Information per Serving:
Calories: 199 | Fat: 14g|Sat Fat: 8g|Carbohydrates: 17g|Fiber: 2g|Sugar: 4g|Protein: 5g

Air Fryer Ravioli

Prep Time: 5 minutes
Cook Time: 10 minutes
Serves: 2
Ingredients:
- 12 frozen ravioli
- ½ cup buttermilk
- ½ cup Italian breadcrumbs
- Cooking oil

Preparation:
1. Place two bowls next to each other. In one bowl, put the buttermilk, and in the other, put the breadcrumbs.
2. Dip Each ravioli piece in buttermilk and then breadcrumbs, making sure it is well coated.
3. Place each breaded ravioli in a single layer in the air fry basket and spritz the tops halfway through with oil.
4. Turn on Ninja Foodi XL Pro Air Oven and select "Air Fry".
5. Select the timer for 7 minutes and the temperature for 400 degrees F.
6. When the unit beeps to signify it has preheated, open the oven and slide the air fry basket into the rail of Level 3. Close the oven and let it cook.
7. Remove from the Ninja Foodi XL Pro Air Oven to serve hot.

Serving Suggestions: Top with fresh parsley.
Variation Tip: You can serve with garlic sauce.
Nutritional Information per Serving:
Calories: 481 | Fat: 20g|Sat Fat: 7g|Carbohydrates: 56g|Fiber: 4g|Sugar: 9g|Protein: 20g

French Toast Bites

Prep Time: 5 minutes
Cook Time: 10 minutes
Serves: 2
Ingredients:
- ½ loaf of brioche bread
- 3 eggs
- 1 tablespoon milk
- 1 teaspoon vanilla
- ½ teaspoon cinnamon

Preparation:
1. In a large mixing bowl, cut half a loaf of bread into cubes.
2. Combine the eggs, milk, vanilla, and cinnamon in a small mixing dish.
3. Pour the mixture over the slices and toss to coat.
4. In a greased air fry basket, arrange bread slices in a single layer.
5. Place on the Level 3 in the oven.
6. Turn on Ninja Foodi XL Pro Air Oven and select "Air Fry".
7. Select the timer for 10 minutes and the temperature for 390 degrees F.
8. Remove from the Ninja Foodi XL Pro Air Oven to serve.

Serving Suggestions: Top with maple syrup.
Variation Tip: Sprinkle sugar on top before placing it in the oven.
Nutritional Information per Serving:
Calories: 107 | Fat: 6.8g|Sat Fat: 2.1g|Carbohydrates: 1.9g|Fiber: 0.3g|Sugar: 1.1g|Protein: 8.6g

Sweet Potato Fries

Prep Time: 10 minutes
Cook Time: 15 minutes
Serves: 4
Ingredients:
- 3 sweet potatoes, cut into fries
- 2 tablespoons olive oil
- ½ teaspoon salt
- ¼ teaspoon black pepper
- ½ teaspoon garlic powder

Preparation:
1. Slice sweet potatoes into 1/2- to 1/4-inch-thick French fry slices.
2. Using olive oil cooking spray, lightly coat the air fry basket.
3. Pour the olive oil, salt, pepper, paprika, and garlic powder over the sweet potatoes in a mixing bowl.

4. To coat them, combine them thoroughly.
5. Place each sweet potato fry in the roast tray in a uniform layer.
6. Place the roast tray on sheet pan into rail of Level 3.
7. Turn on Ninja Foodi XL Pro Air Oven and select "Broil".
8. Select the unit for 12 minutes at LO.
9. Serve immediately after cooking.

Serving Suggestions: Serve with favorite dipping sauce.
Variation Tip: Sprinkle fresh parsley on top.
Nutritional Information per Serving:
Calories: 230 | Fat: 11|Sat Fat: 2g|Carbohydrates: 30g|Fiber: 4g|Sugar: 6g|Protein: 3g

Butternut Squash

Prep Time: 10 minutes
Cook Time: 20 minutes
Serves: 4

Ingredients:

- 4 cups butternut squash, cubed
- 1 teaspoon cinnamon
- Olive oil cooking spray

Preparation:

1. Spray the air fry basket or line it with foil and spray it with olive oil cooking spray.
2. Place the butternut squash in the basket.
3. Coat with olive oil and sprinkle with cinnamon.
4. Insert the wire rack on Level 3.Turn on Ninja Foodi XL Pro Air Oven and select "Bake".
5. Select the timer for 20 minutes and the temperature for 390 degrees F.
6. When the unit beeps to signify it has preheated, open the oven and place the air fry basket on the wire rack. Close the oven and let it cook.
7. Serve immediately after cooking.

Serving Suggestions: Top with freshly grounded cinnamon.
Variation Tip: You can skip the cinnamon.
Nutritional Information per Serving:
Calories: 57 | Fat: 2g|Sat Fat: 0g|Carbohydrates: 11g|Fiber: 3g|Sugar: 2g|Protein: 1g

Chicken & Parmesan Nuggets

Prep Time: 15 minutes
Cook Time: 10 minutes
Serves: 6

Ingredients:

- 2 large chicken breasts, cut into 1-inch cubes
- 1 cup breadcrumbs
- ⅓ tablespoon Parmesan cheese, shredded
- 1 teaspoon onion powder
- ¼ teaspoon smoked paprika
- Salt and ground black pepper, as required

Preparation:

1. In a large resealable bag, add all the ingredients.
2. Seal the bag and shake well to coat completely.
3. Press "Power" button of Ninja Foodi XL Pro Air Oven and select "Air Fry" function. Select 2 LEVEL.
4. Press TEMP/SHADE +/- buttons to set the temperature at 400 degrees F.
5. Now press TIME/SLICES +/- buttons to set the cooking time to 10 minutes.
6. Press "Start/Stop" button to start.
7. When the unit beeps to show that it is preheated, open the oven door.
8. Separate the nuggets into the air fry basket on Level 3 and Ninja sheet pan on Level 1.
9. When cooking time is completed, open the oven door and transfer the nuggets onto a platter.
10. Serve warm.

Serving Suggestions: Serve with mustard sauce.
Variation Tip: Prefer to use freshly grated cheese.
Nutritional Information per Serving:
Calories: 218 | Fat: 6.6g|Sat Fat: 1.8g|Carbohydrates: 13.3g|Fiber: 0.9g|Sugar: 1.3g|Protein: 24.4g

Primavera Chicken

Prep Time: 15 minutes.
Cook Time: 25 minutes.
Serves: 4

Ingredients:

- 4 chicken breasts, boneless
- 1 zucchini, sliced
- 3 medium tomatoes, sliced
- 2 yellow bell peppers, sliced
- ½ red onion, sliced
- 2 tablespoons olive oil
- 1 teaspoon Italian seasoning
- Kosher salt, to taste
- Freshly ground black pepper, to taste
- 1 cup shredded mozzarella
- Freshly chopped parsley for garnish

Preparation:

1. Carve one side slit in the chicken breasts and stuff them with all the veggies.
2. Place these stuffed chicken breasts in a casserole dish, then drizzle oil, Italian seasoning, black pepper, salt, and Mozzarella over the chicken.
3. Transfer the dish to the 2nd rack position of Ninja Foodi XL Pro Air Oven and close the door.
4. Select the "Bake" Mode using FUNCTION +/- buttons and select Rack Level 2.
5. Set its cooking time to 25 minutes and temperature to 370 degrees F, then press "START/STOP" to initiate cooking.
6. Garnish with parsley and serve warm.

Serving Suggestion: Serve chicken with a kale salad on the side.

Variation Tip: Brush the chicken with pesto before baking.

Nutritional Information Per Serving:
Calories 445 | Fat 25g |Sodium 122mg | Carbs 13g | Fiber 0.4g | Sugar 1g | Protein 33g

Roasted Duck

Prep Time: 15 minutes.
Cook Time: 3 hours
Serves: 6

Ingredients:

- 6 pounds whole Pekin duck
- Salt, to taste
- 5 garlic cloves chopped
- 1 lemon, chopped

Glaze

- ½ cup balsamic vinegar
- 1 lemon, juiced
- ¼ cup honey

Preparation:

1. Place the Pekin duck in a baking tray and add garlic, lemon, and salt on top.
2. Whisk honey, vinegar, and lemon juice in a bowl.
3. Brush this glaze over the duck liberally. Marinate overnight in the refrigerator.
4. Remove the duck from the marinade and move the duck to a sheet pan in the Ninja Foodi Air Fryer Oven.
5. Transfer the sandwich to the 1st rack position of Ninja Foodi XL Pro Air Oven and close the door.
6. Select the "Air Roast" Mode using FUNCTION +/- buttons and select Rack Level 1.
7. Set its cooking time to 3 hours and temperature to 350 degrees F, then press "START/STOP" to initiate cooking.
8. Serve warm.

Serving Suggestion: Serve the duck with roasted green beans and mashed potatoes.

Variation Tip: Stuff the duck with the bread stuffing before baking.

Nutritional Information Per Serving:
Calories 465 | Fat 5g |Sodium 422mg | Carbs 16g | Fiber 0g | Sugar 1g | Protein 25g

Blackened Chicken Bake

Prep Time: 15 minutes.
Cook Time: 18 minutes.
Serves: 4

Ingredients:
- 4 chicken breasts
- 2 teaspoons olive oil

Seasoning:
- 1 ½ tablespoons brown sugar
- 1 teaspoon paprika
- 1 teaspoon dried oregano
- ¼ teaspoons garlic powder
- ½ teaspoons salt and pepper

Garnish:
- Chopped parsley

Preparation:

1. Mix olive oil with brown sugar, paprika, oregano, garlic powder, salt, and black pepper in a bowl.
2. Place the chicken breasts in the sheet pan of the Ninja Foodi XL Pro Air Oven.
3. Transfer the sheet pan to the 2nd rack position of Ninja Foodi XL Pro Air Oven and close the door.
4. Select the "Bake" Mode using FUNCTION +/- buttons and select Rack Level 2.
5. Set its cooking time to 18 minutes and temperature to 425 degrees F, then press "START/STOP" to initiate cooking.
6. Serve warm.

Serving Suggestion: Serve the chicken bake with roasted veggies.

Variation Tip: Sprinkle the breadcrumbs on top of the chicken before baking.

Nutritional Information Per Serving:
Calories 419 | Fat 14g |Sodium 442mg | Carbs 23g | Fiber 0.4g | Sugar 2g | Protein 32.3g

Parmesan Chicken Meatballs

Prep Time: 15 minutes.
Cook Time: 12 minutes.
Serves: 4

Ingredients:
- 1 pound ground chicken
- 1 large egg, beaten
- ½ cup Parmesan cheese, grated
- ½ cup pork rinds, ground
- 1 teaspoon garlic powder
- 1 teaspoon paprika
- 1 teaspoon kosher salt
- ½ teaspoon pepper

Crust:
- ½ cup pork rinds, ground

Preparation:

1. Toss all the meatball ingredients in a bowl and mix well.
2. Make small meatballs out of this mixture and roll them in the pork rinds.
3. Place the coated meatballs in the air fry basket.
4. Transfer the basket to the 2nd rack position of Ninja Foodi XL Pro Air Oven and close the door.
5. Select the "Bake" Mode using FUNCTION +/- buttons and select Rack Level 2.
6. Set its cooking time to 12 minutes and temperature to 400 degrees F, then press "START/STOP" to initiate cooking.
7. Serve warm.

Serving Suggestion: Serve the meatballs with fresh herbs on top and a bowl of steamed rice.

Variation Tip: Use crushed oats to the meatballs for a crispy texture.

Nutritional Information Per Serving:
Calories 486 | Fat 13g |Sodium 611mg | Carbs 15g | Fiber 0g | Sugar g4 | Protein 26g

Brine-Soaked Turkey

Prep Time: 15 minutes.
Cook Time: 60 minutes.
Serves: 4

Ingredients:

- 7 pounds bone-in, skin-on turkey breast

Brine

- ½ cup salt
- 1 lemon
- ½ onion
- 3 cloves garlic, smashed
- 5 sprigs fresh thyme
- 3 bay leaves
- black pepper

Turkey Breast

- 4 tablespoons butter, softened
- ½ teaspoon black pepper
- ½ teaspoon garlic powder
- ¼ teaspoon dried thyme
- ¼ teaspoon dried oregano

Preparation:

1. Mix the turkey brine ingredients in a pot and soak the turkey in the brine overnight.
2. The next day, remove the soaked turkey from the brine.
3. Whisk the butter, black pepper, garlic powder, oregano, and thyme.
4. Brush the butter mixture over the turkey, then place it in a roast tray.
5. Transfer the tray to the 2nd rack position of Ninja Foodi XL Pro Air Oven and close the door.
6. Select the "Air Roast" Mode using FUNCTION +/- buttons and select Rack Level 2.
7. Set its cooking time to 60 minutes and temperature to 375 degrees F, then press "START/STOP" to initiate cooking.
8. Slice and serve warm.

Serving Suggestion: Serve the turkey with fresh cucumber and couscous salad.

Variation Tip: Brush the turkey with orange juice for a refreshing taste.

Nutritional Information Per Serving:
Calories 553 | Fat 2.4g |Sodium 216mg | Carbs 18g | Fiber 2.3g | Sugar 1.2g | Protein 23.2g

Deviled Chicken

Prep Time: 15 minutes.
Cook Time: 40 minutes.
Serves: 8

Ingredients:

- 2 tablespoons butter
- 2 cloves garlic, chopped
- 1 cup Dijon mustard
- ½ teaspoon cayenne pepper
- 1 ½ cups panko breadcrumbs
- ¾ cup Parmesan, freshly grated
- ¼ cup chives, chopped
- 2 teaspoons paprika
- 8 small bone-in chicken thighs, skin removed

Preparation:

1. Toss the chicken thighs with crumbs, cheese, chives, butter, and spices in a bowl and mix well to coat.
2. Transfer the chicken along with its spice mix to a sheet pan.
3. Transfer the pan to the 3rd rack position of Ninja Foodi XL Pro Air Oven and close the door.
4. Select the "Air Fry" Mode using FUNCTION +/- buttons and select Rack Level 3.
5. Set its cooking time to 40 minutes and temperature to 375 degrees F, then press "START/STOP" to initiate cooking.
6. Serve warm.

Serving Suggestion: Serve the chicken fried rice or sautéed vegetable.

Variation Tip: Coat the chicken with crushed cornflakes for a crispy texture.

Nutritional Information Per Serving:
Calories 497 | Fat 14g |Sodium 364mg | Carbs 8g | Fiber 1g | Sugar 3g | Protein 32g

Herbed Turkey Legs

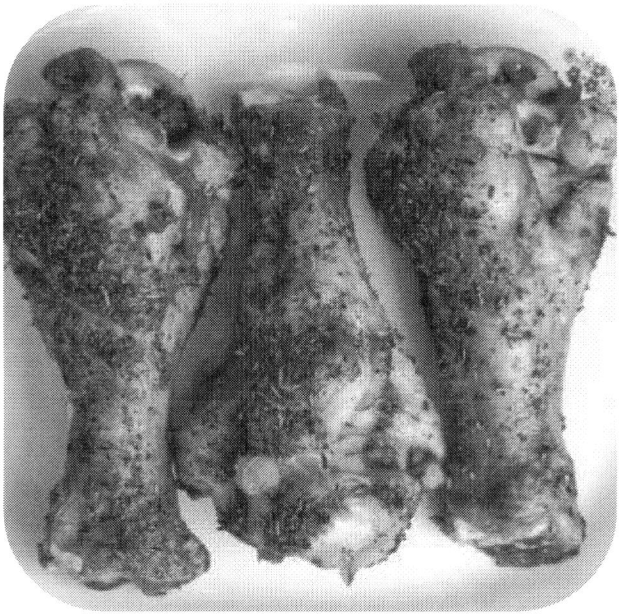

Prep Time: 15 minutes
Cook Time: 30 minutes
Serves: 2

Ingredients:

- 1 tablespoon butter, melted
- 2 garlic cloves, minced
- ¼ teaspoon dried rosemary
- ¼ teaspoon dried thyme
- ¼ teaspoon dried oregano
- Salt and ground black pepper, as required
- 2 turkey legs

Preparation:

1. In a large bowl, mix together the butter, garlic, herbs, salt, and black pepper.
2. Add the turkey legs and coat with mixture generously.
3. Press "Power" button of Ninja Foodi XL Pro Air Oven and select "Air Fry" function.
4. Press TEMP/SHADE +/- buttons to set the temperature at 350 degrees F.
5. Now press TIME/SLICES +/- buttons to set the cooking time to 27 minutes.
6. Press "Start/Stop" button to start.
7. When the unit beeps to show that it is preheated, open the oven door.
8. Arrange the turkey wings into the greased air fry basket and insert into rail of Level 3.
9. When the cooking time is completed, open the oven door and serve hot.

Serving Suggestions: Serve with cabbage slaw.
Variation Tip: Use unsalted butter.
Nutritional Information per Serving:
Calories: 592 | Fat: 22g|Sat Fat: 8.7g|Carbohydrates: 1.3g|Fiber: 0.3g|Sugar: 0g|Protein: 91.6g

Feta Turkey Burgers

Prep Time: 10 minutes
Cook Time: 15 minutes
Serves: 2

Ingredients:

- 8 ounces ground turkey breast
- 1½ tablespoons extra-virgin olive oil
- 2 garlic cloves, grated
- 2 teaspoons fresh oregano, chopped
- ½ teaspoon red pepper flakes, crushed
- Salt, as required
- ¼ cup feta cheese, crumbled

Preparation:

1. In a large bowl, add all the ingredients except for cheese and mix until well combined.
2. Make 2 (½-inch-thick) patties from the mixture.
3. Press "Power" button of Ninja Foodi XL Pro Air Oven and select "Air Fry" function.
4. Press TEMP/SHADE +/- buttons to set the temperature at 360 degrees F.
5. Now press TIME/SLICES +/- buttons to set the cooking time to 15 minutes.
6. Press "Start/Stop" button to start.
7. When the unit beeps to show that it is preheated, open the oven door.
8. Arrange the patties into the greased air fry basket and insert into the rail of Level 3.
9. Flip the turkey burgers once halfway through.
10. When the cooking time is completed, open the oven door and serve hot with the topping of feta.

Serving Suggestions: Serve with fresh greens.
Variation Tip: Try adding some dry breadcrumbs to the turkey mixture before you shape the patties.
Nutritional Information per Serving:
Calories: 364 | Fat: 23.1g|Sat Fat: 6.7g|Carbohydrates: 3g|Fiber: 0.8g|Sugar: 0.9g|Protein: 35.6g

Spiced Turkey Breast

Prep Time: 10 minutes
Cook Time: 45 minutes
Serves: 8

Ingredients:

- 2 tablespoons fresh rosemary, chopped
- 1 teaspoon ground cumin
- 1 teaspoon ground cinnamon
- 1 teaspoon smoked paprika
- 1 teaspoon cayenne pepper
- Salt and ground black pepper, as required
- 1 (3-pound) turkey breast

Preparation:

1. In a bowl, mix together the rosemary, spices, salt and black pepper.
2. Rub the turkey breast with rosemary mixture evenly.
3. With kitchen twines, tie the turkey breast to keep it compact.
4. Press "Power" button of Ninja Foodi XL Pro Air Oven and select "Air Fry" function.
5. Press TEMP/SHADE +/- buttons to set the temperature at 360 degrees F.
6. Now press TIME/SLICES +/- buttons to set the cooking time to 45 minutes.
7. Press "Start/Stop" button to start.
8. When the unit beeps to show that it is preheated, open the oven door.
9. Arrange the turkey breast into the greased air fry basket on Level 3.
10. When the cooking time is completed, open the oven door and place the turkey breast onto a platter for about 5-10 minutes before slicing.
11. With a sharp knife, cut the turkey breast into desired sized slices and serve.

Serving Suggestions: Serve alongside the cranberry sauce.

Variation Tip: Season the turkey breast generously.

Nutritional Information per Serving:

Calories: 190 | Fat: 0.9g|Sat Fat: 0.1g|Carbohydrates: 0.9g|Fiber: 0.5g|Sugar: 6g|Protein: 29.5g

Simple Turkey Wings

Prep Time: 10 minutes
Cook Time: 26 minutes
Serves: 4

Ingredients:

- 2 pounds turkey wings
- 4 tablespoons chicken rub
- 3 tablespoons olive oil

Preparation:

1. In a large bowl, add the turkey wings, chicken rub and olive oil and toss to coat well.
2. Press "Power" button of Ninja Foodi XL Pro Air Oven and select "Air Fry" function.
3. Press TEMP/SHADE +/- buttons to set the temperature at 380 degrees F.
4. Now press TIME/SLICES +/- buttons to set the cooking time to 26 minutes.
5. Press "Start/Stop" button to start.
6. When the unit beeps to show that it is preheated, open the oven door.
7. Arrange the turkey wings into the greased air fry basket on Level 3.
8. Flip the turkey wings once halfway through.
9. When the cooking time is completed, open the oven door and serve hot.

Serving Suggestions: Serve alongside the yogurt sauce.

Variation Tip: You can use seasoning of your choice.

Nutritional Information per Serving:

Calories: 558 | Fat: 38.9g|Sat Fat: 1.5g|Carbohydrates: 3g|Fiber: 0g|Sugar: 0g|Protein: 46.6g

Chicken and Rice Casserole

Prep Time: 15 minutes.
Cook Time: 25 minutes.
Serves: 4

Ingredients:

- 2 pounds bone-in chicken thighs
- Salt and black pepper
- 1 teaspoon olive oil
- 5 cloves garlic, chopped
- 2 large onions, chopped
- 2 large red bell peppers, chopped
- 1 tablespoon sweet Hungarian paprika
- 1 teaspoon hot Hungarian paprika
- 2 tablespoons tomato paste
- 2 cups chicken broth
- 3 cups brown rice, thawed
- 2 tablespoons parsley, chopped
- 6 tablespoons sour cream

Preparation:

1. Season and rub the chicken with black pepper, salt, and olive oil.
2. Sear the chicken in a skillet for 5 minutes per side, then transfer to a casserole dish.
3. Sauté onion in the same skillet until soft.
4. Toss in garlic, peppers, and paprika, then sauté for 3 minutes.
5. Stir in tomato paste, chicken broth, and rice.
6. Mix well and cook until rice is soft, then add sour cream and parsley.
7. Spread the mixture over the chicken in the casserole dish.
8. Transfer the dish to the 2nd rack position of Ninja Foodi XL Pro Air Oven and close the door.
9. Transfer the sandwich to the 2nd rack position of Ninja Foodi XL Pro Air Oven and close the door.
10. Select the "Bake" Mode using FUNCTION +/- buttons and select Rack Level 2.
11. Set its cooking time to 10 minutes and temperature to 375 degrees F, then press "START/STOP" to initiate cooking.
12. Serve warm.

Serving Suggestion: Serve the chicken casserole with toasted bread slices.
Variation Tip: Add corn kernels to the chicken casserole.
Nutritional Information Per Serving:
Calories 454 | Fat 25g |Sodium 412mg | Carbs 22g | Fiber 0.2g | Sugar 1g | Protein 28.3g

Roasted Goose

Prep Time: 15 minutes.
Cook Time: 40 minutes.
Serves: 12

Ingredients:

- 8 pounds goose
- Juice of a lemon
- Salt and pepper
- ½ yellow onion, peeled and chopped
- 1 head garlic, peeled and chopped
- ½ cup wine
- 1 teaspoon dried thyme

Preparation:

1. Place the goose in a roast tray and whisk the rest of the ingredients in a bowl.
2. Pour this thick sauce over the goose and brush it liberally.
3. Transfer the goose to the 2nd rack position of Ninja Foodi XL Pro Air Oven and close the door.
4. Select the "Air Roast" Mode using FUNCTION +/- buttons and select Rack Level 2.
5. Set its cooking time to 40 minutes and temperature to 355 degrees F, then press "START/STOP" to initiate cooking.
6. Serve warm.

Serving Suggestion: Serve the Goose with cucumber salad and toasted bread slices.
Variation Tip: Add butter sauce on top of the goose before cooking.
Nutritional Information Per Serving:
Calories 449 | Fat 13g |Sodium 432mg | Carbs 31g | Fiber 3g | Sugar 1g | Protein 23g

Chicken Potato Bake

Prep Time: 15 minutes.
Cook Time: 25 minutes.
Serves: 4

Ingredients:

- 4 potatoes, diced
- 1 tablespoon garlic, minced
- 1.5 tablespoons olive oil
- ⅛ teaspoon salt
- ⅛ teaspoon pepper
- 1.5 pounds boneless skinless chicken
- ¾ cup mozzarella cheese, shredded
- parsley, chopped

Preparation:

1. Toss chicken and potatoes with all the spices and oil in a sheet pan.
2. Drizzle the cheese on top of the chicken and potato.
3. Transfer the pan to the 2nd rack position of Ninja Foodi XL Pro Air Oven and close the door.
4. Select the "Bake" Mode using FUNCTION +/- buttons and select Rack Level 2.
5. Set its cooking time to 25 minutes and temperature to 375 degrees F, then press "START/STOP" to initiate cooking.
6. Serve warm.

Serving Suggestion: Serve the chicken potato bake with avocado guacamole.

Variation Tip: Add sliced eggplant instead of potatoes for a change of taste.

Nutritional Information Per Serving:
Calories 462 | Fat 14g |Sodium 220mg | Carbs 16g | Fiber 0.2g | Sugar 1g | Protein 26g

Spanish Chicken Bake

Prep Time: 15 minutes.
Cook Time: 25 minutes.
Serves: 4

Ingredients:

- ½ onion, quartered
- ½ red onion, quartered
- ½ pound potatoes, quartered
- 4 garlic cloves
- 4 tomatoes, quartered
- ⅛ cup chorizo
- ¼ teaspoons paprika powder
- 4 chicken thighs, boneless
- ¼ teaspoons dried oregano
- ½ green bell pepper, julienned
- Salt, to taste
- Black pepper, to taste

Preparation:

1. Toss chicken, veggies, and all the ingredients in a roast tray.
2. Transfer the tray to the 2nd rack position of Ninja Foodi XL Pro Air Oven and close the door.
3. Select the "Bake" Mode using FUNCTION +/- buttons and select Rack Level 2.
4. Set its cooking time to 25 minutes and temperature to 425 degrees F, then press "START/STOP" to initiate cooking.
5. Serve warm.

Serving Suggestion: Serve the chicken bake with warmed pita bread.

Variation Tip: Add canned corns to the casserole before cooking.

Nutritional Information Per Serving:
Calories 478 | Fat 8g |Sodium 339mg | Carbs 28g | Fiber 1g | Sugar 2g | Protein 33g

Creamy Chicken Casserole

Prep Time: 15 minutes.
Cook Time: 47 minutes.
Serves: 4

Ingredients:

Chicken Mushroom Casserole

- 2 ½ pounds chicken breasts, sliced
- 1 ½ teaspoons salt
- ¼ teaspoon black pepper
- 1 cup all-purpose flour
- 6 tablespoons olive oil
- 1 pound white mushrooms, sliced
- 1 medium onion, diced
- 3 garlic cloves, minced

Sauce

- 3 tablespoons unsalted butter
- 3 tablespoons all-purpose flour
- 1 ½ cups chicken broth/½ cup milk, optional
- 1 tablespoon lemon juice
- 1 cup half and half cream

Preparation:

1. Butter a casserole dish and toss in chicken with mushrooms and all the casserole ingredients.
2. Prepare its sauce in a suitable pan. Add butter and melt over moderate heat.
3. Stir in flour and whisk well for 2 minutes, then pour in milk/chicken broth, lemon juice, and cream.
4. Mix well and pour this creamy white sauce over the chicken mix in the casserole dish.
5. Transfer the dish to the 2nd rack position of Ninja Foodi XL Pro Air Oven and close the door.
6. Select the "Bake" Mode using FUNCTION +/- buttons and select Rack Level 2.
7. Set its cooking time to 45 minutes and temperature to 350 degrees F, then press "START/STOP" to initiate cooking.
8. Serve warm.

Serving Suggestion: Serve the creamy chicken casserole with steaming white rice.

Variation Tip: Drizzle breadcrumbs on top of the casserole before baking.

Nutritional Information Per Serving:
Calories 601 | Fat 16g |Sodium 189mg | Carbs 32g | Fiber 0.3g | Sugar 0.1g | Protein 28.2g

Gingered Chicken Drumsticks

Prep Time: 10 minutes
Cook Time: 25 minutes
Serves: 3

Ingredients:

- ¼ cup full-fat coconut milk
- 2 teaspoons fresh ginger, minced
- 2 teaspoons galangal, minced
- 2 teaspoons ground turmeric
- Salt, as required
- 3 (6-ounce) chicken drumsticks

Preparation:

1. Place the coconut milk, galangal, ginger, and spices in a large bowl and mix well.
2. Add the chicken drumsticks and coat with the marinade generously.
3. Refrigerate to marinate for at least 6-8 hours.
4. Now press TIME/SLICES +/- buttons to set the cooking time to 25 minutes.
5. Press "Power" button of Ninja Foodi XL Pro Air Oven and select "Air Fry" function.
6. Press TEMP/SHADE +/- buttons to set the temperature at 375 degrees F.
7. Press "START/STOP" button to start.
8. When the unit beeps to show that it is preheated, open the lid and grease the air fry basket.
9. Place the chicken drumsticks into the prepared air fry basket and insert in the oven.
10. When cooking time is completed, open the lid and serve hot.

Serving Suggestions: Serve alongside the lemony couscous.

Variation Tip: Coconut milk can be replaced with cream.

Nutritional Information per Serving:
Calories: 347 | Fat: 14.8g|Sat Fat: 6.9g|Carbohydrates: 3.8g|Fiber: 1.1g|Sugar: 0.8g|Protein: 47.6g

Parmesan Crusted Chicken Breasts

Prep Time: 15 minutes
Cook Time: 15 minutes
Serves: 4

Ingredients:

- 2 large chicken breasts
- 1 cup mayonnaise
- 1 cup Parmesan cheese, shredded
- 1 cup panko breadcrumbs

Preparation:

1. Cut each chicken breast in half and then with a meat mallet pound each into even thickness.
2. Spread the mayonnaise on both sides of each chicken piece evenly.
3. In a shallow bowl, mix together the Parmesan and breadcrumbs.
4. Coat the chicken piece Parmesan mixture evenly.
5. Press "Power" button of Ninja Foodi XL Pro Air Oven and select "Air Fry" function.
6. Press TEMP/SHADE +/- buttons to set the temperature at 390 degrees F.
7. Now press TIME/SLICES +/- buttons to set the cooking time to 15 minutes.
8. Press "Start/Stop" button to start.
9. When the unit beeps to show that it is pre-heated, open the oven door.
10. Arrange the chicken pieces into the greased air fry basket and slide the basket into the rail of Level 3.
11. After 10 minutes of cooking, flip the chicken pieces once.
12. When the cooking time is completed, open the oven door and serve hot.

Serving Suggestions: Serve with ranch dip.
Variation Tip: Use real mayonnaise.
Nutritional Information per Serving:
Calories: 625 | Fat: 35.4g|Sat Fat: 9.4g|Carbohydrates: 18.8g|Fiber: 0.1g|Sugar: 3.8g|Protein: 41.6g

Bacon-Wrapped Chicken Breasts

Prep Time: 10 minutes
Cook Time: 35 minutes
Serves: 2

Ingredients:

- 2 (5- to 6-ounce) boneless, skinless chicken breasts
- ½ teaspoon smoked paprika
- ½ teaspoon garlic powder
- Salt and ground black pepper, as required
- 4 thin bacon slices

Preparation:

1. With a meat mallet, pound each chicken breast into ¾-inch thickness.
2. In a bowl, mix together the paprika, garlic powder, salt and black pepper.
3. Rub the chicken breasts with spice mixture evenly.
4. Wrap each chicken breast with bacon strips.
5. Press "Power" button of Ninja Foodi XL Pro Air Oven and select "Air Fry" function.
6. Press TEMP/SHADE +/- buttons to set the temperature at 400 degrees F.
7. Now press TIME/SLICES +/- buttons to set the cooking time to 35 minutes.
8. Press "Start/Stop" button to start.
9. When the unit beeps to show that it is pre-heated, open the oven door.
10. Arrange the chicken pieces into the greased air fry basket and slide the basket into rail of Level 3.
11. When the cooking time is completed, open the oven door and serve hot.

Serving Suggestions: Serve with fresh baby greens.
Variation Tip: Secure the wrapping of bacon with toothpicks.
Nutritional Information per Serving:
Calories: 293 | Fat: 17.4g|Sat Fat: 5.4g|Carbohydrates: 0.8g|Fiber: 0.1g|Sugar: 0.1g|Protein: 31.3g

Herbed Chicken Thighs

Prep Time: 10 minutes
Cook Time: 20 minutes
Serves: 4

Ingredients:

- ½ tablespoon fresh rosemary, minced
- ½ tablespoon fresh thyme, minced
- Salt and ground black pepper, as required
- 4 (5-ounce) chicken thighs
- 2 tablespoons olive oil

Preparation:

1. In a large bowl, add the herbs, salt and black pepper and mix well.
2. Coat the chicken thighs with oil and then, rub with herb mixture.
3. Arrange the chicken thighs onto the greased sheet pan.
4. Press "Power" button of Ninja Foodi XL Pro Air Oven and select "Air Fry" function.
5. Press TEMP/SHADE +/- buttons to set the temperature at 400 degrees F.
6. Now press TIME/SLICES +/- buttons to set the cooking time to 20 minutes.
7. Press "Start/Stop" button to start.
8. When the unit beeps to show that it is preheated, open the oven door and insert the sheet pan into rail of Level 3.
9. Flip the chicken thighs once halfway through.
10. When the cooking time is completed, open the oven door and serve hot.

Serving Suggestions: Serve with couscous salad.

Variation Tip: Cook the chicken thighs until it reaches an internal temperature of 165° F.

Nutritional Information per Serving:
Calories: 332 | Fat: 17.6g|Sat Fat: 2.9g|Carbohydrates: 0.5g|Fiber: 0.3g|Sugar: 0g|Protein: 41.1g

Spiced Chicken Breasts

Prep Time: 10 minutes
Cook Time: 35 minutes
Serves: 4

Ingredients:

- 1½ tablespoons smoked paprika
- 1 teaspoon ground cumin
- Salt and ground black pepper, as required
- 2 (12-ounce) chicken breasts
- 1 tablespoon olive oil

Preparation:

1. In a small bowl, mix together the paprika, cumin, salt and black pepper.
2. Coat the chicken breasts with oil evenly and then season with the spice mixture generously.
3. Press "Power" button of Ninja Foodi XL Pro Air Oven and select "Air Fry" function.
4. Press TEMP/SHADE +/- buttons to set the temperature at 375 degrees F.
5. Now press TIME/SLICES +/- buttons to set the cooking time to 35 minutes.
6. Press "Start/Stop" button to start.
7. When the unit beeps to show that it is preheated, open the oven door.
8. Arrange the chicken breasts into the air fry basket into the rail of Level 3.
9. When the cooking time is completed, open the oven door and place the chicken breasts onto a cutting board for about 5 minutes.
10. Cut each breast in 2 equal-sized pieces and serve.

Serving Suggestions: Serve with sautéed kale.

Variation Tip: Fat of chicken breasts should always be white or deep yellow and never pale or gray.

Nutritional Information per Serving:
Calories: 363 | Fat: 16.6g|Sat Fat: 4g|Carbohydrates: 1.7g|Fiber: 1g|Sugar: 0.3g|Protein: 49.7g

Chicken Kebabs

Prep Time: 15 minutes.
Cook Time: 20 minutes.
Serves: 6

Ingredients:

- 16 ounces skinless chicken breasts, cubed
- 2 tablespoons soy sauce
- ½ zucchini sliced
- 1 tablespoon chicken seasoning
- 1 teaspoon BBQ seasoning
- Salt and pepper to taste
- ½ green pepper sliced
- ½ red pepper sliced
- ½ yellow pepper sliced
- ¼ red onion sliced
- 4 cherry tomatoes
- Cooking spray

Preparation:

1. Toss chicken and veggies with all the spices and seasoning in a bowl.
2. Alternatively, thread them on skewers and place these skewers in the air fry basket.
3. Transfer the basket to the 3rd rack position of Ninja Foodi XL Pro Air Oven and close the door.
4. Select the "Air Fry" Mode using FUNCTION +/- buttons and select Rack Level 3.
5. Set its cooking time to 20 minutes and temperature to 350 degrees F, then press "START/STOP" to initiate cooking.
6. Flip the skewers when cooked halfway through, then resume cooking.
7. Serve warm.

Serving Suggestion: Serve the kebabs with roasted veggies on the side.

Variation Tip: Add mozzarella balls to the skewers.

Nutritional Information Per Serving:
Calories 434 | Fat 16g |Sodium 462mg | Carbs 13g | Fiber 0.4g | Sugar 3g | Protein 35.3g

Duck a la Orange

Prep Time: 15 minutes.
Cook Time: 60 minutes.
Serves: 8

Ingredients:

- 1 tablespoon salt
- 1 teaspoon ground coriander
- ½ teaspoon ground cumin
- 1 teaspoon black pepper
- 1 (5- to 6-pound) duck, skinned
- 1 juice orange, halved
- 4 fresh thyme sprigs
- 4 fresh marjoram sprigs
- 2 parsley sprigs
- 1 small onion, cut into wedges
- ½ cup dry white wine
- ½ cup chicken broth
- ½ carrot
- ½ celery rib

Preparation:

1. Place the Pekin duck in a roast tray and whisk orange juice and the rest of the ingredients in a bowl.
2. Pour the herb sauce over the duck and brush it liberally
3. Transfer the duck to the 1st rack position of Ninja Foodi XL Pro Air Oven and close the door.
4. Select the "Air Fry" Mode using FUNCTION +/- buttons and select Rack Level 1.
5. Set its cooking time to 60 minutes and temperature to 350 degrees F, then press "START/STOP" to initiate cooking.
6. Continue basting the duck during baking.
7. Serve warm.

Serving Suggestion: Serve the duck with chili garlic sauce.

Variation Tip: Add asparagus sticks around the duck and roast.

Nutritional Information Per Serving:
Calories 531 | Fat 20g |Sodium 941mg | Carbs 30g | Fiber 0.9g | Sugar 1.4g | Protein 24.6g

Baked Duck

Prep Time: 15 minutes.
Cook Time: 2 hours 20 minutes.
Serves: 4
Ingredients:

- 1 ½ sprigs fresh rosemary
- ½ nutmeg
- Black pepper
- Juice from 1 orange
- 1 whole duck
- 4 cloves garlic, chopped
- 1 ½ red onions, chopped
- a few stalks celery
- 1 ½ carrot
- 2 cm piece fresh ginger
- 1 ½ bay leaves
- 2 pounds Piper potatoes
- 4 cups chicken stock

Preparation:

1. Place duck in a large cooking pot and add broth along with all the ingredients.
2. Cook this duck for 2 hours on a simmer, then transfer to the roast tray.
3. Transfer the roast tray to the 1st rack position of Ninja Foodi XL Pro Air Oven and close the door.
4. Select the "Air Fry" Mode using FUNCTION +/- buttons and select Rack Level 1.
5. Set its cooking time to 20 minutes and temperature to 350 degrees F, then press "START/STOP" to initiate cooking.
6. Serve warm.

Serving Suggestion: Serve the duck with a fresh crouton salad.
Variation Tip: Stuff the duck with the bread stuffing and cheese.
Nutritional Information Per Serving:
Calories 505 | Fat 7.9g |Sodium 581mg | Carbs 21.8g | Fiber 2.6g | Sugar 7g | Protein 37.2g

Crispy Chicken Cutlets

Prep Time: 15 minutes
Cook Time: 30 minutes
Serves: 4
Ingredients:

- ¾ cup flour
- 2 large eggs
- 1½ cups breadcrumbs
- ¼ cup Parmesan cheese, grated
- 1 tablespoon mustard powder
- Salt and ground black pepper, as required
- 4 (6-ounce) (¼-inch-thick) skinless, boneless chicken cutlets

Preparation:

1. In a shallow bowl, add the flour.
2. In a second bowl, crack the eggs and beat well.
3. In a third bowl, mix the breadcrumbs, cheese, mustard powder, salt, and black pepper together.
4. Season the chicken with salt, and black pepper.
5. Coat the chicken with flour, then dip into beaten eggs and finally coat with the breadcrumb mixture.
6. Press "Power" button of Ninja Foodi XL Pro Air Oven and select "Air Fry" function.
7. Press TEMP/SHADE +/- buttons to set the temperature at 355 degrees F.
8. Now press TIME/SLICES +/- buttons to set the cooking time to 30 minutes.
9. Press "START/STOP" button to start.
10. When the unit beeps to show that it is preheated, open the lid and grease the air fry basket.
11. Place the chicken cutlets into the prepared air fry basket and insert in the oven.
12. When cooking time is completed, open the lid and serve hot.

Serving Suggestions: Serve with favorite greens.
Variation Tip: Parmesan cheese can be replaced with your favorite cheese.
Nutritional Information per Serving:
Calories: 526 | Fat: 13g|Sat Fat: 4.2g|Carbohydrates: 48.6g|Fiber: 3g|Sugar: 3g|Protein: 51.7g

Simple Turkey Breast

Prep Time: 10 minutes
Cook Time: 1 hour 20 minutes
Serves: 6

Ingredients:

- 1 (2¾-pound) bone-in, skin-on turkey breast half
- Salt and ground black pepper, as required

Preparation:

1. Rub the turkey breast with the salt and black pepper evenly.
2. Arrange the turkey breast into a greased baking pan.
3. Press "Power" button of Ninja Foodi XL Pro Air Oven and select "Bake" function.
4. Press TEMP/SHADE +/- buttons to set the temperature at 450 degrees F.
5. Now press TIME/SLICES +/- buttons to set the cooking time to 1 hour 20 minutes.
6. Press "START/STOP" button to start.
7. When the unit beeps to show that it is preheated, open the lid.
8. Arrange the pan over the wire rack and insert in the oven.
9. When cooking time is completed, open the lid and place the turkey breast onto a cutting board.
10. With a piece of foil, cover the turkey breast for about 20 minutes before slicing.
11. With a sharp knife, cut the turkey breast into desired size slices and serve.

Serving Suggestions: Serve alongside the steamed veggies.
Variation Tip: Beware of flat spots on meat, which can indicate thawing and refreezing.
Nutritional Information per Serving:
Calories: 221 | Fat: 0.8g|Sat Fat: 0g|Carbohydrates: 0g|Fiber: 0g|Sugar: 0g|Protein: 51.6g

Brie Stuffed Chicken Breasts

Prep Time: 15 minutes
Cook Time: 15 minutes
Serves: 4

Ingredients:

- 2 (8-ounce) skinless, boneless chicken fillets
- Salt and ground black pepper, as required
- 4 brie cheese slices
- 1 tablespoon fresh chive, minced
- 4 bacon slices

Preparation:

1. Cut each chicken fillet in 2 equal-sized pieces.
2. Carefully, make a slit in each chicken piece horizontally about ¼-inch from the edge.
3. Open chicken pieces and slightly season with salt and black pepper.
4. Place 1 cheese slice in the open area of each chicken piece and sprinkle with chives.
5. Close the chicken pieces and wrap each one with a bacon slice.
6. Secure with toothpicks.
7. Press "Power" button of Ninja Foodi XL Pro Air Oven and select "Air Fry" function.
8. Press TEMP/SHADE +/- buttons to set the temperature at 355 degrees F.
9. Now press TIME/SLICES +/- buttons to set the cooking time to 15 minutes.
10. Press "START/STOP" button to start.
11. When the unit beeps to show that it is preheated, open the lid and grease the air fry basket.
12. Place the chicken pieces into the prepared air fry basket and insert in the oven.
13. When cooking time is completed, open the lid and place the rolled chicken breasts onto a cutting board.
14. Cut into desired-sized slices and serve.

Serving Suggestions: Serve with creamy mashed potatoes.
Variation Tip: Add some seasoning as you like.
Nutritional Information per Serving:
Calories: 394 | Fat: 24g|Sat Fat: 10.4g|Carbohydrates: 0.6g|Fiber: 0g|Sugar: 0.1g|Protein: 42g

Marinated Spicy Chicken Legs

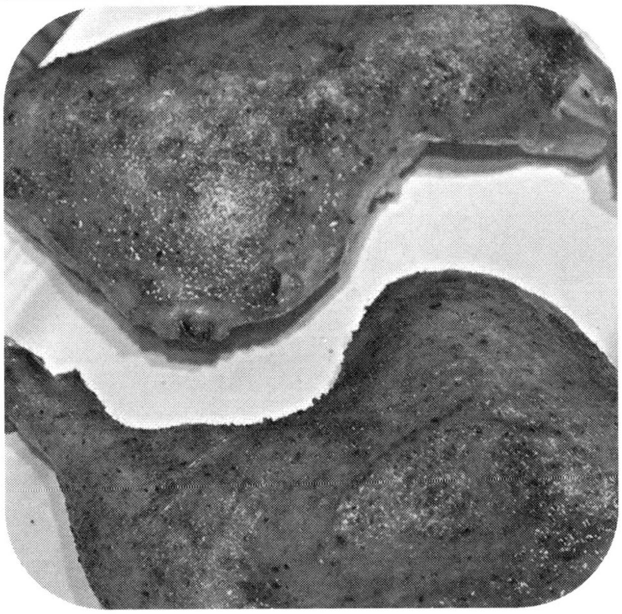

Prep Time: 10 minutes
Cook Time: 20 minutes
Serves: 4

Ingredients:

- 4 chicken legs
- 3 tablespoons fresh lemon juice
- 3 teaspoons ginger paste
- 3 teaspoons garlic paste
- Salt, as required
- 4 tablespoons plain yogurt
- 2 teaspoons red chili powder
- 1 teaspoon ground cumin
- 1 teaspoon ground coriander
- 1 teaspoon ground turmeric
- Ground black pepper, as required

Preparation:

1. In a bowl, mix the chicken legs, lemon juice, ginger, garlic, and salt together. Set aside for about 15 minutes.
2. Meanwhile, in another bowl, mix the yogurt and spices together.
3. Add the chicken legs and coat with the spice mixture generously.
4. Cover the bowl and refrigerate for at least 10-12 hours.
5. Press "Power" button of Ninja Foodi XL Pro Air Oven and select "Air Fry" function.
6. Press TEMP/SHADE +/- buttons to set the temperature at 440 degrees F.
7. Now press TIME/SLICES +/- buttons to set the cooking time to 20 minutes.
8. Press "START/STOP" button to start.
9. When the unit beeps to show that it is preheated, open the lid and grease the air fry basket.
10. Place the chicken legs into the prepared air fry basket and insert in the oven.
11. When cooking time is completed, open the lid and serve hot.

Serving Suggestions: Serve with fresh greens.
Variation Tip: Lemon juice can be replaced with vinegar.
Nutritional Information per Serving:
Calories: 461| Fat: 17.6g|Sat Fat: 5g|Carbohydrates: 4.3g|Fiber: 0.9g|Sugar: 1.5g|Protein: 67.1g

Lemony Whole Chicken

Prep Time: 15 minutes
Cook Time: 1 hour 20 minutes
Serves: 8

Ingredients:

- 1 (5-pound) whole chicken, neck and giblets removed
- Salt and ground black pepper, as required
- 2 fresh rosemary sprigs
- 1 small onion, peeled and quartered
- 1 garlic clove, peeled and cut in half
- 4 lemon zest slices
- 1 tablespoon extra-virgin olive oil
- 1 tablespoon fresh lemon juice

Preparation:

1. Rub the inside and outside of chicken with salt and black pepper evenly.
2. Place the rosemary sprigs, onion quarters, garlic halves and lemon zest in the cavity of the chicken.
3. With kitchen twine, tie off wings and legs.
4. Arrange the chicken onto a greased baking pan and drizzle with oil and lemon juice.
5. Press "Power" button of Ninja Foodi XL Pro Air Oven and select "Bake" function.
6. Press TEMP/SHADE +/- buttons to set the temperature at 400 degrees F.
7. Now press TIME/SLICES +/- buttons to set the cooking time to 20 minutes.
8. Press "START/STOP" button to start.
9. When the unit beeps to show that it is preheated, open the lid.
10. Arrange the pan over the wire rack and insert in the oven.
11. After 20 minutes of cooking, set the temperature to 375 degrees F for 60 minutes.
12. When cooking time is completed, open the lid and place the chicken onto a platter for about 10 minutes before carving.
13. Cut into desired sized pieces and serve.

Serving Suggestions: Serve alongside the steamed veggies.
Variation Tip: Lemon can be replaced with lime.
Nutritional Information per Serving:
Calories: 448 | Fat: 10.4g|Sat Fat: 2.7g|Carbohydrates: 1g|Fiber: 0.4g|Sugar: 0.2g|Protein: 82g

Buttered Turkey Breast

Prep Time: 15 minutes
Cook Time: 1¼ hours
Serves: 10

Ingredients:

- ¼ cup butter
- 5 carrots, peeled and cut into chunks
- 1 (6-pound) boneless turkey breast
- Salt and ground black pepper, as required
- 1 cup chicken broth

Preparation:

1. In a pan, heat the oil over medium heat and the carrots for about 4-5 minutes.
2. Add the turkey breast and cook for about 10 minutes or until golden brown from both sides.
3. Remove from the heat and stir in salt, black pepper and broth.
4. Transfer the mixture into a baking dish.
5. Press "Power" button of Ninja Foodi XL Pro Air Oven and select "Bake" function.
6. Press TEMP/SHADE +/- buttons to set the temperature at 375 degrees F.
7. Now press TIME/SLICES +/- buttons to set the cooking time to 60 minutes.
8. Press "Start/Stop" button to start.
9. When the unit beeps to show that it is pre-heated, open the oven door.
10. Arrange the baking dish over the wire rack and insert into rail of Level 3.
11. When the cooking time is completed, open the oven door and with tongs, place the turkey onto a cutting board for about 5 minutes before slicing.
12. Cut into desired-sized slices and serve alongside carrots.

Serving Suggestions: Serve with fresh salad.
Variation Tip: You can also cook fennel and parsnip alongside the carrot in this recipe.
Nutritional Information per Serving:
Calories: 322 | Fat: 6g|Sat Fat: 3g|Carbohydrates: 3.1g|Fiber: 0.8g|Sugar: 1.6g|Protein: 6.2g

Simple Chicken Thighs

Prep Time: 10 minutes
Cook Time: 20 minutes
Serves: 4

Ingredients:

- 4 (4-ounce) skinless, boneless chicken thighs
- Salt and ground black pepper, as required
- 2 tablespoons butter, melted

Preparation:

1. Line a sheet pan with a lightly greased piece of foil.
2. Rub the chicken thighs with salt and black pepper evenly and then, brush with melted butter.
3. Place the chicken thighs into the prepared sheet pan.
4. Press "Power" button of Ninja Foodi XL Pro Air Oven and select "Bake" function.
5. Press TEMP/SHADE +/- buttons to set the temperature at 450 degrees F.
6. Now press TIME/SLICES +/- buttons to set the cooking time to 20 minutes.
7. Press "Start/Stop" button to start.
8. When the unit beeps to show that it is pre-heated, open the oven door and insert the sheet pan on Level 3.
9. When the cooking time is completed, open the oven door and serve hot.

Serving Suggestions: Serve alongside the creamy mashed potatoes.
Variation Tip: Pat the chicken thighs dry with a paper towel.
Nutritional Information per Serving:
Calories: 193 | Fat: 9.8g|Sat Fat: 5.2g|Carbohydrates: 0g|Fiber: 0g|Sugar: 0g|Protein: 25.4g

Crispy Chicken Drumsticks

Prep Time: 15 minutes
Cook Time: 25 minutes
Serves: 4

Ingredients:
- 4 chicken drumsticks
- 1 tablespoon adobo seasoning
- Salt, as required
- 1 tablespoon onion powder
- 1 tablespoon garlic powder
- ½ tablespoon paprika
- Ground black pepper, as required
- 2 eggs
- 2 tablespoons milk
- 1 cup all-purpose flour
- ¼ cup cornstarch

Preparation:
1. Season chicken drumsticks with adobo seasoning and a pinch of salt.
2. Set aside for about 5 minutes.
3. In a small bowl, add the spices, salt and black pepper and mix well.
4. In a shallow bowl, add the eggs, milk and 1 teaspoon of spice mixture and beat until well combined.
5. In another shallow bowl, add the flour, cornstarch and remaining spice mixture.
6. Coat the chicken drumsticks with flour mixture completely and tap off the excess.
7. Now, dip the chicken drumsticks in egg mixture.
8. Again coat the chicken drumsticks with flour mixture.
9. Arrange the chicken drumsticks onto a wire rack lined baking sheet and set aside for about 15 minutes.
10. Now, arrange the chicken drumsticks onto a sheet pan and spray the chicken with cooking spray lightly.
11. Press "Power" button of Ninja Foodi XL Pro Air Oven and select "Air Fry" function.
12. Press TEMP/SHADE +/- buttons to set the temperature at 350 degrees F.
13. Now press TIME/SLICES +/- buttons to set the cooking time to 25 minutes.
Press "START/STOP" button to start.
14. When the unit beeps to show that it is preheated, open the lid and grease the air fry basket.
15. Place the chicken drumsticks into the prepared air fry basket and insert in the oven.
16. When cooking time is completed, open the lid and serve hot.

Serving Suggestions: Serve with French fries.
Variation Tip: Feel free to add some seasoning as you like.
Nutritional Information per Serving:
Calories: 483 | Fat: 12.5g|Sat Fat: 3.4g|Carbohydrates: 35.1g|Fiber: 1.6g|Sugar: 1.8g|Protein: 53.7g

Cajun Spiced Whole Chicken

Prep Time: 15 minutes
Cook Time: 1 hour 10 minutes
Serves: 6

Ingredients:
- ¼ cup butter, softened
- 2 teaspoons dried rosemary
- 2 teaspoons dried thyme
- 1 tablespoon Cajun seasoning
- 1 tablespoon onion powder
- 1 tablespoon garlic powder
- 1 tablespoon paprika
- 1 teaspoon cayenne pepper
- Salt, as required
- 1 (3-pound) whole chicken, neck and giblets removed

Preparation:
1. In a bowl, add the butter, herbs, spices and salt and mix well.
2. Rub the chicken with spicy mixture generously.
3. With kitchen twine, tie off wings and legs.
4. Press "Power" button of Ninja Foodi XL Pro Air Oven and select "Bake" function.
5. Press TEMP/SHADE +/- buttons to set the temperature at 380 degrees F.
6. Now press TIME/SLICES +/- buttons to set the cooking time to 70 minutes.
7. Press "START/STOP" button to start.
8. When the unit beeps to show that it is preheated, open the lid.
9. Arrange the chicken over the wire rack and insert in the oven.
10. When cooking time is completed, open the lid and place the chicken onto a platter for about 10 minutes before carving.
11. Cut into desired sized pieces and serve.

Serving Suggestions: Serve alongside a fresh green salad.
Variation Tip: You can adjust the ratio of spices according to your choice.
Nutritional Information per Serving:
Calories: 421 | Fat: 14.8g|Sat Fat: 6.9g|Carbohydrates: 2.3g|Fiber: 0.9g|Sugar: 0.5g|Protein: 66.3g

Crispy Chicken Thighs

Prep Time: 15 minutes
Cook Time: 25 minutes
Serves: 4

Ingredients:

- ½ cup all-purpose flour
- 1½ tablespoons Cajun seasoning
- 1 teaspoon seasoning salt
- 1 egg
- 4 (4-ounce) skin-on chicken thighs

Preparation:

1. In a shallow bowl, mix the flour, Cajun seasoning, and salt together.
2. In another bowl, crack the egg and beat well.
3. Coat each chicken thigh with the flour mixture, then dip into beaten egg and finally, coat with the flour mixture again.
4. Shake off the excess flour thoroughly.
5. Press "Power" button of Ninja Foodi XL Pro Air Oven and select "Air Fry" function.
6. Press TEMP/SHADE +/- buttons to set the temperature at 390 degrees F.
7. Now press TIME/SLICES +/- buttons to set the cooking time to 25 minutes.
8. Press "START/STOP" button to start.
9. When the unit beeps to show that it is preheated, open the lid and grease the air fry basket.
10. Place the chicken thighs into the prepared air fry basket and insert in the oven.
11. When cooking time is completed, open the lid and serve hot.

Serving Suggestions: Serve with ketchup.
Variation Tip: Feel free to use seasoning of your choice.
Nutritional Information per Serving:
Calories: 288 | Fat: 9.6g|Sat Fat: 2.7g|Carbohydrates: 12g|Fiber: 0.4g|Sugar: 0.1g|Protein: 35.9g

Herbed Duck Breast

Prep Time: 15 minutes
Cook Time: 20 minutes
Serves: 2

Ingredients:

- 1 (10-ounce) duck breast
- Olive oil cooking spray
- ½ tablespoon fresh thyme, chopped
- ½ tablespoon fresh rosemary, chopped
- 1 cup chicken broth
- 1 tablespoon fresh lemon juice
- Salt and ground black pepper, as required

Preparation:

1. Spray the duck breast with cooking spray evenly.
2. In a bowl, mix well the remaining ingredients.
3. Add the duck breast and coat with the marinade generously.
4. Refrigerate, covered for about 4 hours.
5. With a piece of foil, cover the duck breast.
6. Press "Power" button of Ninja Foodi XL Pro Air Oven and select "Air Fry" function.
7. Press TEMP/SHADE +/- buttons to set the temperature at 390 degrees F.
8. Now press TIME/SLICES +/- buttons to set the cooking time to 15 minutes.
9. Press "START/STOP" button to start.
10. When the unit beeps to show that it is preheated, open the lid and grease the air fry basket.
11. Place the duck breast into the prepared air fry basket and insert in the oven.
12. After 15 minutes of cooking, set the temperature to 355 degrees F for 5 minutes.
13. When cooking time is completed, open the lid and serve hot.

Serving Suggestions: Serve with spiced potatoes.
Variation Tip: Feel free to add some seasoning as you like.
Nutritional Information per Serving:
Calories: 209 | Fat: 6.6g|Sat Fat: 0.3g|Carbohydrates: 1.6g|Fiber: 0.6g|Sugar: 0.5g|Protein: 33.8g

Chicken Kabobs

Prep Time: 15 minutes
Cook Time: 9 minutes
Serves: 2

Ingredients:

- 1 (8-ounce) chicken breast, cut into medium-sized pieces
- 1 tablespoon fresh lemon juice
- 3 garlic cloves, grated
- 1 tablespoon fresh oregano, minced
- ½ teaspoon lemon zest, grated
- Salt and ground black pepper, as required
- 1 teaspoon plain Greek yogurt
- 1 teaspoon olive oil

Preparation:

1. In a large bowl, add the chicken, lemon juice, garlic, oregano, lemon zest, salt and black pepper and toss to coat well.
2. Cover the bowl and refrigerate overnight.
3. Remove the bowl from the refrigerator and stir in the yogurt and oil.
4. Thread the chicken pieces onto the metal skewers.
5. Press "Power" button of Ninja Foodi XL Pro Air Oven and select "Air Fry" function.
6. Press TEMP/SHADE +/- buttons to set the temperature at 350 degrees F.
7. Now press TIME/SLICES +/- buttons to set the cooking time to 9 minutes.
8. Press "START/STOP" button to start.
9. When the unit beeps to show that it is preheated, open the lid and grease the air fry basket.
10. Place the skewers into the prepared air fry basket and insert in the oven.
11. Flip the skewers once halfway through.
12. When cooking time is completed, open the lid and serve hot.

Serving Suggestions: Serve alongside fresh salad.

Variation Tip: Feel free to add some seasoning as you like.

Nutritional Information per Serving:
Calories: 167 | Fat: 5.5g|Sat Fat: 0.5g|Carbohydrates: 3.4g|Fiber: 0.5g|Sugar: 1.1g|Protein: 24.8g

Chinese Chicken Drumsticks

Prep Time: 10 minutes
Cook Time: 20 minutes
Serves: 4

Ingredients:

- 1 tablespoon oyster sauce
- 1 teaspoon light soy sauce
- ½ teaspoon sesame oil
- 1 teaspoon Chinese five-spice powder
- Salt and ground white pepper, as required
- 4 (6-ounce) chicken drumsticks
- 1 cup corn flour

Preparation:

1. In a bowl, mix the sauces, oil, five-spice powder, salt, and black pepper together.
2. Add the chicken drumsticks and generously coat with the marinade.
3. Refrigerate for at least 30-40 minutes.
4. In a shallow dish, place the corn flour.
5. Remove the chicken from marinade and lightly coat with corn flour.
6. Press "Power" button of Ninja Foodi XL Pro Air Oven and select "Air Fry" function.
7. Press TEMP/SHADE +/- buttons to set the temperature at 390 degrees F.
8. Now press TIME/SLICES +/- buttons to set the cooking time to 20 minutes.
9. Press "START/STOP" button to start.
10. When the unit beeps to show that it is preheated, open the lid and grease the air fry basket.
11. Place the chicken drumsticks into the prepared air fry basket and insert in the oven.
12. When cooking time is completed, open the lid and serve hot.

Serving Suggestions: Serve with fresh greens.

Variation Tip: Add seasoning or sauces as you like.

Nutritional Information per Serving:
Calories: 287 | Fat: 13.8g|Sat Fat: 7.1g|Carbohydrates: 1.6g|Fiber: 0.2g|Sugar: 0.1g|Protein: 38.3g

Oat Crusted Chicken Breasts

Prep Time: 15 minutes
Cook Time: 12 minutes
Serves: 2

Ingredients:

- 2 (6-ounce) chicken breasts
- Salt and ground black pepper, as required
- ¾ cup oats
- 2 tablespoons mustard powder
- 1 tablespoon fresh parsley
- 2 medium eggs

Preparation:

1. Check the meat "best by" date. Place the chicken breasts onto a cutting board and with a meat mallet, flatten each into even thickness.
2. Then, cut each breast in half.
3. Sprinkle the chicken pieces with salt and black pepper and set aside.
4. In a blender, add the oats, mustard powder, parsley, salt and black pepper and pulse until a coarse breadcrumb-like mixture is formed.
5. Transfer the oat mixture into a shallow bowl.
6. In another bowl, crack the eggs and beat well.
7. Coat the chicken with oats mixture and then, dip into beaten eggs and again, coat with the oats mixture.
8. Press "Power" button of Ninja Foodi XL Pro Air Oven and select "Air Fry" function.
9. Press TEMP/SHADE +/- buttons to set the temperature at 350 degrees F.
10. Now press TIME/SLICES +/- buttons to set the cooking time to 12 minutes.
11. Press "START/STOP" button to start.
12. When the unit beeps to show that it is pre-heated, open the lid and grease the air fry basket.
13. Place the chicken breasts into the prepared air fry basket and insert in the oven.
14. Flip the chicken breasts once halfway through.
15. When cooking time is completed, open the lid and serve hot.

Serving Suggestions: Serve with mashed potatoes.

Variation Tip: Feel free to add some seasoning as you like.

Nutritional Information per Serving:
Calories: 556 | Fat: 22.2g|Sat Fat: 5.3g|Carbohydrates: 25.1g|Fiber: 4.8g|Sugar: 1.4g|Protein: 61.6g

Lemony Chicken Thighs

Prep Time: 15 minutes
Cook Time: 20 minutes
Serves: 6

Ingredients:

- 6 (6-ounce) chicken thighs
- 2 tablespoons olive oil
- 2 tablespoons fresh lemon juice
- 1 tablespoon Italian seasoning
- Salt and ground black pepper, as required
- 1 lemon, sliced thinly

Preparation:

1. In a large bowl, add all the ingredients except for lemon slices and toss to coat well.
2. Refrigerate to marinate for 30 minutes to overnight.
3. Remove the chicken thighs and let any excess marinade drip off.
4. Press "Power" button of Ninja Foodi XL Pro Air Oven and select "Air Fry" function.
5. Press TEMP/SHADE +/- buttons to set the temperature at 350 degrees F.
6. Now press TIME/SLICES +/- buttons to set the cooking time to 20 minutes.
7. Press "START/STOP" button to start.
8. When the unit beeps to show that it is pre-heated, open the lid and grease the air fry basket.
9. Place the chicken thighs into the prepared air fry basket and insert in the oven.
10. After 10 minutes of cooking, flip the chicken thighs.
11. When cooking time is completed, open the lid and serve hot alongside the lemon slices.

Serving Suggestions: Serve alongside your favorite dipping sauce.

Variation Tip: Select chicken with a pinkish hue.

Nutritional Information per Serving:
Calories: 472 | Fat: 18g|Sat Fat: 4.3g|Carbohydrates: 0.6g|Fiber: 0.1g|Sugar: 0.4g|Protein: 49.3g

Buttermilk Whole Chicken

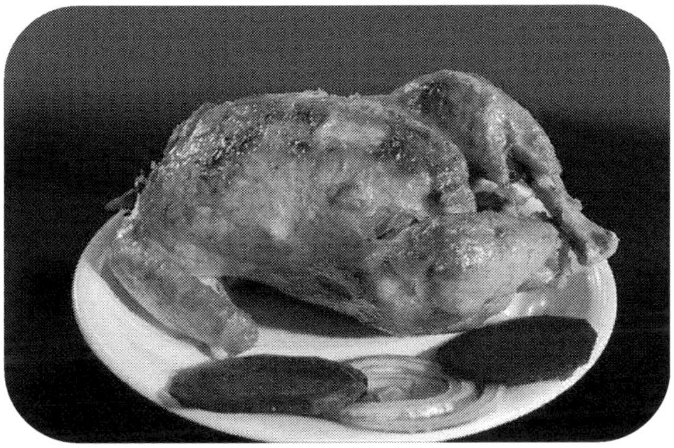

Prep Time: 15 minutes
Cook Time: 50 minutes
Serves: 6

Ingredients:

- 2 cups buttermilk
- ¼ cup olive oil
- 1 teaspoon garlic powder
- Salt, as required
- 1 (3-pound) whole chicken, neck and giblets removed
- Ground black pepper, as required

Preparation:

1. In a large resealable bag, mix together the buttermilk, oil, garlic powder and 1 tablespoon of salt.
2. Add the whole chicken and seal the bag tightly.
3. Refrigerate to marinate for 24 hours up to 2 days.
4. Remove the chicken from bag and pat dry with paper towels.
5. Season the chicken with salt and black pepper.
6. With kitchen twine, tie off wings and legs.
7. Press "Power" button of Ninja Foodi XL Pro Air Oven and select "Air Fry" function.
8. Press TEMP/SHADE +/- buttons to set the temperature at 380 degrees F.
9. Now press TIME/SLICES +/- buttons to set the cooking time to 50 minutes.
10. Press "Start/Stop" button to start.
11. When the unit beeps to show that it is preheated, open the oven door.
12. Arrange the chicken into the greased air fry basket, breast-side down on sheet pan into rails of Level 3.
13. When the cooking time is completed, open the oven door and place the chicken onto a cutting board for about 10 minutes before carving.
14. With a sharp knife, cut the chicken into desired sized pieces and serve.

Serving Suggestions: Serve with steamed veggies

Variation Tip: Kitchen shears are very useful for trimming excess fat from the chicken's cavity.

Nutritional Information per Serving:
Calories: 449 | Fat: 16g|Sat Fat: 3.6g|Carbohydrates: 68.5g|Fiber: 4.3g|Sugar: 0.1g|Protein: 4g

Cheesy Chicken Cutlets

Prep Time: 10 minutes
Cook Time: 30 minutes
Serves: 2

Ingredients:

- 1 large egg
- 6 tablespoons flour
- ¾ cup panko breadcrumbs
- 2 tablespoons parmesan cheese, grated
- 2 chicken cutlets, skinless and boneless
- ½ tablespoon mustard powder
- Salt and black pepper, to taste

Preparation:

1. Take a shallow bowl, add the flour.
2. In a second bowl, crack the egg and beat well.
3. Take a third bowl and mix together breadcrumbs, cheeses, mustard powder, salt and black pepper.
4. Season the chicken with salt and black pepper.
5. Coat the chicken with flour, then dip into beaten egg and then finally coat with the breadcrumbs mixture.
6. Turn on your Ninja Foodi XL Pro Air Oven and select "Air Fry".
7. Select the timer for about 30 minutes and temperature for 355 degrees F. Press START/STOP to begin preheating.
8. When the unit beeps to signify it has preheated, open the oven and slide an air fry basket into the rail of Level 3.
9. Grease the air fry basket and place the chicken cutlets into the prepared basket. Close the oven and let it cook.
10. Remove from the oven and serve on a platter.
11. Serve hot and enjoy!

Serving Suggestions: Serve with a topping of lemon slices.

Variation Tip: You can also use mozzarella cheese instead.

Nutritional Information per Serving:
Calories: 510 | Fat: 16.3g|Sat Fat: 7.5g|Carbohydrates: 26.2g|Fiber: 1.2g|Sugar: 0.5g|Protein: 41.4g

Herbed Whole Chicken

Prep Time: 15 minutes
Cook Time: 1 hour
Serves: 8

Ingredients:

- 1 tablespoon fresh basil, chopped
- 1 tablespoon fresh oregano, chopped
- 1 tablespoon fresh thyme, chopped
- Salt and ground black pepper, as required
- 1 (4½-pound) whole chicken, necks and giblets removed
- 3 tablespoons olive oil, divided

Preparation:

1. In a bowl, mix together the herbs, salt and black pepper.
2. Coat the chicken with 2 tablespoons of oil and then, rub inside, outside and underneath the skin with half of the herb mixture generously.
3. Press "Power" button of Ninja Foodi XL Pro Air Oven and select "Air Fry" function.
4. Press TEMP/SHADE +/- buttons to set the temperature at 360 degrees F.
5. Now press TIME/SLICES +/- buttons to set the cooking time to 60 minutes.
6. Press "Start/Stop" button to start.
7. When the unit beeps to show that it is preheated, open the oven door.
8. Arrange the chicken into the greased air fry basket, breast-side down and slide the basket into rails of Level 3.
9. After 30 minutes of cooking, arrange the chicken, breast-side up and coat with the remaining oil.
10. Then rub with the remaining herb mixture.
11. When the cooking time is completed, open the oven door and place the chicken onto a cutting board for about 10 minutes before carving.
12. With a sharp knife, cut the chicken into desired sized pieces and serve.

Serving Suggestions: Serve with roasted vegetables.
Variation Tip: Dried herbs can be used instead of fresh herbs.
Nutritional Information per Serving:
Calories: 533 | Fat: 24.3g|Sat Fat: 6g|Carbohydrates: 0.6g|Fiber: 0.4g|Sugar: 0g|Protein: 73.9g

Breaded Chicken Tenderloins

Prep Time: 10 minutes
Cook Time: 15 minutes
Serves: 2

Ingredients:

- 4 chicken tenderloins, skinless and boneless
- ½ egg, beaten
- 1 tablespoon vegetable oil
- ¼ cup breadcrumbs

Preparation:

1. Take a shallow dish and add the beaten egg.
2. Take another dish and mix together oil and breadcrumbs until you have a crumbly mixture.
3. Dip the chicken tenderloins into the beaten egg and then coat with the breadcrumbs mixture.
4. Shake off the excess coating.
5. Turn on your Ninja Foodi XL Pro Air Oven and select "Air Fry".
6. Select the timer for about 15 minutes and temperature for 355 degrees F. Press START/STOP to begin preheating.
7. When the unit beeps to signify it has preheated, open the oven and place an air fry basket on Level 3.
8. Grease the air fry basket and place the chicken tenderloins into the prepared basket. Close the oven and let it cook.
9. Remove from the oven and serve on a platter.
10. Serve hot and enjoy!

Serving Suggestions: Serve with red chili sauce or ketchup.
Variation Tip: You can use foil to cover the chicken.
Nutritional Information per Serving:
Calories: 409 | Fat: 16.6g|Sat Fat: 4.8g|Carbohydrates: 9.8g|Fiber: 0.6g|Sugar: 0.9g|Protein: 53.2g

Crispy Chicken Legs

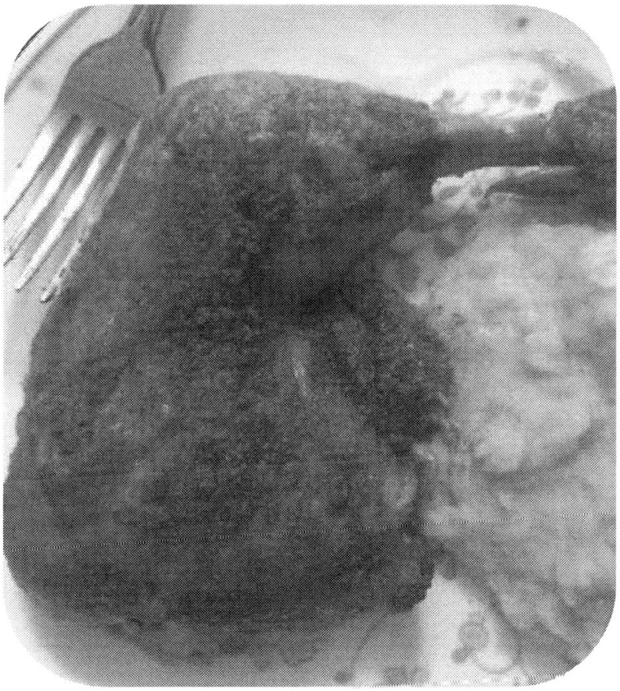

Prep Time: 15 minutes
Cook Time: 20 minutes
Serves: 3

Ingredients:

- 3 (8-ounce) chicken legs
- 1 cup buttermilk
- 2 cups white flour
- 1 teaspoon garlic powder
- 1 teaspoon onion powder
- 1 teaspoon ground cumin
- 1 teaspoon paprika
- Salt and ground black pepper, as required
- 1 tablespoon olive oil

Preparation:

1. In a bowl, place the chicken legs and buttermilk and refrigerate for about 2 hours.
2. In a shallow dish, mix together the flour and spices.
3. Remove the chicken from buttermilk.
4. Coat the chicken legs with flour mixture, then dip into buttermilk and finally, coat with the flour mixture again.
5. Press "Power" button of Ninja Foodi XL Pro Air Oven and select "Air Fry" function.
6. Press TEMP/SHADE +/- buttons to set the temperature at 355 degrees F.
7. Now press TIME/SLICES +/- buttons to set the cooking time to 20 minutes.
8. Press "START/STOP" button to start.
9. When the unit beeps to show that it is preheated, open the lid and grease the air fry basket.
10. Arrange chicken legs into the prepared air fry basket and drizzle with the oil.
11. Insert the basket in the oven.
12. When cooking time is completed, open the lid and serve hot.

Serving Suggestions: Serve with your favorite dip.

Variation Tip: White flour can be replaced with almond flour too.

Nutritional Information per Serving:
Calories: 817 | Fat: 23.3g|Sat Fat: 5.9g|Carbohydrates: 69.5g|Fiber: 2.7g|Sugar: 4.7g|Protein: 77.4g

Herbed Cornish Game Hen

Prep Time: 15 minutes
Cook Time: 35 minutes
Serves: 4

Ingredients:

- 2 tablespoons avocado oil
- ½ teaspoon dried oregano
- ½ teaspoon dried rosemary
- ½ teaspoon dried thyme
- ½ teaspoon dried basil
- Salt and ground black pepper, as required
- 2 Cornish game hens

Preparations:

1. In a bowl, mix the oil, dried herbs, salt and black pepper together.
2. Rub each hen with herb mixture evenly.
3. Press "Power" button of Ninja Foodi XL Pro Air Oven and select "Air Fry" function.
4. Press TEMP/SHADE +/- buttons to set the temperature at 360 degrees F.
5. Now press TIME/SLICES +/- buttons to set the cooking time to 35 minutes.
6. Press "START/STOP" button to start.
7. When the unit beeps to show that it is preheated, open the lid and grease the air fry basket.
8. Arrange the hens into the prepared basket, breast side down and insert in the oven.
9. When cooking time is completed, open the lid and transfer the hens onto a platter.
10. Cut each hen in pieces and serve.

Serving Suggestions: Serve alongside roasted veggies.

Variation Tip: You can use fresh herbs instead of dried herbs.

Nutritional Information per Serving:
Calories: 895 | Fat: 62.9g|Sat Fat: 17.4g|Carbohydrates: 0.7g|Fiber: 0.5g|Sugar: 0g|Protein: 75.9g

Molasses Glazed Duck Breast

Prep Time: 15 minutes
Cook Time: 44 minutes
Serves: 3

Ingredients:

- 2 cups fresh pomegranate juice
- 2 tablespoons fresh lemon juice
- 3 tablespoons brown sugar
- 1 pound boneless duck breast
- Salt and ground black pepper, as required

Preparation:

1. For pomegranate molasses: in a medium saucepan, add the pomegranate juice, lemon and brown sugar over medium heat and bring to a boil.
2. Reduce the heat to low and simmer for about 25 minutes until the mixture is thick.
3. Remove from the hat and set aside to cool slightly
4. Meanwhile, with a knife, make the slit on the duck breast.
5. Season the duck breast with salt and black pepper generously.
6. Press "Power" button of Ninja Foodi XL Pro Air Oven and select "Air Fry" function.
7. Press TEMP/SHADE +/- buttons to set the temperature at 400 degrees F.
8. Now press TIME/SLICES +/- buttons to set the cooking time to 14 minutes.
9. Press "Start/Stop" button to start.
10. When the unit beeps to show that it is pre-heated, open the oven door.
11. Arrange the duck breast into the greased air fry basket, skin side up and insert in the rail of Level 3.
12. After 6 minutes of cooking, flip the duck breast.
13. When the cooking time is completed, open the oven door and place the duck breast onto a platter for about 5 minutes before slicing.
14. With a sharp knife, cut the duck breast into desired sized slices and transfer onto a platter.
15. Drizzle with warm molasses and serve.

Serving Suggestions: Serve alongside the garlicky sweet potatoes.
Variation Tip: You can also use store-bought pomegranate molasses.
Nutritional Information per Serving:
Calories: 332 | Fat: 6.1g|Sat Fat: 0.1g|Carbohydrates: 337g|Fiber: 0g|Sugar: 31.6g|Protein: 34g

Crispy Roasted Chicken

Prep Time: 15 minutes
Cook Time: 40 minutes
Serves: 8

Ingredients:

- 1 (3½-pound) whole chicken, cut into 8 pieces
- Salt and ground black pepper, as required
- 2 cups buttermilk
- 2 cups all-purpose flour
- 1 tablespoon ground mustard
- 1 tablespoon garlic powder
- 1 tablespoon onion powder
- 1 tablespoon paprika

Preparation:

1. Rub the chicken pieces with salt and black pepper.
2. In a large bowl, add the chicken pieces and buttermilk and refrigerate to marinate for at least 1 hour.
3. Meanwhile, in a large bowl, place the flour, mustard, spices, salt and black pepper and mix well.
4. Remove the chicken pieces from bowl and drip off the excess buttermilk.
5. Coat the chicken pieces with the flour mixture, shaking any excess off.
6. Insert wire rack on Level 2. Press "Power" button of Ninja Foodi XL Pro Air Oven and select "Air Fry" function. Select 2 Level.
7. Press TEMP/SHADE +/- buttons to set the temperature at 390 degrees F.
8. Now press TIME/SLICES +/- buttons to set the cooking time to 20 minutes.
9. Press "Start/Stop" button to start.
10. When the unit beeps to show that it is pre-heated, open the oven door and grease air fry basket.
11. Arrange half of the chicken pieces into air fry basket and insert into the rail of Level 4. And the other on roast tray over wire rack into the rail of Level 2.
12. When the cooking time is completed, open the oven door and serve immediately.

Serving Suggestions: Serve alongside the French fries.
Variation Tip: Adjust the ratio of spices according to your taste.
Nutritional Information per Serving:
Calories: 518 | Fat: 8.5g|Sat Fat: 2.4g|Carbohydrates: 33.4g|Fiber: 1.8|Sugar: 4.3g|Protein: 72.6g

Parmesan Chicken Tenders

Prep Time: 15 minutes
Cook Time: 15 minutes
Serves: 4

Ingredients:

- ½ cup flour
- Salt and ground black pepper, as required
- 2 eggs, beaten
- ¾ cup panko breadcrumbs
- ¾ cup Parmesan cheese, grated finely
- 1 teaspoon Italian seasoning
- 8 chicken tenders

Preparation:

1. In a shallow dish, mix together the flour, salt and black pepper.
2. In a second shallow dish, place the beaten eggs.
3. In a third shallow dish, mix together the breadcrumbs, parmesan cheese and Italian seasoning.
4. Coat the chicken tenders with flour mixture, then dip into the beaten eggs and finally coat with breadcrumb mixture.
5. Arrange the tenders onto a greased sheet pan in a single layer and a greased air fryer basket.
6. Insert wire rack into rail of Level 2. Press "Power" button of Ninja Foodi XL Pro Air Oven and select "Air Fry" function.
7. Press TEMP/SHADE +/- buttons to set the temperature at 360 degrees F.
8. Now press TIME/SLICES +/- buttons to set the cooking time to 15 minutes.
9. Press "Start/Stop" button to start.
10. When the unit beeps to show that it is preheated, open the oven door and slide the basket on Level 4 and the sheet pan over wire rack on Level 2.
11. When the cooking time is completed, open the oven door and serve hot.

Serving Suggestions: Serve with blue cheese dip.

Variation Tip: Use dry breadcrumbs.

Nutritional Information per Serving:
Calories: 435 | Fat: 16.1g|Sat Fat: 5.4g|Carbohydrates: 15.3g|Fiber: 0g|Sugar: 0.5g|Protein: 0.4g

Spiced Roasted Chicken

Prep Time: 10 minutes
Cook Time: 1 hour
Serves: 3

Ingredients:

- 1 teaspoon paprika
- ½ teaspoon cayenne pepper
- ½ teaspoon ground white pepper
- ½ teaspoon garlic powder
- 1 teaspoon dried thyme
- ½ teaspoon onion powder
- Salt and black pepper, to taste
- 2 tablespoons oil
- ½ whole chicken, necks and giblets removed

Preparation:

1. Take a bowl and mix together the thyme and spices.
2. Coat the chicken with oil and rub it with the spice mixture.
3. Turn on your Ninja Foodi XL Pro Air Oven and select "Air Fry".
4. Select the timer for about 30 minutes and temperature for 350 degrees F.
5. Place the chicken in the air fry basket on Level 3 in oven and air fry for 30 minutes.
6. After that, take out the chicken, flip it over and let it air fry for another 30 minutes.
7. When cooked, let it sit for 10 minutes on a large plate and then carve to desired pieces.
8. Serve and enjoy!

Serving Suggestions: Top with chopped celery leaves and hot sauce.

Variation Tip: You can also add shredded mozzarella cheese on top.

Nutritional Information per Serving:
Calories: 113 | Fat: 8.7g|Sat Fat: 1.4g|Carbohydrates: 1.9g|Fiber: 0.7g|Sugar: 0.4g|Protein: 7.1g

Sweet and Spicy Chicken Drumsticks

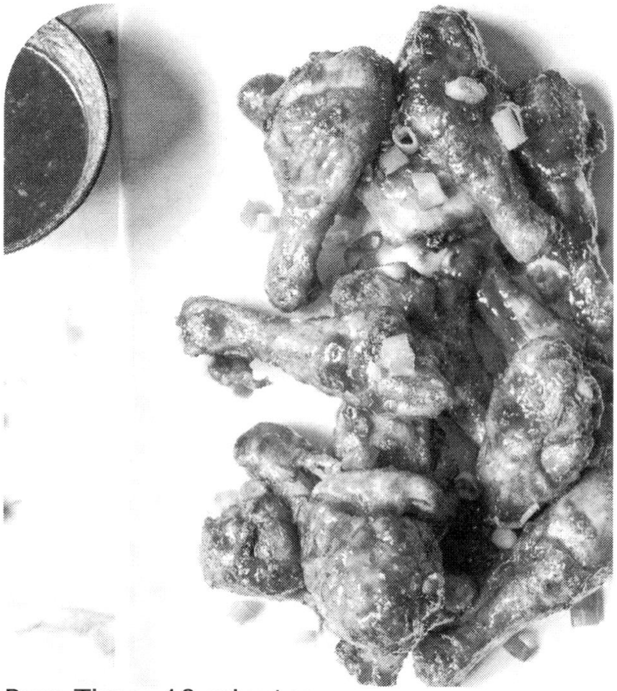

Prep Time: 10 minutes
Cook Time: 20 minutes
Serves: 2

Ingredients:

- 2 chicken drumsticks
- ½ garlic clove, crushed
- 1 teaspoon ginger, crushed
- 1 teaspoon brown sugar
- ½ tablespoon mustard
- ½ teaspoon red chili powder
- ½ teaspoon cayenne pepper
- ½ tablespoon vegetable oil
- Salt and black pepper, to taste

Preparation:

1. Take a bowl and mix together mustard, ginger, brown sugar, oil and spices.
2. Add chicken drumsticks to the bowl for well coating.
3. Refrigerate for at least 20 to 30 minutes.
4. Turn on your Ninja Foodi XL Pro Air Oven and select "Air Fry".
5. Select the timer for about 10 minutes and temperature for 390 degrees F.
6. When the unit beeps to signify it has preheated, open the oven and slide the air fry basket into the rail of Level 3.
7. Grease the air fry basket and place the drumsticks into the prepared basket. Close the oven and let it cook.
8. Air fry for about 10 minutes and then 10 more minutes at 300 degrees F.
9. Remove from the oven and serve on a platter.
10. Serve hot and enjoy!

Serving Suggestions: Serve with red chili sauce.

Variation Tip: You can add lemon juice to enhance taste.

Nutritional Information per Serving:
Calories: 131 | Fat: 7g|Sat Fat: 1.4g|Carbohydrates: 3.3g|Fiber: 0.8g|Sugar: 1.8g|Protein: 13.5g

Honey-Glazed Chicken Drumsticks

Prep Time: 10 minutes
Cook Time: 22 minutes
Serves: 2

Ingredients:

- ½ tablespoon fresh thyme, minced
- 2 tablespoons Dijon mustard
- ½ tablespoon honey
- 1 tablespoon olive oil
- 1 teaspoon fresh rosemary, minced
- 2 chicken drumsticks, boneless
- Salt and black pepper, to taste

Preparation:

1. Take a bowl and mix together mustard, honey, herbs, salt, oil and black pepper.
2. Add chicken drumsticks to the bowl and coat them well with the mixture.
3. Cover and refrigerate overnight.
4. Turn on your Ninja Foodi XL Pro Air Oven and select "Air Fry".
5. Select the timer for about 12 minutes and temperature for 320 degrees F.
6. When the unit beeps to signify it has preheated, open the oven and slide an air fry basket on Level 3.
7. Grease the air fry basket and place the drumsticks into the prepared basket. Close the oven and let it cook.
8. Air fry for about 12 minutes and then for about 10 more minutes at 355 degrees F.
9. Remove from the oven and serve on a platter.
10. Serve hot and enjoy!

Serving Suggestions: Serve with red chili sauce.

Variation Tip: You can add lemon juice to enhance taste.

Nutritional Information per Serving:
Calories: 301 | Fat: 19.8g|Sat Fat: 4.4g|Carbohydrates: 6.1g|Fiber: 1g|Sugar: 4.5g|Protein: 23.8g

Sweet and Sour Chicken Thighs

Prep Time: 10 minutes
Cook Time: 20 minutes
Serves: 1

Ingredients:

- ¼ tablespoon soy sauce
- ¼ tablespoon rice vinegar
- ½ teaspoon sugar
- ½ garlic, minced
- ½ scallion, finely chopped
- ¼ cup corn flour
- 1 chicken thigh, skinless and boneless
- Salt and black pepper, to taste

Preparation:

1. Take a bowl and mix all the ingredients together except chicken and corn flour.
2. Add the chicken thigh to the bowl to coat well.
3. Take another bowl and add corn flour.
4. Remove the chicken thighs from marinade and lightly coat with corn flour.
5. Turn on your Ninja Foodi XL Pro Air Oven and select "Air Fry".
6. Select the timer for about 10 minutes and temperature for 390 degrees F. Press START/STOP to begin preheating.
7. When the unit beeps to signify it has preheated, open the oven and place an air fry basket on Level 3.
8. Grease the air fry basket and place the chicken thighs into the prepared basket. Close the oven and let it cook.
9. Air fry for about 10 minutes and then for another to 10 minutes at 355 degrees F.
10. Remove from the oven and serve on a platter.
11. Serve hot and enjoy!

Serving Suggestions: Serve with red chili sauce.
Variation Tip: You can add lemon juice on top.
Nutritional Information per Serving:
Calories: 262 | Fat: 5.2g|Sat Fat: 1.7g|Carbohydrates: 25.8g|Fiber: 2.4g|Sugar: 2.5g|Protein: 27.5g

Spicy Chicken Legs

Prep Time: 20 minutes
Cook Time: 25 minutes
Serves: 6

Ingredients:

- 6 chicken legs
- 4 cups white flour
- 2 cups buttermilk
- 2 teaspoons onion powder
- 2 teaspoons garlic powder
- 2 teaspoons paprika
- 2 teaspoons ground cumin
- Salt and black pepper, to taste
- 2 tablespoons olive oil

Preparation:

1. Take a bowl, add chicken legs and buttermilk. Refrigerate for about 2 hours.
2. Take another bowl, mix together flour and spices.
3. Remove the chicken legs from buttermilk and coat them with the flour mixture.
4. Do it again until we have a fine coating.
5. Turn on your Ninja Foodi XL Pro Air Oven and select "Air Fry".
6. Select the timer for about 20 to 25 minutes and temperature for 360 degrees F.
7. Place an air fry basket on Level 3. Grease the air fry basket and arrange the chicken legs on it.
8. Take it out when chicken legs are brown enough and serve onto a serving platter.

Serving Suggestions: Add hot sauce on top.
Variation Tip: You can also add dried basil.
Nutritional Information per Serving:
Calories: 653 | Fat: 16.9g|Sat Fat: 4.1g|Carbohydrates: 69.5g|Fiber: 2.7g|Sugar: 4.7g|Protein: 52.3g

Chicken Alfredo Bake

Prep Time: 8 minutes
Cook Time: 25 minutes
Serves: 2

Ingredients:

- ¼ cup heavy cream
- ½ cup milk
- 1 tablespoon flour, divided
- ½ clove garlic, minced
- 1 cup penne pasta
- ½ tablespoon butter
- ½ cup cubed rotisserie chicken
- ½ cup Parmigiano-Reggiano cheese, freshly grated
- ½ pinch ground nutmeg

Preparation:

1. Take a large pot of lightly salted water and bring it to a boil.
2. Add penne and cook for about 11 minutes.
3. Insert a wire rack on Level 3. Turn on your Ninja Foodi XL Pro Air Oven and select "Bake".
4. Set time to 10 to 12 minutes and temperature to 375 degrees F. Press START/STOP to begin preheating.
5. In the meanwhile, take a sauce pan and melt butter over medium heat and cook garlic for about a minute.
6. Add in flour and whisk continuously until you have a paste.
7. Pour in milk and cream, whisking continuously.
8. Stir in cheese and nutmeg.
9. Now add drained penne pasta and cooked chicken.
10. Pour the mixture into an oven-safe dish.
11. Sprinkle cheese on top.
12. When the unit beeps to signify that it has preheated, add the dish on the wire rack in the Ninja Foodi XL Pro Air Oven.
13. Close the oven and bake in the preheated Ninja Foodi XL Pro Air Oven for about 10 to 12 minutes at 375 degrees F.
14. Serve and enjoy!

Serving Suggestions: Serve with garlic bread.

Variation Tip: Add salt and black pepper according to taste.

Nutritional Information per Serving:
Calories: 403 | Fat: 16.2g|Sat Fat: 8.3g|Carbohydrates: 43g|Fiber: 0.1g|Sugar: 3.1g|Protein: 22g

Marinated Ranch Broiled Chicken

Prep Time: 5 minutes
Cook Time: 15 minutes
Serves: 1

Ingredients:

- 1 tablespoon olive oil
- ½ tablespoon red wine vinegar
- 2 tablespoons dry Ranch-style dressing mix
- 1 chicken breast half, skinless and boneless

Preparation:

1. Take a bowl and mix together dressing mix, oil and vinegar.
2. Add chicken in it and toss to coat well.
3. Refrigerate for about an hour.
4. Turn on your Ninja Foodi XL Pro Air Oven and select "Broil".
5. Set timer for 15 minutes and temperature level to HI. Press START/STOP button to begin preheating.
6. When the unit beeps to signify that it has preheated, place chicken onto the roast tray on sheet pan into Level 3 and broil for about 15 minutes until chicken is cooked through.
7. Serve warm and enjoy!

Serving Suggestions: Serve with some rice.

Variation Tip: You can use any type of vinegar.

Nutritional Information per Serving:
Calories: 372 | Fat: 28g|Sat Fat: 5.5g|Carbohydrates: 1.1g|Fiber: 0g|Sugar: 0g|Protein: 25g

Lemon-Lime Chicken

Prep Time: 10 minutes
Cook Time: 20 minutes
Serves: 2

Ingredients:

- 2 tablespoons vegetable oil
- 2 tablespoons lime juice
- ¼ cup lemon juice
- 2 skinless, boneless chicken breast halves
- Italian seasoning to taste
- Salt to taste

Preparation:

1. Take a large bowl and add lemon juice, lime juice and oil.
2. Place the chicken in the mixture and refrigerate for at least an hour.
3. Turn on your Ninja Foodi XL Pro Air Oven and select "Broil".
4. Take a sheet pan with a greased wire rack.
5. Arrange the chicken on the sheet pan and season with Italian seasoning and salt.
6. Place the sheet pan with the wire rack on Level 3.
7. Select the unit for 10 minutes and set temperature level to LO.
8. Turn chicken, season again and broil for another 10 minutes.
9. Serve warm and enjoy!

Serving Suggestions: Serve with lemon wedges.
Variation Tip: You can also add honey.
Nutritional Information per Serving:
Calories: 279 | Fat: 18g|Sat Fat: 4.4g|Carbohydrates: 4.4g|Fiber: 0.3g|Sugar: 1.4g|Protein: 25.4g

Parmesan Chicken Bake

Prep Time: 10 minutes
Cook Time: 50 minutes
Serves: 3

Ingredients:

- 3 skinless, boneless chicken breast halves
- 1 cup prepared marinara sauce
- ¼ cup grated Parmesan cheese, divided
- ½ package garlic croutons
- ½ package shredded mozzarella cheese, divided
- 2 tablespoons chopped fresh basil
- 1 tablespoon olive oil
- 1 clove garlic, crushed and finely chopped
- Red pepper flakes, to taste

Preparation:

1. Insert a wire rack on Level 3. Turn on your Ninja Foodi XL Pro Air Oven and select "Bake".
2. Preheat by selecting the timer for 3 minutes and temperature for 350 degrees F.
3. Grease the dish and sprinkle garlic and red pepper flakes.
4. Arrange the chicken breasts on an oven-safe dish and pour marinara sauce over chicken.
5. Also, top with half of the mozzarella cheese and Parmesan cheese and then sprinkle the croutons.
6. Lastly, add remaining mozzarella cheese on top, followed by half the Parmesan cheese.
7. Select the timer for about 50 minutes and temperature for 160 degrees F.
8. Place the dish on wire rack in oven. Close the oven.
9. Bake until cheese and croutons are golden brown and the chicken is no longer pink inside.
10. Serve and enjoy!

Serving Suggestions: Serve alongside fettuccini noodles.
Variation Tip: Use more marinara sauce if you like.
Nutritional Information per Serving:
Calories: 287 | Fat: 12.7g|Sat Fat: 3.6g|Carbohydrates: 13.7g|Fiber: 2.2g|Sugar: 7.4g|Protein: 29g

Herb Butter Chicken

Prep Time: 10 minutes
Cook Time: 15 minutes
Serves: 2

Ingredients:

- 1½ cloves garlic, minced
- ½ teaspoon dried parsley
- ⅛ teaspoon dried rosemary
- ⅛ teaspoon dried thyme
- 2 skinless, boneless chicken breast halves
- ¼ cup butter, softened

Preparation:

1. Insert a wire rack on Level 3. Turn on your Ninja Foodi XL Pro Air Oven and select "Broil".
2. Cover the sheet pan with aluminum foil and place chicken on it.
3. Take a small bowl and mix together parsley, rosemary, thyme, butter and garlic.
4. Spread the mixture on top of chicken.
5. Place the sheet pan onto the wire rack. Close the oven.
6. Broil in the oven with the coating of butter and herbs for at least 30 minutes at LO.
7. Serve warm and enjoy!

Serving Suggestions: Top with some extra herbs before serving.

Variation Tip: You can also use chopped onions.

Nutritional Information per Serving:
Calories: 354 | Fat: 27.2g|Sat Fat: 16.1g|Carbohydrates: 2.6g|Fiber: 1.2g|Sugar: 0g|Protein: 25.3g

Sauce Glazed Meatloaf

Prep Time: 15 minutes.
Cook Time: 60 minutes.
Serves: 6

Ingredients:

- 1 pound ground beef
- ½ onion chopped
- 1 egg
- 1 ½ garlic clove, minced
- 1 ½ tablespoons ketchup
- 1 ½ tablespoons fresh parsley, chopped
- ¼ cup breadcrumbs
- 2 tablespoons milk
- Salt to taste
- 1 ½ teaspoons herb seasoning
- ¼ teaspoon black pepper
- ½ teaspoon ground paprika

Glaze

- ¾ cup ketchup
- 1 ½ teaspoons white vinegar
- 2 ½ tablespoons brown sugar
- 1 teaspoon garlic powder
- ½ teaspoon onion powder
- ¼ teaspoon ground black pepper
- ¼ teaspoon salt

Preparation:

1. Thoroughly mix ground beef with egg, onion, garlic, crumbs, and all the ingredients in a bowl.
2. Grease a meatloaf pan with oil or butter and spread the minced beef in the pan.
3. Transfer the pan to the 3rd rack position of Ninja Foodi XL Pro Air Oven and close the door.
4. Select the "Air Fry" Mode using FUNCTION +/- buttons and select Rack Level 3.
5. Set its cooking time to 40 minutes and temperature to 375 degrees F, then press "START/STOP" to initiate cooking.
6. Meanwhile, prepare the glaze by whisking its ingredients in a suitable saucepan.
7. Stir cook for 5 minutes until it thickens.
8. Brush this glaze over the meatloaf and bake it again for 15 minutes.
9. Slice and serve.

Serving Suggestion: Serve the meatloaf with mashed potatoes.

Variation Tip: Wrap the bacon over the meatloaf before baking.

Nutritional Information Per Serving:
Calories 435 | Fat 25g |Sodium 532mg | Carbs 23g | Fiber 0.4g | Sugar 2g | Protein 28.3g

Zucchini Beef Meatloaf

Prep Time: 15 minutes.
Cook Time: 40 minutes.
Serves: 4

Ingredients:

- 2 pounds ground beef
- 1 cup zucchini, shredded
- 2 eggs
- ½ cup onion, chopped
- 3 garlic cloves, minced
- 3 tablespoons Worcestershire sauce
- 3 tablespoons fresh parsley, chopped
- ¾ cup Panko breadcrumbs
- ⅓ cup beef broth
- Salt to taste
- ¼ teaspoon ground black pepper
- ½ teaspoon ground paprika

Preparation:

1. Thoroughly mix ground beef with egg, zucchini, onion, garlic, crumbs, and all the ingredients in a bowl.
2. Grease a meatloaf pan with oil and spread the minced beef in the pan.
3. Transfer the pan to the 2nd rack position of Ninja Foodi XL Pro Air Oven and close the door.
4. Select the "Air Fry" Mode using FUNCTION +/- buttons and select Rack Level 2.
5. Set its cooking time to 40 minutes and temperature to 375 degrees F, then press "START/STOP" to initiate cooking.
6. Slice and serve.

Serving Suggestion: Serve the meatloaf with toasted bread slices.

Variation Tip: Add crumbled bacon on top for a crispy texture.

Nutritional Information Per Serving:
Calories 325 | Fat 16g |Sodium 431mg | Carbs 22g | Fiber 1.2g | Sugar 4g | Protein 23g

Lamb Chops with Rosemary Sauce

Prep Time: 15 minutes.
Cook Time: 45 minutes.
Serves: 8

Ingredients:

- 8 lamb loin chops
- 1 small onion, peeled and chopped
- Salt and black pepper, to taste

For its sauce:

- 1 onion, peeled and chopped
- 1 tablespoon rosemary leaves
- 1 ounce butter
- 1 ounce plain flour
- 6 ounces milk
- 6 ounces vegetable stock
- 2 tablespoons cream, whipping
- Salt and black pepper, to taste

Preparation:

1. Place the lamb loin chops and onion in a roast tray, then drizzle salt and black pepper on top.
2. Transfer the tray to the 2nd rack position of Ninja Foodi XL Pro Air Oven and close the door.
3. Select the "Air Fry" Mode using FUNCTION +/- buttons and select Rack Level 2.
4. Set its cooking time to 45 minutes and temperature to 350 degrees F, then press "START/STOP" to initiate cooking.
5. Prepare the white sauce by melting butter in a suitable saucepan, then stir in onions.
6. Sauté for 5 minutes, then stir flour and stir cook for 2 minutes.
7. Stir in the rest of the sauce ingredients and mix well.
8. Pour its sauce over baked chops and serve.

Serving Suggestion: Serve the chops with a fresh green's salad.

Variation Tip: Wrap the lamb chops with a foil sheet before baking for a rich taste.

Nutritional Information Per Serving:
Calories 450 | Fat 20g |Sodium 686mg | Carbs 3g | Fiber 1g | Sugar 1.2g | Protein 31g

Garlicky Lamb Chops

Prep Time: 15 minutes.
Cook Time: 45 minutes.
Serves: 8

Ingredients:

- 8 medium lamb chops
- ¼ cup olive oil
- 3 thin lemon slices
- 2 garlic cloves, crushed
- 1 teaspoon dried oregano
- 1 teaspoon salt
- ½ teaspoon black pepper

Preparation:

1. Place the lamb chops in a suitable baking tray and rub them with olive oil.
2. Add garlic, lemon slices, salt, oregano, and black pepper on top of the lamb chops.
3. Transfer the tray to the 2nd rack position of Ninja Foodi XL Pro Air Oven and close the door.
4. Select the "Air Roast" Mode using FUNCTION +/- buttons and select Rack Level 2.
5. Set its cooking time to 45 minutes and temperature to 400 degrees F, then press "START/STOP" to initiate cooking.
6. Serve warm.

Serving Suggestion: Serve the chops with boiled rice or cucumber salad.

Variation Tip: Cook the lamb chops with potatoes and asparagus

Nutritional Information Per Serving:
Calories 461 | Fat 16g |Sodium 515mg | Carbs 3g | Fiber 0.1g | Sugar 1.2g | Protein 21.3g

Lamb Kebabs

Prep Time: 15 minutes.
Cook Time: 20 minutes.
Serves: 4

Ingredients:

- 18 ounces lamb mince
- 1 teaspoon chili powder
- 1 teaspoon cumin powder
- 1 egg
- 2 ounces onion, chopped
- 2 teaspoons sesame oil

Preparation:

1. Whisk onion with egg, chili powder, oil, cumin powder, and salt in a bowl.
2. Add lamb to coat well, then thread it on the skewers.
3. Place these lamb skewers in the air fry basket.
4. Transfer the basket to the 3rd rack position of Ninja Foodi XL Pro Air Oven and close the door.
5. Select the "Air Fry" Mode using FUNCTION +/- buttons and select Rack Level 3.
6. Set its cooking time to 20 minutes and temperature to 395 degrees F, then press "START/STOP" to initiate cooking.
7. Serve warm.

Serving Suggestion: Serve the lamb kebabs with garlic bread slices and fresh herbs on top.
Variation Tip: Add chopped green chilis to the meat mixture.
Nutritional Information Per Serving:
Calories 405 | Fat 22.7g |Sodium 227mg | Carbs 6.1g | Fiber 1.4g | Sugar 0.9g | Protein 45.2g

Beef Short Ribs

Prep Time: 15 minutes.
Cook Time: 35 minutes.
Serves: 4

Ingredients:

- 1 ⅔ pounds short ribs
- Salt and black pepper, to taste
- 1 teaspoon grated garlic
- ½ teaspoon salt
- 1 teaspoon cumin seeds
- ¼ cup panko crumbs
- 1 teaspoon ground cumin
- 1 teaspoon avocado oil
- ½ teaspoon orange zest
- 1 egg, beaten

Preparation:

1. Place the beef ribs in a baking tray and pour the whisked egg on top.
2. Whisk the rest of the crusting ingredients in a bowl and spread over the beef.
3. Transfer the tray to the 2nd rack position of Ninja Foodi XL Pro Air Oven and close the door.
4. Select the "Air Fry" Mode using FUNCTION +/- buttons and select Rack Level 2.
5. Set its cooking time to 35 minutes and temperature to 350 degrees F, then press "START/STOP" to initiate cooking.
6. Serve warm.

Serving Suggestion: Serve the short ribs with white rice or warmed bread.
Variation Tip: Add orange juice to the marinade for a refreshing taste.
Nutritional Information Per Serving:
Calories 425 | Fat 14g |Sodium 411mg | Carbs 44g | Fiber 0.3g | Sugar 1g | Protein 23g

Garlic Braised Ribs

Prep Time: 15 minutes.
Cook Time: 20 minutes.
Serves: 8

Ingredients:

- 2 tablespoons vegetable oil
- 5 pounds bone-in short ribs
- Salt and black pepper, to taste
- 2 heads garlic, halved
- 1 medium onion, chopped
- 4 ribs celery, chopped
- 2 medium carrots, chopped
- 3 tablespoons tomato paste
- ¼ cup dry red wine
- ¼ cup beef stock
- 4 sprigs thyme
- 1 cup parsley, chopped
- ½ cup chives, chopped
- 1 tablespoon lemon zest, grated

Preparation:

1. Toss everything in a large bowl, then add short ribs.
2. Mix well to soak the ribs and marinate for 30 minutes.
3. Transfer the soaked ribs to the baking pan and add the marinade around them.
4. Transfer the pan to the 2nd rack position of Ninja Foodi XL Pro Air Oven and close the door.
5. Select the "Air Fry" Mode using FUNCTION +/- buttons and select Rack Level 2.
6. Set its cooking time to 20 minutes and temperature to 400 degrees F, then press "START/STOP" to initiate cooking.
7. Serve warm.

Serving Suggestion: Serve the ribs with mashed potatoes.

Variation Tip: Add barbecue sauce to season the ribs.

Nutritional Information Per Serving:
Calories 441 | Fat 5g |Sodium 88mg | Carbs 13g | Fiber 0g | Sugar 0g | Protein 24g

Mint Lamb with Toasted Hazelnuts

Prep Time: 15 minutes.
Cook Time: 25 minutes.
Serves: 2

Ingredients:

- ¼ cup hazelnuts, toasted
- ⅔ pound shoulder lamb, cut into strips
- 1 tablespoon hazelnut oil
- 2 tablespoons mint leaves, chopped
- ½ cup frozen peas
- ¼ cup of water
- ½ cup white wine
- Salt and black pepper to taste

Preparation:

1. Toss lamb with hazelnuts, spices, and all the ingredients in a baking pan.
2. Transfer the pan to the 3rd rack position of Ninja Foodi XL Pro Air Oven and close the door.
3. Select the "Air Fry" Mode using FUNCTION +/- buttons and select Rack Level 3.
4. Set its cooking time to 25 minutes and temperature to 370 degrees F, then press "START/STOP" to initiate cooking.
5. Serve warm.

Serving Suggestion: Serve the lamb with carrots and potatoes on the side.

Variation Tip: Use chimichurri sauce to season the lamb.

Nutritional Information Per Serving:
Calories 445 | Fat 36g |Sodium 272mg | Carbs 1g | Fiber 0.2g | Sugar 0.1g | Protein 22.5g

Greek lamb Farfalle

Prep Time: 15 minutes.
Cook Time: 20 minutes.
Serves: 6

Ingredients:

- 1 tablespoon olive oil
- 1 onion, chopped
- 2 garlic cloves, chopped
- 2 teaspoons dried oregano
- 1 pound pack lamb mince
- ¾ pound tin tomatoes, chopped
- ¼ cup black olives pitted
- ½ cup frozen spinach, defrosted
- 2 tablespoons dill, removed and chopped
- 9 ounces farfalle, boiled
- 1 ball half-fat mozzarella, torn

Preparation:

1. Sauté onion and garlic with oil in a pan over moderate heat for 5 minutes.
2. Stir in tomatoes, spinach, dill, oregano, lamb, and olives, then stir cook for 5 minutes.
3. Spread the lamb in a casserole dish and toss in the boiled Farfelle pasta.
4. Top the pasta lamb mix with mozzarella cheese.
5. Transfer the dish to the 2nd rack position of Ninja Foodi XL Pro Air Oven and close the door.
6. Select the "Air Fry" Mode using FUNCTION +/- buttons and select Rack Level 2.
7. Set its cooking time to 10 minutes and temperature to 350 degrees F, then press "START/STOP" to initiate cooking.
8. Serve warm.

Serving Suggestion: Serve the lamb farfalle with fresh green and mashed potatoes.

Variation Tip: Add shredded cheddar cheese to the meat mixture, then bake.

Nutritional Information Per Serving:
Calories 461 | Fat 5g |Sodium 340mg | Carbs 24.7g | Fiber 1.2g | Sugar 1.3g | Protein 15.3g

Beef Zucchini Shashliks

Prep Time: 15 minutes.
Cook Time: 25 minutes.
Serves: 4

Ingredients:

- 1 pound beef, boned and diced
- 1 lime, juiced, and chopped
- 3 tablespoons olive oil
- 20 garlic cloves, chopped
- 1 handful rosemary, chopped
- 3 green peppers, cubed
- 2 zucchinis, cubed
- 2 red onions, cut into wedges

Preparation:

1. Toss the beef with the rest of the skewer's ingredients in a bowl.
2. Thread the beef, peppers, zucchini, and onion on the skewers.
3. Place these beef skewers in the air fry basket.
4. Transfer the basket to the 3rd rack position of Ninja Foodi XL Pro Air Oven and close the door.
5. Select the "Air Fry" Mode using FUNCTION +/- buttons and select Rack Level 3.
6. Set its cooking time to 25 minutes and temperature to 370 degrees F, then press "START/STOP" to initiate cooking.
7. Flip the skewers when cooked halfway through, then resume cooking.
8. Serve warm.

Serving Suggestion: Serve the shashlik with crispy bacon and sautéed vegetables.

Variation Tip: Season the beef with yogurt and spice marinade.

Nutritional Information Per Serving:
Calories 416 | Fat 21g |Sodium 476mg | Carbs 22g | Fiber 3g | Sugar 4g | Protein 20g

Minced Lamb Casserole

Prep Time: 15 minutes.
Cook Time: 31 minutes.
Serves: 6

Ingredients:

- 2 tablespoons olive oil
- 1 medium onion, chopped
- ½ pound ground lamb
- 4 fresh mushrooms, sliced
- 1 cup small pasta shells, cooked
- 2 cups bottled marinara sauce
- 1 teaspoon butter
- 4 teaspoons flour
- 1 cup milk
- 1 egg, beaten
- 1 cup cheddar cheese, grated

Preparation:

1. Put a wok on moderate heat and add oil to heat.
2. Toss in onion and sauté until soft.
3. Stir in mushrooms and lamb, then cook until meat is brown.
4. Add marinara sauce and cook it to a simmer.
5. Stir in pasta, then spread this mixture in a casserole dish.
6. Prepare its sauce by melting butter in a suitable saucepan over moderate heat.
7. Stir in flour and whisk well, pour in the milk.
8. Mix well and whisk ¼ cup sauce with egg, then return it to its saucepan.
9. Stir, cook for 1 minute, then pour this sauce over the lamb.
10. Drizzle cheese over the lamb casserole.
11. Transfer the dish to the 2nd rack position of Ninja Foodi XL Pro Air Oven and close the door.
12. Select the "Bake" Mode using FUNCTION +/- buttons and select Rack Level 2.
13. Set its cooking time to 30 minutes and temperature to 350 degrees F, then press "START/STOP" to initiate cooking.
14. Serve warm.

Serving Suggestion: Serve the lamb casserole with quinoa salad.
Variation Tip: Add shredded cheese to the casserole for a cheesy taste.
Nutritional Information Per Serving:
Calories 448 | Fat 23g |Sodium 350mg | Carbs 18g | Fiber 6.3g | Sugar 1g | Protein 40.3g

Lamb Rack with Lemon Crust

Prep Time: 15 minutes.
Cook Time: 25 minutes.
Serves: 3

Ingredients:

- 1 ⅔ pounds frenched rack of lamb
- Salt and black pepper, to taste
- ¼ pound dry breadcrumbs
- 1 teaspoon garlic, grated
- ½ teaspoon salt
- 1 teaspoon cumin seeds
- 1 teaspoon ground cumin
- 1 teaspoon oil
- ½ teaspoon grated lemon rind
- 1 egg, beaten

Preparation:

1. Place the lamb rack in a baking tray and pour the whisked egg on top.
2. Whisk the rest of the crusting ingredients in a bowl and spread over the lamb.
3. Transfer the baking tray to the 2nd rack position of Ninja Foodi XL Pro Air Oven and close the door.
4. Select the "Air Fry" Mode using FUNCTION +/- buttons and select Rack Level 2.
5. Set its cooking time to 25 minutes and temperature to 350 degrees F, then press "START/STOP" to initiate cooking.
6. Serve warm.

Serving Suggestion: Serve the Lamb rack with sautéed green beans and mashed potatoes.
Variation Tip: Drizzle parmesan cheese on top before cooking.
Nutritional Information Per Serving:
Calories 455 | Fat 9.5g |Sodium 655mg | Carbs 13.4g | Fiber 0.4g | Sugar 0.4g | Protein 28.3g

Pork Chops with Cashew Sauce

Prep Time: 15 minutes.
Cook Time: 52 minutes.
Serves: 8

Ingredients:

- 8 pork loin chops
- 1 small onion, peeled and chopped
- Salt and black pepper, to taste

For its sauce:

- ¼ cup cashews, finely chopped
- 1 cup cashew butter
- 1 ounce wheat flour
- 6 fl. oz. milk
- 6 fl. oz. beef stock
- 2 tablespoons coconut cream, whipping
- Salt and black pepper, to taste

Preparation:

1. Place the pork loin chops and onion in a baking tray, then drizzle salt and black pepper on top.
2. Transfer the tray to the 2nd rack position of Ninja Foodi XL Pro Air Oven and close the door.
3. Select the "Bake" Mode using FUNCTION +/- buttons and select Rack Level 2.
4. Set its cooking time to 45 minutes and temperature to 375 degrees F, then press "START/STOP" to initiate cooking.
5. Prepare the white sauce by first melting butter in a suitable saucepan, then stir in cashews.
6. Sauté for 5 minutes, then stir flour and stir cook for 2 minutes.
7. Stir in the rest of its sauce ingredients and mix well.
8. Pour its sauce over baked chops and serve.

Serving Suggestion: Serve the pork chops with sautéed vegetables and toasted bread slices.
Variation Tip: Add crushed cashews on top before baking.

Nutritional Information Per Serving:
Calories 309 | Fat 25g |Sodium 463mg | Carbs 9g | Fiber 0.3g | Sugar 0.3g | Protein 18g

Za'atar Chops

Prep Time: 15 minutes.
Cook Time: 20 minutes.
Serves: 8

Ingredients:

- 8 pork loin chops, bone-in
- 1 tablespoon Za'atar
- 3 garlic cloves, crushed
- 1 teaspoon avocado oil
- 2 tablespoons lemon juice
- 1 ¼ teaspoons salt
- Black pepper, to taste

Preparation:

1. Rub the pork chops with oil, za'atar, salt, lemon juice, garlic, and black pepper.
2. Place these chops in the air fry basket.
3. Transfer the basket to the 2nd rack position of Ninja Foodi XL Pro Air Oven and close the door.
4. Select the "Air Fry" Mode using FUNCTION +/- buttons and select Rack Level 2.
5. Set its cooking time to 20 minutes and temperature to 400 degrees F, then press "START/STOP" to initiate cooking.
6. Flip the chops when cooked halfway through, then resume cooking.
7. Serve warm.

Serving Suggestion: Serve the chops with mashed potatoes.
Variation Tip: Add dried herbs to season the chops.

Nutritional Information Per Serving:
Calories 437 | Fat 20g |Sodium 719mg | Carbs 5.1g | Fiber 0.9g | Sugar 1.4g | Protein 37.8g

Bacon-Wrapped Pork Tenderloin

Prep Time: 15 minutes
Cook Time: 30 minutes
Serves: 4

Ingredients:

- 1 (1½-pound) pork tenderloin
- 2 tablespoons Dijon mustard
- 1 tablespoon honey
- 4 bacon strips

Preparation:

1. Coat the tenderloin with mustard and honey.
2. Wrap the pork tenderloin with bacon strips.
3. Press "Power" button of Ninja Foodi XL Pro Air Oven and select "Air Fry" function.
4. Press TEMP/SHADE +/- buttons to set the temperature at 360 degrees F.
5. Now press TIME/SLICES +/- buttons to set the cooking time to 30 minutes.
6. Press "START/STOP" button to start.
7. When the unit beeps to show that it is preheated, open the lid and grease the air fry basket.
8. Place the pork tenderloin into the prepared air fry basket and insert in the oven.
9. Flip the pork tenderloin once halfway through.
10. When cooking time is completed, open the lid and place the pork loin onto a cutting board for about 10 minutes before slicing.
11. With a sharp knife, cut the tenderloin into desired sized slices and serve.

Serving Suggestions: Enjoy with mashed potatoes.

Variation Tip: Make sure to remove the silver skin from the tenderloin.

Nutritional Information per Serving:
Calories: 386 | Fat: 16.1g|Sat Fat: 5.7g|Carbohydrates: 4.8g|Fiber: 0.3g|Sugar: 4.4g|Protein: 52g

Spiced Pork Shoulder

Prep Time: 15 minutes
Cook Time: 55 minutes
Serves: 4

Ingredients:

- 1 teaspoon ground cumin
- 1 teaspoon cayenne pepper
- ½ teaspoon garlic powder
- ½ teaspoon onion powder
- Salt and ground black pepper, as required
- 2 pounds skin-on pork shoulder

Preparation:

1. In a small bowl, place the spices, salt and black pepper and mix well.
2. Arrange the pork shoulder onto a cutting board, skin-side down.
3. Season the inner side of pork shoulder with salt and black pepper.
4. With kitchen twines, tie the pork shoulder into a long round cylinder shape.
5. Season the outer side of pork shoulder with spice mixture.
6. Press "Power" button of Ninja Foodi XL Pro Air Oven and select the "Air Roast" function.
7. Press TEMP/SHADE +/- buttons to set the temperature at 350 degrees F.
8. Now press TIME/SLICES +/- buttons to set the cooking time to 55 minutes.
9. Press "START/STOP" button to start.
10. When the unit beeps to show that it is preheated, open the lid and grease the air fry basket.
11. Arrange the pork shoulder into air fry basket and insert in the oven.
12. When cooking time is completed, open the lid and place the pork shoulder onto a platter for about 10 minutes before slicing.
13. With a sharp knife, cut the pork shoulder into desired sized slices and serve.

Serving Suggestions: Choose a pork shoulder with pinkish-red color. Serve with southern-style grits.

Variation Tip: Add some seasoning of your choice.

Nutritional Information per Serving:
Calories: 445 | Fat: 32.5g|Sat Fat: 11.9g|Carbohydrates: 0.7g|Fiber: 0.2g|Sugar: 0.2g|Protein: 35.4g

Garlicky Lamb Steaks

Prep Time: 15 minutes
Cook Time: 15 minutes
Serves: 4

Ingredients:

- ½ onion, roughly chopped
- 5 garlic cloves, peeled
- 1 tablespoon fresh ginger, peeled
- 1 teaspoon ground fennel
- ½ teaspoon ground cumin
- ½ teaspoon ground cinnamon
- ½ teaspoon cayenne pepper
- Salt and ground black pepper, as required
- 1½ pounds boneless lamb sirloin steaks

Preparation:

1. In a blender, add the onion, garlic, ginger, and spices and pulse until smooth.
2. Transfer the mixture into a large bowl.
3. Add the lamb steaks and coat with the mixture generously.
4. Refrigerate to marinate for about 24 hours.
5. Press "Power" button of Ninja Foodi XL Pro Air Oven and select "Air Fry" function.
6. Press TEMP/SHADE +/- buttons to set the temperature at 330 degrees F.
7. Now press TIME/SLICES +/- buttons to set the cooking time to 15 minutes.
8. Press "START/STOP" button to start.
9. When the unit beeps to show that it is preheated, open the lid and grease the air fry basket.
10. Allow the lamb steaks to reach room temperature before cooking. Place the lamb steaks into the prepared air fry basket and insert in the oven.
11. Flip the steaks once halfway through.
12. When cooking time is completed, open the lid and serve hot.

Serving Suggestions: Serve with your favorite greens.
Variation Tip: Feel free to add some seasoning as you like.
Nutritional Information per Serving:
Calories: 336 | Fat: 12.8g|Sat Fat: 4.5g|Carbohydrates: 4.2g|Fiber: 1g|Sugar: 0.7g|Protein: 8.4g

Rosemary Lamb Chops

Prep Time: 10 minutes
Cook Time: 6 minutes
Serves: 2

Ingredients:

- 1 tablespoon olive oil, divided
- 2 garlic cloves, minced
- 1 tablespoon fresh rosemary, chopped
- Salt and ground black pepper, as required
- 4 (4-ounce) fresh lamb chops

Preparation:

1. In a large bowl, mix the oil, garlic, rosemary, salt and black pepper together.
2. Dry out the edges of lamb chops. Coat the chops with half of the garlic mixture.
3. Press "Power" button of Ninja Foodi XL Pro Air Oven and select "Air Fry" function.
4. Press TEMP/SHADE +/- buttons to set the temperature at 390 degrees F.
5. Now press TIME/SLICES +/- buttons to set the cooking time to 6 minutes.
6. Press "START/STOP" button to start.
7. When the unit beeps to show that it is preheated, open the lid and grease the air fry basket.
8. Place the lamb chops into the prepared air fry basket and insert in the oven.
9. Flip the chops once halfway through.
10. When cooking time is completed, open the lid and serve hot with the topping of the remaining garlic mixture.

Serving Suggestions: Serve with yogurt sauce.
Variation Tip: Feel free to add some seasoning of your choice.
Nutritional Information per Serving:
Calories: 492 | Fat: 23.9g|Sat Fat: 7.1g|Carbohydrates: 2.1g|Fiber: 0.8g|Sugar: 0g|Protein: 64g

Seasoned Sirloin Steak

Prep Time: 10 minutes
Cook Time: 12 minutes
Serves: 2

Ingredients:

- 2 (7-ounce) top sirloin steaks
- 1 tablespoon steak seasoning
- Salt and ground black pepper, as required

Preparation:

1. Make sure the surface of the steak be moist but not wet or sticky.
2. Season each steak with steak seasoning, salt and black pepper.
3. Arrange the steaks onto the greased cooking pan.
4. Press "Power" button of Ninja Foodi XL Pro Air Oven and select "Air Fry" function.
5. Press TEMP/SHADE +/- buttons to set the temperature at 400 degrees F.
6. Now press TIME/SLICES +/- buttons to set the cooking time to 12 minutes.
7. Press "START/STOP" button to start.
8. When the unit beeps to show that it is preheated, open the lid and insert the baking pan in the oven.
9. Flip the steaks once halfway through.
10. When cooking time is completed, open the lid and serve hot.

Serving Suggestions: Serve with cheesy scalloped potatoes.

Variation Tip: Feel free to add some seasoning of your choice.

Nutritional Information per Serving:
Calories: 369 | Fat: 12.4g|Sat Fat: 4.7g|Carbohydrates: 0g|Fiber: 0g|Sugar: 0g|Protein: 60.2g

Breaded Pork Chops

Prep Time: 15 minutes
Cook Time: 15 minutes
Serves: 3

Ingredients:

- 3 (6-ounce) pork chops
- Salt and ground black pepper, as required
- ¼ cup plain flour
- 1 egg
- 4 ounces seasoned breadcrumbs
- 1 tablespoon canola oil

Preparation:

1. Season each pork chop with salt and black pepper.
2. In a shallow bowl, place the flour.
3. In a second bowl, crack the egg and beat well.
4. In a third bowl, add the breadcrumbs and oil and mix until a crumbly mixture forms.
5. Coat the pork chop with flour, then dip into beaten egg and finally, coat with the breadcrumbs mixture.
6. Press "Power" button of Ninja Foodi XL Pro Air Oven and select "Air Fry" function.
7. Press TEMP/SHADE +/- buttons to set the temperature at 400 degrees F.
8. Now press TIME/SLICES +/- buttons to set the cooking time to 15 minutes.
9. Press "START/STOP" button to start.
10. When the unit beeps to show that it is preheated, open the lid and grease the air fry basket.
11. Place the lamb chops into the prepared air fry basket and insert in the oven.
12. Flip the chops once halfway through.
13. When cooking time is completed, open the lid and serve hot.

Serving Suggestions: Don't cook chops straight from the refrigerator. Serve with your favorite dipping sauce.

Variation Tip: Replace the black pepper with some other peppers of your choice.

Nutritional Information per Serving:
Calories: 413 | Fat: 20.2g|Sat Fat: 4.4g|Carbohydrates: 31g|Fiber: 1.6g|Sugar: 0.1g|Protein: 28.3g

Pork Stuffed Bell Peppers

Prep Time: 20 minutes
Cook Time: 1 hour 10 minutes
Serves: 4

Ingredients:

- 4 medium green bell peppers
- ⅔ pound ground pork
- 2 cups cooked white rice
- 1½ cups marinara sauce, divided
- 1 teaspoon Worcestershire sauce
- 1 teaspoon Italian seasoning
- Salt and ground black pepper, as required
- ½ cup mozzarella cheese, shredded

Preparation:

1. Cut the tops from bell peppers and then carefully remove the seeds.
2. Heat a large skillet over medium heat and cook the pork for about 6-8 minutes, breaking into crumbles.
3. Add the rice, ¾ cup of marinara sauce, Worcestershire sauce, Italian seasoning, salt and black pepper and stir to combine.
4. Remove from the heat.
5. Arrange the bell peppers into the greased baking pan.
6. Carefully, stuff each bell pepper with the pork mixture and top each with the remaining sauce.
7. Press "Power" button of Ninja Foodi XL Pro Air Oven and select the "Bake" function.
8. Press TEMP/SHADE +/- buttons to set the temperature at 350 degrees F.
9. Now press TIME/SLICES +/- buttons to set the cooking time to 60 minutes.
10. Press "START/STOP" button to start.
11. When the unit beeps to show that it is preheated, open the lid.
12. Insert the baking pan in oven.
13. After 50 minute of cooking, top each bell pepper with cheese.
14. When cooking time is completed, open the lid and transfer the bell peppers onto a platter.
15. Serve warm.

Serving Suggestions: Serve with baby greens.
Variation Tip: Feel free to add some seasoning as you like.
Nutritional Information per Serving:
Calories: 580 | Fat: 7.1g|Sat Fat: 2.2g|Carbohydrates: 96.4g|Fiber: 5.2g|Sugar: 14.8g|Protein: 30.3g

Steak with Bell Peppers

Prep Time: 15 minutes
Cook Time: 11 minutes
Serves: 4

Ingredients:

- 1 teaspoon dried oregano, crushed
- 1 teaspoon onion powder
- 1 teaspoon garlic powder
- 1 teaspoon red chili powder
- 1 teaspoon paprika
- Salt, as required
- 1¼ pounds flank steak, cut into thin strips
- 3 green bell peppers, seeded and cubed
- 1 red onion, sliced
- 2 tablespoons olive oil
- 3-4 tablespoons feta cheese, crumbled

Preparation:

1. In a large bowl, mix the oregano and spices together.
2. Add the steak strips, bell peppers, onion, and oil and mix until well combined.
3. Press "Power" button of Ninja Foodi XL Pro Air Oven and select "Air Fry" function.
4. Press TEMP/SHADE +/- buttons to set the temperature at 390 degrees F.
5. Now press TIME/SLICES +/- buttons to set the cooking time to 11 minutes.
6. Press "START/STOP" button to start.
7. When the unit beeps to show that it is preheated, open the lid and grease the air fry basket.
8. Place the steak mixture into the prepared air fry basket and insert in the oven.
9. When cooking time is completed, open the lid and transfer the steak mixture onto serving plates.
10. Serve immediately with the topping of feta.

Serving Suggestions: Serve with plain rice.
Variation Tip: Adjust the ratio of spices according to your taste.
Nutritional Information per Serving:
Calories: 732 | Fat: 35g|Sat Fat: 12.9g|Carbohydrates: 11.5g|Fiber: 2.5g|Sugar: 6.5g|Protein: 89.3g

Simple Beef Tenderloin

Prep Time: 10 minutes
Cook Time: 50 minutes
Serves: 10

Ingredients:

- 1 (3½-pound) beef tenderloin, trimmed
- 2 tablespoons olive oil
- Salt and ground black pepper, as required

Preparation:

1. With kitchen twine, tie the tenderloin.
2. Rub the tenderloin with oil and season with salt and black pepper.
3. Place the tenderloin into the greased baking pan.
4. Press "Power" button of Ninja Foodi XL Pro Air Oven and select the "Air Roast" function.
5. Press TEMP/SHADE +/- buttons to set the temperature at 400 degrees F.
6. Now press TIME/SLICES +/- buttons to set the cooking time to 50 minutes.
7. Press "START/STOP" button to start.
8. When the unit beeps to show that it is preheated, open the lid and insert the baking pan in the oven.
9. When cooking time is completed, open the lid and place the tenderloin onto a platter for about 10 minutes before slicing.
10. With a sharp knife, cut the tenderloin into desired sized slices and serve.

Serving Suggestions: Serve with lemony herbed couscous.

Variation Tip: Add some seasoning as you like.

Nutritional Information per Serving:
Calories: 351 | Fat: 17.3g|Sat Fat: 5.9g|Carbohydrates: 0g|Fiber: 0g|Sugar: 0g|Protein: .46g

Herbed Chuck Roast

Prep Time: 10 minutes
Cook Time: 45 minutes
Serves: 6

Ingredients:

- 1 (2-pound) beef chuck roast
- 1 tablespoon olive oil
- 1 teaspoon dried rosemary, crushed
- 1 teaspoon dried thyme, crushed
- Salt, as required

Preparation:

1. In a bowl, add the oil, herbs and salt and mix well.
2. Coat the beef roast with herb mixture generously.
3. Arrange the beef roast onto the greased cooking pan.
4. Press "Power" button of Ninja Foodi XL Pro Air Oven and select "Air Fry" function.
5. Press TEMP/SHADE +/- buttons to set the temperature at 360 degrees F.
6. Now press TIME/SLICES +/- buttons to set the cooking time to 45 minutes.
7. Press "START/STOP" button to start.
8. When the unit beeps to show that it is preheated, open the lid and insert the baking pan in the oven.
9. When cooking time is completed, open the lid and place the roast onto a cutting board.
10. With a piece of foil, cover the beef roast for about 20 minutes before slicing.
11. With a sharp knife, cut the beef roast into desired size slices and serve.

Serving Suggestions: Serve with roasted Brussels sprouts.

Variation Tip: Dried herbs can be replaced with fresh herbs.

Nutritional Information per Serving:
Calories: 304 | Fat: 14g|Sat Fat: 4.5g|Carbohydrates: 0.2g|Fiber: 0.2g|Sugar: 0g|Protein: 41.5g

Herb-Crumbed Rack of Lamb

Prep Time: 15 minutes
Cook Time: 30 minutes
Serves: 5

Ingredients:

- 1 tablespoon butter, melted
- 1 garlic clove, finely chopped
- 1¾ pounds rack of lamb
- Salt and ground black pepper, as required
- 1 egg
- ½ cup panko breadcrumbs
- 1 tablespoon fresh thyme, minced
- 1 tablespoon fresh rosemary, minced

Preparation:

1. In a bowl, mix the butter, garlic, salt, and black pepper together.
2. Coat the rack of lamb evenly with garlic mixture.
3. In a shallow dish, beat the egg.
4. In another dish, mix the breadcrumbs and herbs together.
5. Dip the rack of lamb in beaten egg and then coat with breadcrumbs mixture.
6. Press "Power" button of Ninja Foodi XL Pro Air Oven and select "Air Fry" function.
7. Press TEMP/SHADE +/- buttons to set the temperature at 215 degrees F.
8. Now press TIME/SLICES +/- buttons to set the cooking time to 25 minutes.
9. Press "START/STOP" button to start.
10. When the unit beeps to show that it is preheated, open the lid and grease the air fry basket.
11. Place the rack of lamb into the prepared air fry basket and insert in the oven.
12. After 25 minutes of cooking, flip the rack of lamb.
13. When cooking time is completed, open the lid and set the temperature at 390 degrees F for 5 minutes.
14. When cooking time is completed, open the lid and place the rack of lamb onto a cutting board for about 5-10 minutes for a more delicious taste.
15. With a sharp knife, cut the rack of lamb into individual chops and serve.

Serving Suggestions: Serve with a drizzling of lemon juice.
Variation Tip: Add some seasoning as you like.
Nutritional Information per Serving:
Calories: 331 | Fat: 17.2g|Sat Fat: 6.7g|Carbohydrates: 2.6g|Fiber: 0.5g|Sugar: 0g|Protein: 32.7g

Lamb Burgers

Prep Time: 10 minutes
Cook Time: 8 minutes
Serves: 6

Ingredients:

- 2 pounds ground lamb
- ½ tablespoon onion powder
- ½ tablespoon garlic powder
- ¼ teaspoon ground cumin
- Salt and ground black pepper, as required

Preparation:

1. In a bowl, add all the ingredients and mix well.
2. Make 6 equal-sized patties from the mixture.
3. Arrange the patties onto the greased sheet pan in a single layer.
4. Press "Power" button of Ninja Foodi XL Pro Air Oven and select "Air Fry" function.
5. Press TEMP/SHADE +/- buttons to set the temperature at 360 degrees F.
6. Now press TIME/SLICES +/- buttons to set the cooking time to 8 minutes.
7. Press "START/STOP" button to start.
8. When the unit beeps to show that it is preheated, open the lid.
9. Insert the sheet pan in oven.
10. Flip the burgers once halfway through.
11. When cooking time is completed, open the lid and serve hot.

Serving Suggestions: Serve with fresh salad.
Variation Tip: Feel free to add some seasoning or sauces of your choice.
Nutritional Information per Serving:
Calories: 286 | Fat: 11.1g|Sat Fat: 4g|Carbohydrates: 1g|Fiber: 0.1g|Sugar: 0.4g|Protein: 42.7g

Buttered Strip Steak

Prep Time: 10 minutes
Cook Time: 15 minutes
Serves: 4

Ingredients:

- 2 (14-ounce) New York strip steaks
- 2 tablespoons butter, melted
- Salt and ground black pepper, as required

Preparation:

1. Brush each steak with the melted butter evenly and then season with salt and black pepper.
2. Press "Power" button of Ninja Foodi XL Pro Air Oven and select the "Broil" function.
3. Press the TEMP/SHADE +/- buttons to select HI.
4. Now press TIME/SLICES +/- buttons to set the cooking time to 15 minutes.
5. Press "Start/Stop" button to start.
6. When the unit beeps to show that it is preheated, open the oven door.
7. Place the steaks on the sheet pan over the wire rack and insert into the rail of Level 3.
8. When cooking time is completed, open the oven door and place the steaks onto a cutting board for about 5 minutes before slicing.
9. Cut each steak into 2 portions and serve.

Serving Suggestions: Serve alongside the spiced potatoes.

Variation Tip: Use freshly ground black pepper.

Nutritional Information per Serving:
Calories: 296 | Fat: 12.7g|Sat Fat: 6.6g|Carbohydrates: 0g|Fiber: 0g|Sugar: 0g|Protein: 44.5g

Crispy Sirloin Steaks

Prep Time: 10 minutes
Cook Time: 14 minutes
Serves: 2

Ingredients:

- ½ cup flour
- Salt and ground black pepper, as required
- 2 eggs
- ¾ cup breadcrumbs
- 3 (6-ounce) sirloin steaks, pounded

Preparation:

1. In a shallow bowl, place the flour, salt and black pepper and mix well.
2. In a second shallow bowl, beat the eggs.
3. In a third shallow bowl, place the breadcrumbs.
4. Coat the steak with flour, then dip into eggs, and finally coat with the panko mixture.
5. Press "Power" button of Ninja Foodi XL Pro Air Oven and select "Air Fry" function.
6. Press TEMP/SHADE +/- buttons to set the temperature at 360 degrees F.
7. Now press TIME/SLICES +/- buttons to set the cooking time to 14 minutes.
8. Press "Start/Stop" button to start.
9. When the unit beeps to show that it is preheated, open the oven door.
10. Arrange the steaks into the greased air fry basket and insert into the rail of Level 3.
11. When the cooking time is completed, open the oven door and serve hot.

Serving Suggestions: Serve with your favorite dipping sauce.

Variation Tip: Feel free to use breadcrumbs of your choice.

Nutritional Information per Serving:
Calories: 540 | Fat: 15.2g|Sat Fat: 5.3g|Carbohydrates: 35.6g|Fiber: 1.8g|Sugar: 2g|Protein: 61g

Balsamic Beef Top Roast

Prep Time: 10 minutes
Cook Time: 45 minutes
Serves: 10

Ingredients:

- 1 tablespoon butter, melted
- 1 tablespoon balsamic vinegar
- ½ teaspoon ground cumin
- ½ teaspoon smoked paprika
- ½ teaspoon red pepper flakes, crushed
- Salt and ground black pepper, as required
- 3 pounds beef top roast

Preparation:

1. In a bowl, add butter, vinegar, spices, salt and black pepper and mix well.
2. Coat the roast with spice mixture generously.
3. With kitchen twines, tie the roast to keep it compact.
4. Arrange the roast onto the greased sheet pan and greased air fry basket.
5. Press "Power" button of Ninja Foodi XL Pro Air Oven and select "Air Fry" function. Select 2 LEVEL.
6. Press TEMP/SHADE +/- buttons to set the temperature at 360 degrees F.
7. Now press TIME/SLICES +/- buttons to set the cooking time to 45 minutes.
8. Press "Start/Stop" button to start.
9. When the unit beeps to show that it is pre-heated, open the oven door and insert the sheet pan over wire rack on Level 2 and air fry basket on Level 4.
10. When the cooking time is completed, open the oven door and place the roast onto a cutting board for about 10 minutes before slicing.
11. With a sharp knife, cut the roast into desired sized slices and serve.

Serving Suggestions: Serve alongside the buttered green beans.

Variation Tip: Use unsalted butter.

Nutritional Information per Serving:
Calories: 305 | Fat: 17.1g|Sat Fat: 6.1g|Carbohydrates: 0.1g|Fiber: 0.1g|Sugar: 0g|Protein: 35.1g

Tarragon Beef Shanks

Prep Time: 15 minutes.
Cook Time: 15 minutes.
Serves: 4

Ingredients:

- 2 tablespoons olive oil
- 2 pounds beef shank
- Salt and black pepper to taste
- 1 onion, diced
- 2 stalks celery, diced
- 1 cup Marsala wine
- 2 tablespoons dried tarragon

Preparation:

1. Place the beef shanks in a baking pan.
2. Whisk the rest of the ingredients in a bowl and pour over the shanks.
3. Place these shanks in the air fry basket.
4. Transfer the basket to the 2nd rack position of Ninja Foodi XL Pro Air Oven and close the door.
5. Select the "Air Fry" Mode using FUNCTION +/- buttons and select Rack Level 2.
6. Set its cooking time to 15 minutes and temperature to 375 degrees F, then press "START/STOP" to initiate cooking.
7. Serve warm.

Serving Suggestion: Serve the beef shanks with sweet potato casserole.

Variation Tip: Cook the beef shanks with the mushrooms sauce.

Nutritional Information Per Serving:
Calories 425 | Fat 15g |Sodium 345mg | Carbs 12.3g | Fiber 1.4g | Sugar 3g | Protein 23.3g

Glazed Beef Short Ribs

Prep Time: 15 minutes
Cook Time: 8 minutes
Serves: 4

Ingredients:

- 2 pounds bone-in beef short ribs
- 3 tablespoons scallions, chopped
- ½ tablespoon fresh ginger, finely grated
- ½ cup low-sodium soy sauce
- ¼ cup balsamic vinegar
- ½ tablespoon Sriracha
- 1 tablespoon sugar
- ½ teaspoon ground black pepper

Preparation:

1. In a resealable bag, place all the ingredients.
2. Seal the bag and shake to coat well.
3. Refrigerate overnight.
4. Press "Power" button of Ninja Foodi XL Pro Air Oven and select "Air Fry" function.
5. Press TEMP/SHADE +/- buttons to set the temperature at 380 degrees F.
6. Now press TIME/SLICES +/- buttons to set the cooking time to 8 minutes.
7. Press "Start/Stop" button to start.
8. When the unit beeps to show that it is pre-heated, open the oven door.
9. Place the ribs into the greased roast tray on sheet pan and place them into rail of Level 3.
10. Flip the ribs once halfway through.
11. When the cooking time is completed, open the oven door and serve hot.

Serving Suggestions: Serve with cucumber salad.

Variation Tip: Brown sugar can also be used in this recipe.

Nutritional Information per Serving:
Calories: 496 | Fat: 20.5g|Sat Fat: 7.8g|Carbohydrates: 6.5g|Fiber: 0.3g|Sugar: 5.2g|Protein: 67.7g

Simple Pork Chops

Prep Time: 10 minutes
Cook Time: 18 minutes
Serves: 2

Ingredients:

- 2 (6-ounce) (½-inch thick) pork chops
- Salt and ground black pepper, as required

Preparation:

1. Season the pork chops with salt and black pepper evenly.
2. Arrange the pork chops onto a greased sheet pan.
3. Press "Power" button of Ninja Foodi XL Pro Air Oven and select the "Broil" function.
4. Press the TEMP/SHADE +/- buttons to select HI.
5. Now press TIME/SLICES +/- buttons to set the cooking time to 18 minutes.
6. Press "Start/Stop" button to start.
7. When the unit beeps to show that it is pre-heated, open the oven door and insert the sheet pan over wire rack into the rail of Level 3.
8. After 12 minutes of cooking, flip the chops once.
9. When cooking time is completed, open the oven door and serve hot.

Serving Suggestions: Serve alongside the mashed potato.

Variation Tip: Season the chops generously.

Nutritional Information per Serving:
Calories: 544 | Fat: 42.3g|Sat Fat: 15.8g|Carbohydrates: 0g|Fiber: 0g|Sugar: 0g|Protein: 38.2g

Citrus Pork Chops

Prep Time: 15 minutes
Cook Time: 15 minutes
Serves: 6
Ingredients:
- ½ cup olive oil
- 1 teaspoon fresh orange zest, grated
- 3 tablespoons fresh orange juice
- 1 teaspoon fresh lime zest, grated
- 3 tablespoons fresh lime juice
- 8 garlic cloves, minced
- 1 cup fresh cilantro, chopped finely
- ¼ cup fresh mint leaves, chopped finely
- 1 teaspoon dried oregano, crushed
- 1 teaspoon ground cumin
- Salt and ground black pepper, as required
- 6 thick-cut pork chops

Preparation:
1. In a bowl, place the oil, orange zest, orange juice, lime zest, lime juice, garlic, fresh herbs, oregano, cumin, salt and black pepper and beat until well combined.
2. In a small bowl, reserve ¼ cup of the marinade.
3. In a large zip lock bag, place the remaining marinade and pork chops.
4. Seal the bag and shake to coat well.
5. Refrigerate to marinate overnight.
6. Remove the pork chops from the bag and shake off to remove the excess marinade.
7. Press "Power" button of Ninja Foodi XL Pro Air Oven and select the "Broil" function.
8. Press TEMP/SHADE button to select HI.
9. Now press TIME/SLICES +/- buttons to set the cooking time to 15 minutes.
10. Press "Start/Stop" button to start.
11. When the unit beeps to show that it is preheated, open the oven door.
12. Place the pork chops over the wire rack on Level 3.
13. After 8 minutes of cooking, flip the chops once.
14. When the cooking time is completed, open the oven door and serve hot.

Serving Suggestions: Serve with steamed broccoli.
Variation Tip: Use fresh orange juice and zest.
Nutritional Information per Serving:
Calories: 700 | Fat: 59.3g|Sat Fat: 18.3g|Carbohydrates: 2.1g|Fiber: 0.4g|Sugar: 0.3g|Protein: 38.7g

BBQ Pork Chops

Prep Time: 10 minutes
Cook Time: 16 minutes
Serves: 6
Ingredients:
- 6 (8-ounce) pork loin chops
- Salt and ground black pepper, as required
- ½ cup BBQ sauce

Preparation:
1. With a meat tenderizer, tenderize the chops completely.
2. Sprinkle the chops with a little salt and black pepper.
3. In a large bowl, add the BBQ sauce and chops and mix well.
4. Refrigerate, covered for about 6-8 hours.
5. Press "Power" button of Ninja Foodi XL Pro Air Oven and select "Air Fry" function. Select 2 LEVEL.
6. Press TEMP/SHADE +/- buttons to set the temperature at 355 degrees F.
7. Now press TIME/SLICES +/- buttons to set the cooking time to 16 minutes.
8. Press "Start/Stop" button to start.
9. When the unit beeps to show that it is preheated, open the oven door.
10. Arrange the pork chops into the greased air fry basket on Level 4 and sheet pan over wire rack on Level 2.
11. Flip the chops once halfway through.
12. When the cooking time is completed, open the oven door and serve hot.

Serving Suggestions: Serve with roasted veggies.
Variation Tip: Make sure to use good quality BBQ sauce.
Nutritional Information per Serving:
Calories: 757 | Fat: 56.4g|Sat Fat: 21.1g|Carbohydrates: 7.6g|Fiber: 0.1g|Sugar: 5.4g|Protein: 51g

Herbed Leg of Lamb

Prep Time: 10 minutes
Cook Time: 1¼ hours
Serves: 6

Ingredients:

- 2¼ pounds boneless leg of lamb
- 2 tablespoons olive oil
- Salt and ground black pepper, as required
- 2 fresh rosemary sprigs
- 2 fresh thyme sprigs

Preparation:

1. Coat the leg of lamb with oil and sprinkle with salt and black pepper.
2. Wrap the leg of lamb with herb sprigs.
3. Press "Power" button of Ninja Foodi XL Pro Air Oven and select "Air Fry" function.
4. Press TEMP/SHADE +/- buttons to set the temperature at 300 degrees F.
5. Now press TIME/SLICES +/- buttons to set the cooking time to 75 minutes.
6. Press "Start/Stop" button to start.
7. When the unit beeps to show that it is preheated, open the oven door.
8. Arrange the leg of lamb into the greased air fry basket on Level 3.
9. Immediately set the temperature at 355 degrees F.
10. When the cooking time is completed, open the oven door and place the leg of lamb onto a cutting board for about 10 minutes.
11. Cut the leg of lamb into desired-sized pieces and serve.

Serving Suggestions: Serve alongside the roasted Brussels sprout.
Variation Tip: Always slice the meat against the grain.
Nutritional Information per Serving:
Calories: 360 | Fat: 17.3g|Sat Fat: 5.2g|Carbohydrates: 0.7g|Fiber: 0.5g|Sugar: 0g|Protein: 47.8g

Lamb Chops with Carrots

Prep Time: 15 minutes
Cook Time: 10 minutes
Serves: 4

Ingredients:

- 2 tablespoons fresh rosemary, minced
- 2 tablespoons fresh mint leaves, minced
- 1 garlic clove, minced
- 3 tablespoons olive oil
- Salt and ground black pepper, as required
- 4 (6-ounce) lamb chops
- 2 large carrots, peeled and cubed

Preparation:

1. In a large bowl, mix together the herbs, garlic, oil, salt, and black pepper.
2. Add the chops and generously coat with mixture.
3. Refrigerate to marinate for about 3 hours.
4. In a large pan of water, soak the carrots for about 15 minutes.
5. Drain the carrots completely.
6. Press "Power" button of Ninja Foodi XL Pro Air Oven and select "Air Fry" function.
7. Press TEMP/SHADE +/- buttons to set the temperature at 390 degrees F.
8. Now press TIME/SLICES +/- buttons to set the cooking time to 10 minutes.
9. Press "Start/Stop" button to start.
10. When the unit beeps to show that it is preheated, open the oven door.
11. Arrange chops into the greased air fry basket in a single layer and insert into the rail of Level 3.
12. After 2 minutes of cooking, arrange carrots into the air fry basket and top with the chops in a single layer.
13. Insert the basket in oven.
14. When the cooking time is completed, open the oven door and transfer the chops and carrots onto serving plates.
15. Serve hot.

Serving Suggestions: Serve with fresh greens.
Variation Tip: You can use herbs of your choice.
Nutritional Information per Serving:
Calories: 429 | Fat: 23.2g|Sat Fat: 6.1g|Carbohydrates: 5.1g|Fiber: 1.8g|Sugar: 1.8g|Protein: 48.3g

Mustard Lamb Loin Chops

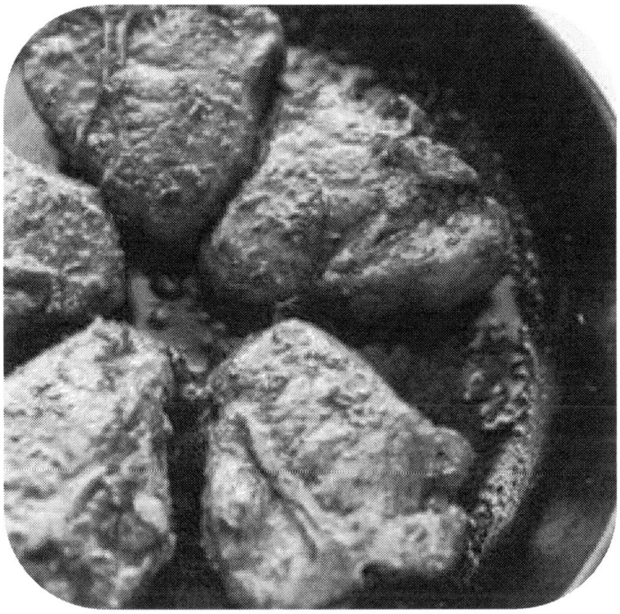

Prep Time: 10 minutes
Cook Time: 15 minutes
Serves: 2

Ingredients:

- 1 tablespoon Dijon mustard
- ½ tablespoon white wine vinegar
- 1 teaspoon olive oil
- ½ teaspoon dried tarragon
- Salt and ground black pepper, as required
- 4 (4-ounce) lamb loin chops

Preparation:

1. In a large bowl, mix together the mustard, vinegar, oil, tarragon, salt, and black pepper.
2. Add the chops and coat with the mixture generously.
3. Arrange the chops onto the greased sheet pan.
4. Press "Power" button of Ninja Foodi XL Pro Air Oven and select "Bake" function.
5. Press TEMP/SHADE +/- buttons to set the temperature at 390 degrees F.
6. Now press TIME/SLICES +/- buttons to set the cooking time to 15 minutes.
7. Press "Start/Stop" button to start.
8. When the unit beeps to show that it is preheated, open the oven door and insert the sheet pan into rail of Level 3.
9. When the cooking time is completed, open the oven door and serve hot.

Serving Suggestions: Serve alongside the feta spinach.

Variation Tip: Remember to bring the chops to room temperature.

Nutritional Information per Serving:
Calories: 44 | Fat: 19.3g|Sat Fat: 6.3g|Carbohydrates: 0.5g|Fiber: 0.3g|Sugar: 0.1g|Protein: 64.1g

Herbed Lamb Loin Chops

Prep Time: 10 minutes
Cook Time: 12 minutes
Serves: 2

Ingredients:

- 4 (4-ounce) (½-inch-thick) lamb loin chops
- 1 teaspoon fresh thyme, minced
- 1 teaspoon fresh rosemary, minced
- 1 teaspoon fresh oregano, minced
- 2 garlic cloves, crushed
- Salt and ground black pepper, as required

Preparation:

1. In a large bowl, place all ingredients and mix well.
2. Refrigerate to marinate overnight.
3. Arrange the chops onto the greased sheet pan.
4. Press "Power" button of Ninja Foodi XL Pro Air Oven and select "Bake" function.
5. Press TEMP/SHADE +/- buttons to set the temperature at 400 degrees F.
6. Now press TIME/SLICES +/- buttons to set the cooking time to 12 minutes.
7. Press "Start/Stop" button to start.
8. When the unit beeps to show that it is preheated, open the oven door and insert the sheet pan over wire rack into rail of Level 3.
9. Flip the chops once halfway through.
10. When the cooking time is completed, open the oven door and serve hot.

Serving Suggestions: Serve with steamed cauliflower.

Variation Tip: Season the chops nicely.

Nutritional Information per Serving:
Calories: 432 | Fat: 16.9g|Sat Fat: 6g|Carbohydrates: 2.2g|Fiber: 0.8g|Sugar: 0.1g|Protein: 64g

Simple New York Strip Steak

Prep Time: 5 minutes
Cook Time: 8 minutes
Serves: 1

Ingredients:

- ½ teaspoon olive oil
- ½ New York strip steak
- Kosher salt and ground black pepper, to taste

Preparation:

1. Coat the steak with oil and then, generously season with salt and black pepper.
2. Grease an air fry basket.
3. Place steak into the prepared air fry basket on Level 3 in oven.
4. Turn on your Ninja Foodi XL Pro Air Oven and select "Air Fry".
5. Select the timer for about 7 to 8 minutes and temperature for 400 degrees F.
6. Remove from the oven and place the steak onto a cutting board for about 10 minutes before slicing.
7. Cut the steak into desired-size slices and transfer onto serving plates.
8. Serve immediately.

Serving Suggestions: Add your favorite sauce or mushroom sauce on top.

Variation Tip: You can also add chopped rosemary.

Nutritional Information per Serving:
Calories: 245 | Fat: 16.3g|Sat Fat: 5.8g|Carbohydrates: 0g|Fiber: 0g|Sugar: 0g|Protein: 25g

Roast Beef and Yorkshire Pudding

Prep Time: 20 minutes
Cook Time: 1 hour 50 minutes
Serves: 2

Ingredients:

- 1 egg, beaten
- ½ cup milk
- ½ cup flour
- ⅛ teaspoon salt
- Salt, to taste
- Freshly ground pepper, to taste
- 1 pound rump roast
- Garlic powder, to taste

Preparation:

1. Turn on your Ninja Foodi XL Pro Air Oven and select "Air Roast".
2. Preheat by selecting the timer for 3 minutes and temperature for 375 degrees F.
3. Place beef in a sheet pan on Level 3 in oven and season with salt, garlic powder and pepper.
4. Roast in oven for about 90 minutes until the thickest part of the beef is at 135 degrees F.
5. Remove from oven, reserving drippings.
6. Take a small bowl, beat egg until foamy.
7. Take another bowl, stir salt and flour. Pour in the beaten egg and add milk.
8. Now, preheat by selecting the timer for 3 minutes and temperature for 400 degrees F on "Air Roast" mode.
9. Pour the reserved drippings to a tin. Place in the preheated oven for about 3 minutes.
10. Remove from oven, add the flour mixture into the hot drippings.
11. Return to oven and set the timer for 20 minutes or until brown.
12. Serve warm and enjoy!

Serving Suggestions: Serve it with your favorite sauce.

Variation Tip: You can add an extra egg if you like.

Nutritional Information per Serving:
Calories: 582 | Fat: 17.4g|Sat Fat: 1.5g|Carbohydrates: 27.2g|Fiber: 0.9g|Sugar: 3g|Protein: 78.4g

Baked Pork Chops

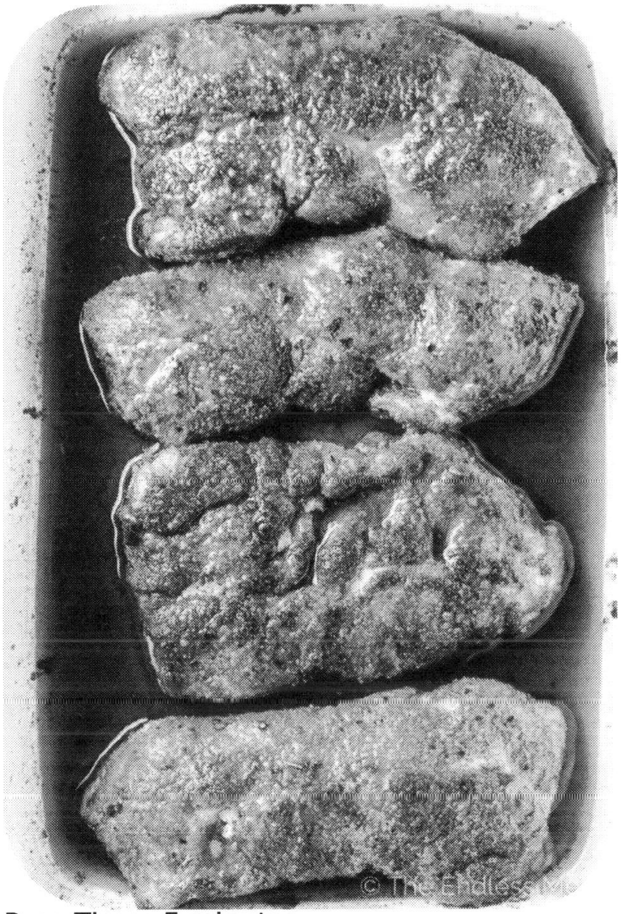

Prep Time: 5 minutes
Cook Time: 20 minutes
Serves: 2

Ingredients:

- 2 boneless pork chops
- ½ tablespoon olive oil
- ¾ tablespoon brown sugar
- ½ teaspoon onion powder
- 1 teaspoon paprika
- ½ teaspoon dried thyme
- ¼ teaspoon black pepper
- ½ teaspoon salt

Preparation:

1. Turn on your Ninja Foodi XL Pro Air Oven and select "Bake".
2. Take a dish and line sheet pan with parchment paper.
3. Arrange the pork chops on the prepared dish.
4. Take a small bowl and combine the brown sugar, onion powder, dried thyme, salt, pepper and paprika.
5. Rub the prepared mixture over pork chops evenly.
6. Place the sheet pan on Level 3 in oven.
7. Select the timer for 20 minutes and temperature for 425 degrees F.
8. Bake the pork chops in the preheated Ninja Foodi XL Pro Air Oven for 20 minutes at 425 degrees F.
9. After done, set them aside for 5 minutes and then serve.
10. Enjoy!

Serving Suggestions: Serve with mashed potatoes and salad.

Variation Tip: Be careful not to overcook the pork chops or they may dry out.

Nutritional Information per Serving:
Calories: 171 | Fat: 6.7g|Sat Fat: 1.6g|Carbohydrates: 4.7g|Fiber: 0.6g|Sugar: 3.6g|Protein: 22.5g

American Roast Beef

Prep Time: 5 minutes
Cook Time: 1 hour
Serves: 3

Ingredients:

- 1½ pounds beef eye of round roast
- ¼ teaspoon kosher salt
- ⅛ teaspoon black pepper, freshly ground
- ¼ teaspoon garlic powder

Preparation:

1. Turn on your Ninja Foodi XL Pro Air Oven and select "Air Roast".
2. Set the timer for 60 minutes and temperature for 375 degrees F.
3. Press START/STOP to begin preheating.
4. When the unit beeps to signify it has preheated, place beef in a sheet pan on Level 3 and season with salt, garlic powder and pepper.
5. Roast in oven for about an hour.
6. Remove from oven and set aside for 10 minutes before slicing.
7. Serve warm and enjoy!

Serving Suggestions: Serve it with mashed potatoes.

Variation Tip: You can add onions on top for a little flavoring.

Nutritional Information per Serving:
Calories: 382 | Fat: 11.1g|Sat Fat: 4g|Carbohydrates: 0.2g|Fiber: 0g|Sugar: 0.1g|Protein: 65.8g

Savory Pork Roast

Prep Time: 10 minutes
Cook Time: 1 hour
Serves: 3

Ingredients:

- ¼ teaspoon dried thyme
- 1 tablespoon fresh rosemary, divided
- 1 teaspoon garlic salt
- ⅛ teaspoon black pepper, freshly ground
- 1½ pounds pork loin roast, boneless

Preparation:

1. Turn on your Ninja Foodi XL Pro Air Oven and select "Air Roast".
2. Select the timer for 60 minutes and temperature for 350 degrees F.
3. Take a bowl mix well rosemary, garlic salt, thyme, and pepper together.
4. Now add pork to coat well.
5. Take a roast tray and place coated pork on it.
6. When the unit beeps to signify it has preheated, open the oven and place the roast tray on sheet pan on Level 3. Close the oven and let it cook.
7. Roast pork for about an hour in preheated Ninja Foodi XL Pro Air Oven at 350 degrees F.
8. Serve and enjoy!

Serving Suggestions: Serve with juice and salad.

Variation Tip: Use foil to avoid dryness.

Nutritional Information per Serving:
Calories: 331 | Fat: 8.2g|Sat Fat: 2.8g|Carbohydrates: 1.4g|Fiber: 0.6g|Sugar: 0.2g|Protein: 59.6g

Czech Roast Pork

Prep Time: 20 minutes
Cook Time: 3 hours and 30 minutes
Serves: 4

Ingredients:

- 1 tablespoon caraway seeds
- ½ tablespoon garlic powder
- 1 tablespoon vegetable oil
- ½ tablespoon prepared mustard
- ½ tablespoon salt
- 1½ medium onions, chopped
- 2 pounds pork shoulder blade roast
- 1 teaspoon ground black pepper
- ¼ cup beer

Preparation:

1. Take a bowl and add garlic powder, mustard, vegetable oil, caraway seeds, salt and pepper to form a paste.
2. Rub the paste over pork roast and let it sit for about 30 minutes.
3. Turn on your Ninja Foodi XL Pro Air Oven and select "Air Roast".
4. Select the timer for 60 minutes and temperature for 350 degrees F.
5. Take a roast tray and add onions, pour in the beer and place pork.
6. Cover it with a foil.
7. When the unit beeps to signify it has preheated, open the oven and place the roast tray on a sheet pan into rail of Level 3.
8. Roast for about an hour in preheated Ninja Foodi XL Pro Air Oven at 350 degrees F.
9. Remove foil, turn roast and let it roast for 2 hours and 30 minutes more.
10. Remove from oven and set aside for 10 minutes before slicing.
11. Serve warm and enjoy!

Serving Suggestions: Serve it with the sprinkle of herbs.

Variation Tip: Do not skip the beer.

Nutritional Information per Serving:
Calories: 722 | Fat: 44.3g|Sat Fat: 15.4g|Carbohydrates: 6.4g|Fiber: 1.8g|Sugar: 2g|Protein: 69.8g

Ground Beef Casserole

Prep Time: 8 minutes
Cook Time: 25 minutes
Serves: 3

Ingredients:

- ¼ medium onion, chopped
- ½ pound extra lean ground beef
- ½ pound penne
- ½ tablespoon olive oil
- ½ clove garlic, minced
- ½ cup marinara sauce
- 1 cup cheddar cheese, shredded
- Salt and pepper to taste

Preparation:

1. Take a large pot with lightly salted water and bring it to a boil. Add penne and let it cook for about 10 minutes.
2. Take a pan and add oil, beef and onion.
3. Fry for about 10 minutes over medium-high heat and add garlic.
4. Stir in the marinara sauce and add salt and pepper according to taste.
5. Drain the pasta and pour into the sheet pan.
6. Add the beef-marinara mixture on top of the penne pasta. Lastly, add cheese with cheese.
7. Insert a wire rack on Level 3. Turn on your Ninja Foodi XL Pro Air Oven and select "Bake".
8. Select the timer for 10 minutes and temperature for 400 degrees F.
9. When the unit beeps to signify it has preheated, open the oven and place the sheet pan on wire rack.
10. Close the oven and bake for about 10 minutes in preheated Ninja Foodi XL Pro Air Oven until the cheese is nicely melted.
11. Serve immediately.

Serving Suggestions: Serve it with your favorite soda.

Variation Tip: You can add more marinara sauce if you want.

Nutritional Information per Serving:
Calories: 560 | Fat: 22.6g|Sat Fat: 11.1g|Carbohydrates: 48.6g|Fiber: 1.3g|Sugar: 4.3g|Protein: 38.7g

Herby Pork Bake

Prep Time: 10 minutes
Cook Time: 40 minutes
Serves: 2

Ingredients:

- 1 pork loin steak, cut into bite-sized pieces
- ½ red onion, cut into wedges
- 1 potato, halved
- ½ carrot, halved
- ½ tablespoon olive oil
- 1 tablespoon mixed dried herbs
- 4 tablespoons Cider Pour Over Sauce

Preparation:

1. Turn on your Ninja Foodi XL Pro Air Oven and select "Bake".
2. Select the timer for 25 minutes and temperature for 420 degrees F.
3. Take a roast tray and toss pork, onion, potatoes and carrots with herbs and olive oil.
4. When the unit beeps to signify it has preheated, open the oven and place the roast tray on sheet pan into rail of Level 3.
5. Bake for about 25 minutes in preheated Ninja Foodi XL Pro Air Oven at 420 degrees F.
6. Remove from the oven and add sauce on top.
7. Bake for 5 more minutes so that you have a bubbling sauce.
8. Serve and enjoy!

Serving Suggestions: Serve with garlic bread.

Variation Tip: You can also add tomatoes to your like.

Nutritional Information per Serving:
Calories: 269 | Fat: 9.6g|Sat Fat: 2.6g|Carbohydrates: 32g|Fiber: 3.3g|Sugar: 4g|Protein: 14.7g

Baked Beef Stew

Prep Time: 15 minutes
Cook Time: 2 hours
Serves: 4
Ingredients:

- 1 pound beef-stew, cut into cubes
- ½ cup water
- 2 tablespoons instant tapioca
- ½ can dried tomatoes with juice
- 1 teaspoon white sugar
- ½ tablespoon beef bouillon granules
- ¾ teaspoon salt
- ⅛ teaspoon ground black pepper
- 1 strip celery, cut into ¾ inch pieces
- ½ onion, chopped
- 2 carrots, cut into 1-inch pieces
- ½ slice bread, cubed
- 2 potatoes, peeled and cubed

Preparation:
1. Insert a wire rack on Level 3. Turn on your Ninja Foodi XL Pro Air Oven and select "Bake".
2. Select the timer for 2 hours and temperature for 375 degrees F.
3. Grease a sheet pan.
4. Take a large pan over medium heat and brown the stew meat.
5. Meanwhile, take a bowl and mix together tomatoes, water, tapioca, beef bouillon granules, sugar, salt and pepper.
6. Add prepared brown beef, celery, potatoes, carrots, onion and bread cubes.
7. Pour in the greased sheet pan.
8. When the unit beeps to signify it has preheated, open the oven and place the sheet pan on the wire rack.
9. Close the oven and bake for about 2 hours in preheated Ninja Foodi Air Fryer at 375 degrees F.
10. Remove from oven and set aside for 2 minutes.
11. Serve warm and enjoy!

Serving Suggestions: Serve warm with rice.
Variation Tip: You can also add few tablespoons of cornstarch.
Nutritional Information per Serving:
Calories: 378 | Fat: 7.6g|Sat Fat: 2.7g|Carbohydrates: 30.1g|Fiber: 3.9g|Sugar: 5.6g|Protein: 44.8g

Lamb Chops

Prep Time: 5 minutes
Cook Time: 16 minutes
Serves: 4
Ingredients:

- 4 medium lamb chops
- 2 tablespoons olive oil
- 1 garlic clove, crushed
- 3 thin lemon slices
- ½ teaspoon dried oregano
- ¼ teaspoon black pepper, freshly ground
- ½ teaspoon kosher salt

Preparation:
1. Take a dish and mix together salt, pepper, olive oil, lemon slices, garlic, and oregano.
2. Add lamb in the dish and marinate for about 4 hours.
3. Insert a wire rack on Level 3. Turn on your Ninja Foodi XL Pro Air Oven and select "Bake".
4. Select the timer for 10 minutes and temperature for 400 degrees F.
5. Meanwhile, take a pan and add oil and heat over medium heat and cook each side of lamb for 3 minutes until brown.
6. When the unit beeps to signify it has preheated, open the oven and place the lamb in a sheet pan on wire rack. Bake for about 8 to 10 minutes in preheated Ninja Foodi XL Pro Air Oven at 400 degrees F.
7. Remove from oven and set aside for 2 minutes.
8. Serve warm and enjoy!

Serving Suggestions: Serve with roasted carrots.
Variation Tip: You can also use foil.
Nutritional Information per Serving:
Calories: 302 | Fat: 18.5g|Sat Fat: 4.3g|Carbohydrates: 0.5g|Fiber: 0.1g|Sugar: 0g|Protein: 32.6g

Russian Baked Beef

Prep Time: 10 minutes
Cook Time: 1 hour
Serves: 3

Ingredients:

- ½ beef tenderloin
- 1 onion, sliced
- ¾ cup Cheddar cheese, grated
- ½ cup milk
- 1½ tablespoons mayonnaise
- Salt and black pepper, to taste

Preparation:

1. Insert a wire rack on Level 3. Turn on your Ninja Foodi XL Pro Air Oven and select "Bake".
2. Select the timer for 60 minutes and temperature for 350 degrees F.
3. Grease a sheet pan.
4. Cut the beef into thick slices and place in the sheet pan.
5. Season beef with salt and pepper and cover with onion slices. Also, spread cheese on top.
6. Take a bowl and stir together milk and mayonnaise and pour over cheese.
7. When the unit beeps to signify it has preheated, open the oven and place the sheet pan on the wire rack.
8. Close the oven and bake for about an hour in preheated Ninja Foodi XL Pro Air Oven at 350 degrees F.
9. Remove from oven and set aside for 2 minutes.
10. Serve warm and enjoy!

Serving Suggestions: Serve with roasted tomatoes.
Variation Tip: You can use any cheese instead of cheddar cheese.
Nutritional Information per Serving:
Calories: 207 | Fat: 14g|Sat Fat: 7.3g|Carbohydrates: 7.5g|Fiber: 0.8g|Sugar: 4g|Protein: 12.9g

Roasted Pork Belly

Prep Time: 10 minutes
Cook Time: 1 hour and 30 minutes
Serves: 8

Ingredients:

- ¾ teaspoon dried oregano
- ¾ teaspoon ground cumin
- ¾ teaspoon ground black pepper
- ¾ teaspoon salt
- ¾ teaspoon paprika
- ¾ teaspoon onion powder
- ¾ teaspoon ground turmeric
- ¾ teaspoon garlic powder
- 2 pounds whole pork belly
- Cayenne pepper, to taste
- 1 tablespoon lemon juice

Preparation:

1. Take a bowl and add garlic powder, onion powder, turmeric, cayenne pepper, paprika, oregano, cumin, salt and pepper.
2. Rub the mixture onto pork belly.
3. Cover with a plastic wrap and refrigerate for at least 2 hours.
4. Turn on your Ninja Foodi XL Pro Air Oven and select "Air Roast".
5. Preheat by selecting the timer for 3 minutes and temperature for 450 degrees F.
6. Line a sheet pan with parchment paper.
7. Place pork belly onto the prepared roast tray, with shallow cuts.
8. Rub lemon juice on top. Place the roast tray on sheet pan into rail of Level 3.
9. Roast for about 40 minutes in preheated Ninja Foodi XL Pro Air Oven at 350 degrees F until fat is crispy.
10. Remove from oven and set aside for 10 minutes before slicing.
11. Serve warm and enjoy!

Serving Suggestions: Serve it with slices of lemon and savor the taste.
Variation Tip: You can also add mushrooms.
Nutritional Information per Serving:
Calories: 602 | Fat: 61.8g|Sat Fat: 21.9g|Carbohydrates: 1g|Fiber: 0.3g|Sugar: 0.2g|Protein: 8.2g

Lamb and Potato Bake

Prep Time: 8 minutes
Cook Time: 55 minutes
Serves: 2

Ingredients:

- 2 potatoes
- ¾ lean lamb mince
- ½ teaspoon cinnamon
- ½ tablespoon olive oil
- 4 cups tomato pasta sauce
- 1 cup cheese sauce

Preparation:

1. Boil the potatoes for 12 minutes or until half cooked.
2. Meanwhile, take a pan and heat oil over medium heat.
3. Add lamb mince in to brown. Use a spoon to break up lumps.
4. Add cinnamon and fry for about a minute.
5. Pour in the tomato sauce and leave for about 5 minutes.
6. Once the potatoes are done, thinly slice them.
7. Place everything on a sheet pan and spread cheese on top.
8. Inset a wire rack on Level 3. Turn on your Ninja Foodi XL Pro Air Oven and select "Bake".
9. Select the timer for 35 minutes and temperature for 390 degrees F.
10. When the unit beeps to signify it has preheated, open the oven and place the sheet pan on wire rack.
11. Close the oven and bake until well cooked.
12. Serve and enjoy!

Serving Suggestions: Top the peppers with the cheese.

Variation Tip: You can also use green peppers instead.

Nutritional Information per Serving:
Calories: 823 | Fat: 41.4g|Sat Fat: 20.8g|Carbohydrates: 78.1g|Fiber: 13.3g|Sugar: 27.3g|Protein: 34g

Fish and Seafood

Seafood Casserole

Prep Time: 15 minutes.
Cook Time: 20 minutes.
Serves: 8

Ingredients:

- 8 ounces haddock, skinned and diced
- 1 pound scallops
- 1 pound large shrimp, peeled and deveined
- 3-4 garlic cloves, minced
- ½ cup heavy cream
- ½ cup Swiss cheese, shredded
- 2 tablespoons Parmesan, grated
- Paprika, to taste
- Sea salt and black pepper, to taste

Preparation:

1. Toss shrimp, scallops, and haddock chunks in the sheet pan greased with cooking spray.
2. Drizzle salt, black pepper, and minced garlic over the seafood mix.
3. Top this seafood with cream, Swiss cheese, paprika, and Parmesan cheese.
4. Transfer the dish to the Ninja Foodi XL Pro Air Oven and Close its lid.
5. Select the "Bake" Mode using FUNCTION +/- buttons and select Rack Level 2.
6. Set its cooking time to 20 minutes and temperature to 375 degrees F, then press "START/STOP" to initiate cooking.
7. Serve warm.

Serving Suggestion: Serve the seafood casserole with fresh vegetable salad.

Variation Tip: Add alfredo sauce to the casserole for better taste.

Nutritional Information Per Serving:
Calories 548 | Fat 13g |Sodium 353mg | Carbs 31g | Fiber 0.4g | Sugar 1g | Protein 29g

Spicy Bay Scallops

Prep Time: 15 minutes.
Cook Time: 8 minutes.
Serves: 4

Ingredients:

- 1 pound bay scallops rinsed and patted dry
- 2 teaspoons smoked paprika
- 2 teaspoons chili powder
- 2 teaspoons olive oil
- 1 teaspoon garlic powder
- ¼ teaspoon ground black pepper
- ⅛ teaspoon cayenne red pepper

Preparation:

1. Scallops with paprika, chili powder, olive oil, garlic powder, black pepper, and red pepper in a bowl.
2. Place the scallops in the air fry basket.
3. Transfer the basket to the 3rd rack position of Ninja Foodi XL Pro Air Oven and close the door.
4. Select the "Air Fry" Mode using FUNCTION +/- buttons and select Rack Level 3.
5. Set its cooking time to 8 minutes and temperature to 400 degrees F, then press "START/STOP" to initiate cooking.
6. Enjoy.

Serving Suggestion: Serve the scallops with crispy onion rings on the side.

Variation Tip: Coat the scallops with breadcrumbs for a crispy texture.

Nutritional Information Per Serving:
Calories 476 | Fat 17g |Sodium 1127mg | Carbs 4g | Fiber 1g | Sugar 3g | Protein 29g

Buttered Crab Shells

Prep Time: 15 minutes
Cook Time: 20 minutes
Serves: 4

Ingredients:

- 4 soft crab shells, cleaned
- 1 cup buttermilk
- 3 eggs
- 2 cups panko breadcrumb
- 2 teaspoons seafood seasoning
- 1½ teaspoons lemon zest, grated
- 2 tablespoons butter, melted

Preparations:

1. In a shallow bowl, place the buttermilk.
2. In a second bowl, whisk the eggs.
3. In a third bowl, mix the breadcrumbs, seafood seasoning, and lemon zest together.
4. Soak the crab shells into the buttermilk for about 10 minutes.
5. Now, dip the crab shells into beaten eggs and then, coat with the breadcrumb mixture.
6. Press "Power" button of Ninja Foodi XL Pro Air Oven and select "Air Fry" function.
7. Press TEMP/SHADE +/- buttons to set the temperature at 375 degrees F.
8. Now press TIME/SLICES +/- buttons to set the cooking time to 10 minutes.
9. Press "START/STOP" button to start.
10. When the unit beeps to show that it is preheated, open the lid and grease the air fry basket.
11. Place the crab shells into the prepared air fry basket and insert in the oven.
12. When cooking time is completed, open the lid and transfer the crab shells onto serving plates.
13. Drizzle crab shells with the melted butter and serve immediately.

Serving Suggestions: Serve alongside the lemon slices.

Variation Tip: Use seasoning of your choice.

Nutritional Information per Serving:
Calories: 549 | Fat: 17.3g|Sat Fat: 7g|Carbohydrates: 11.5g|Fiber: 0.3g|Sugar: 3.3g|Protein: 53.5g

Nuts Crusted Salmon

Prep Time: 15 minutes
Cook Time: 15 minutes
Serves: 2

Ingredients:

- 2 (6-ounce) skinless salmon fillets
- Salt and ground black pepper, as required
- 3 tablespoons walnuts, chopped finely
- 3 tablespoons quick-cooking oats, crushed
- 2 tablespoons olive oil

Preparation:

1. Rub the salmon fillets with salt and black pepper evenly.
2. In a bowl, mix the walnuts, oats and oil together.
3. Arrange the salmon fillets onto the greased sheet pan in a single layer.
4. Place the oat mixture over salmon fillets and gently, press down.
5. Press "Power" button of Ninja Foodi XL Pro Air Oven and select the "Bake" function.
6. Press TEMP/SHADE +/- buttons to set the temperature at 400 degrees F.
7. Now press TIME/SLICES +/- buttons to set the cooking time to 15 minutes.
8. Press "START/STOP" button to start.
9. When the unit beeps to show that it is preheated, open the lid.
10. Insert the sheet pan in oven.
11. When cooking time is completed, open the lid and serve hot.

Serving Suggestions: Serve with steamed asparagus.

Variation Tip: Walnuts can be replaced with pecans.

Nutritional Information per Serving:
Calories: 446 | Fat: 319g|Sat Fat: 4g|Carbohydrates: 6.4g|Fiber: 1.6g|Sugar: 0.2g|Protein: 36.8g

Scallops with Capers Sauce

Prep Time: 10 minutes
Cook Time: 6 minutes
Serves: 2

Ingredients:

- 10 (1-ounce) sea scallops, cleaned and patted very dry
- Salt and ground black pepper, as required
- ¼ cup extra-virgin olive oil
- 2 tablespoons fresh parsley, finely chopped
- 2 teaspoons capers, finely chopped
- 1 teaspoon fresh lemon zest, finely grated
- ½ teaspoon garlic, finely chopped

Preparation:

1. Season each scallop evenly with salt and black pepper.
2. Press "Power" button of Ninja Foodi XL Pro Air Oven and select "Air Fry" function.
3. Press TEMP/SHADE +/- buttons to set the temperature at 400 degrees F.
4. Now press TIME/SLICES +/- buttons to set the cooking time to 6 minutes.
5. Press "START/STOP" button to start.
6. When the unit beeps to show that it is preheated, open the lid and grease the air fry basket.
7. Place the scallops into the prepared air fry basket and insert in the oven.
8. Meanwhile, for the sauce: in a bowl, mix the remaining ingredients.
9. When cooking time is completed, open the lid and transfer the scallops onto serving plates.
10. Top with the sauce and serve immediately.

Serving Suggestions: Serve with a garnishing of fresh herbs.

Variation Tip: Avoid shiny, wet or soft scallops.

Nutritional Information per Serving:
Calories: 344 | Fat: 26.3g|Sat Fat: 3.7g|Carbohydrates: 4.2g|Fiber: 0.3g|Sugar: 0.1g|Protein: 24g

Cod Parcel

Prep Time: 10 minutes
Cook Time: 23 minutes
Serves: 4

Ingredients:

- 2 (4-ounce) cod fillets
- 6 asparagus stalks
- ¼ cup white sauce
- 1 teaspoon oil
- ¼ cup champagne
- Salt and ground black pepper, as required

Preparation:

1. In a bowl, mix all the ingredients together.
2. Divide the cod mixture over 2 pieces of foil evenly.
3. Seal the foil around the cod mixture to form the packet.
4. Press "Power" button of Ninja Foodi XL Pro Air Oven and select "Air Fry" function.
5. Press TEMP/SHADE +/- buttons to set the temperature at 355 degrees F.
6. Now press TIME/SLICES +/- buttons to set the cooking time to 13 minutes.
7. Press "START/STOP" button to start.
8. When the unit beeps to show that it is preheated, open the lid.
9. Arrange the cod parcels in air fry basket and insert in the oven.
10. When cooking time is completed, open the lid and transfer the parcels onto serving plates. The meat of cod should look translucent fairly.
11. Carefully unwrap the parcels and serve hot.

Serving Suggestions: Serve with mashed potatoes.

Variation Tip: Feel free to add seasoning of your choice.

Nutritional Information per Serving:
Calories: 188 | Fat: 6.6g|Sat Fat: 1.2g|Carbohydrates: 5g|Fiber: 0.8g|Sugar: 2.2g|Protein: 22.2g

Scallops with Spinach

Prep Time: 15 minutes
Cook Time: 10 minutes
Serves: 2

Ingredients:

- ¾ cup heavy whipping cream
- 1 tablespoon tomato paste
- 1 teaspoon garlic, minced
- 1 tablespoon fresh basil, chopped
- Salt and ground black pepper, as required
- 8 jumbo sea scallops
- Olive oil cooking spray
- 1 (12-ounce) package frozen spinach, thawed and drained

Preparation:

1. In a bowl, place the cream, tomato paste, garlic, basil, salt, and black pepper and mix well.
2. Spray each scallop evenly with cooking spray and then, sprinkle with a little salt and black pepper.
3. In the bottom of a baking pan, place the spinach.
4. Arrange scallops on top of the spinach in a single layer and top with the cream mixture evenly.
5. Press "Power" button of Ninja Foodi XL Pro Air Oven and select "Air Fry" function.
6. Press TEMP/SHADE +/- buttons to set the temperature at 350 degrees F.
7. Now press TIME/SLICES +/- buttons to set the cooking time to 10 minutes.
8. Press "START/STOP" button to start.
9. When the unit beeps to show that it is preheated, open the lid.
10. Place the pan into the prepared air fry basket and insert in the oven.
11. When cooking time is completed, open the lid and serve hot.

Serving Suggestions: Serve with crusty bread.
Variation Tip: Spinach can be replaced with kale.
Nutritional Information per Serving:
Calories: 309 | Fat: 18.8g|Sat Fat: 10.6g|Carbohydrates: 12.3g|Fiber: 4.1g|Sugar: 1.7g|Protein: 26.4g

Buttered Trout

Prep Time: 10 minutes
Cook Time: 10 minutes
Serves: 2

Ingredients:

- 2 (6-ounces) trout fillets
- Salt and ground black pepper, as required
- 1 tablespoon butter, melted

Preparation:

1. Rinse the trout thoroughly. Season each trout fillet with salt and black pepper and then coat with the butter.
2. Arrange the trout fillets onto the greased sheet pan in a single layer.
3. Press "Power" button of Ninja Foodi XL Pro Air Oven and select "Air Fry" function.
4. Press TEMP/SHADE +/- buttons to set the temperature at 360 degrees F.
5. Now press TIME/SLICES +/- buttons to set the cooking time to 10 minutes.
6. Press "START/STOP" button to start.
7. When the unit beeps to show that it is preheated, open the lid.
8. Insert the sheet pan in oven.
9. Flip the fillets once halfway through.
10. When cooking time is completed, open the lid and serve hot.

Serving Suggestions: Serve with your favorite salad.
Variation Tip: Feel free to add seasoning as you like.
Nutritional Information per Serving:
Calories: 374 | Fat: 20.2g|Sat Fat: 6.2g|Carbohydrates: 0g|Fiber: 0g|Sugar: 0g|Protein: 45.4g

Cajun Salmon

Prep Time: 10 minutes
Cook Time: 7 minutes
Serves: 2

Ingredients:

- 2 (7-ounce) (¾-inch-thick) salmon fillets
- 1 tablespoon Cajun seasoning
- ½ teaspoon sugar
- 1 tablespoon fresh lemon juice

Preparation:

1. Sprinkle the salmon fillets with Cajun seasoning and sugar evenly.
2. Press "Power" button of Ninja Foodi XL Pro Air Oven and select "Air Fry" function.
3. Press TEMP/SHADE +/- buttons to set the temperature at 360 degrees F.
4. Now press TIME/SLICES +/- buttons to set the cooking time to 7 minutes.
5. Press "START/STOP" button to start.
6. When the unit beeps to show that it is preheated, open the lid.
7. Arrange the salmon fillets, skin-side up in the greased air fry basket and insert in the oven.
8. When cooking time is completed, open the lid and transfer the salmon fillets onto a platter.
9. Drizzle with the lemon juice and serve hot.

Serving Suggestions: Serve with mashed cauliflower.

Variation Tip: Adjust the ratio of Cajun seasoning according to your taste.

Nutritional Information per Serving:
Calories: 268 | Fat: 12.3g|Sat Fat: 1.8g|Carbohydrates: 1.2g|Fiber: 0g|Sugar: 1.2g|Protein: 36.8g

Crab Cakes

Prep Time: 15 minutes
Cook Time: 10 minutes
Serves: 4

Ingredients:

- ¼ cup red bell pepper, seeded and chopped finely
- 2 scallions, chopped finely
- 2 tablespoons mayonnaise
- 2 tablespoons breadcrumbs
- 1 tablespoon Dijon mustard
- 1 teaspoon old bay seasoning
- 8 ounces lump crabmeat, drained

Preparation:

1. In a large bowl, add all the ingredients except crabmeat and mix until well combined.
2. Gently fold in the crabmeat.
3. Make 4 equal-sized patties from the mixture.
4. Arrange the patties onto the lightly greased sheet pan.
5. Press "Power" button of Ninja Foodi XL Pro Air Oven and press FUNCTION +/- buttons to select the "Air Fry" function.
6. Press TEMP/SHADE +/- buttons to set the temperature at 370 degrees F.
7. Now press TIME/SLICES +/- buttons to set the cooking time to 10 minutes.
8. Press "Start/Stop" button to start.
9. When the unit beeps to show that it is preheated, open the oven door and insert the sheet pan in oven.
10. When cooking time is completed, open the oven door and serve hot.

Serving Suggestions: Serve alongside the fresh salad.

Variation Tip: Make sure to remove any cartilage from crabmeat.

Nutritional Information per Serving:
Calories: 91 | Fat: 7.4g|Sat Fat: 0.4g|Carbohydrates: 6.4g|Fiber: 0.6g|Sugar: 1.3g|Protein: 9.1g

Herbed Shrimp

Prep Time: 15 minutes
Cook Time: 7 minutes
Serves: 3

Ingredients:

- 4 tablespoons salted butter, melted
- 1 tablespoon fresh lemon juice
- 1 tablespoon garlic, minced
- 2 teaspoons red pepper flakes, crushed
- 1 pound shrimp, peeled and deveined
- 2 tablespoons fresh basil, chopped
- 1 tablespoon fresh chives, chopped
- 2 tablespoons chicken broth

Preparation:

1. In a 7-inch-round baking pan, place butter, lemon juice, garlic, and red pepper flakes and mix well.
2. Press "Power" button of Ninja Foodi XL Pro Air Oven and select the "Air Fry" function.
3. Press TEMP/SHADE +/- buttons to set the temperature at 325 degrees F.
4. Now press TIME/SLICES +/- buttons to set the cooking time to 7 minutes.
5. Press "Start/Stop" button to start.
6. When the unit beeps to show that it is preheated, open the oven door and place the pan over wire rack on Level 3.
7. Insert the wire rack in oven.
8. After 2 minutes of cooking in the pan, stir in the shrimp, basil, chives and broth.
9. When cooking time is completed, open the oven door and stir the mixture.
10. Serve hot.

Serving Suggestions: Serve with the garnishing of scallion.

Variation Tip: Use fresh shrimp.

Nutritional Information per Serving:
Calories: 327 | Fat: 18.3g|Sat Fat: 10.6g|Carbohydrates: 4.2g|Fiber: 0.5g|Sugar: 0.3g|Protein: 35.3g

Lemony Salmon

Prep Time: 10 minutes
Cook Time: 8 minutes
Serves: 3

Ingredients:

- 1½ pounds salmon
- ½ teaspoon red chili powder
- Salt and ground black pepper, as required
- 1 lemon, cut into slices
- 1 tablespoon fresh dill, chopped

Preparation:

1. Season the salmon with chili powder, salt, and black pepper.
2. Press "Power" button of Ninja Foodi XL Pro Air Oven and select "Air Fry" function.
3. Press TEMP/SHADE +/- buttons to set the temperature at 375 degrees F.
4. Now press TIME/SLICES +/- buttons to set the cooking time to 8 minutes.
5. Press "Start/Stop" button to start.
6. When the unit beeps to show that it is preheated, open the oven door.
7. Arrange the salmon fillets into the greased air fry basket and slide the basket into the rail of Level 3.
8. When cooking time is completed, open the oven door and serve hot with the garnishing of fresh dill.

Serving Suggestions: Serve with the topping of cheese.

Variation Tip: Make sure to pat dry the salmon completely before seasoning.

Nutritional Information per Serving:
Calories: 305 | Fat: 14.1g|Sat Fat: 2g|Carbohydrates: 1.3g|Fiber: 0.4g|Sugar: 0.2g|Protein: 44.3g

Salmon & Asparagus Parcel

Prep Time: 15 minutes
Cook Time: 13 minutes
Serves: 2

Ingredients:

- 2 (4-ounce) salmon fillets
- 6 asparagus stalks
- ¼ cup white sauce
- 1 teaspoon oil
- ¼ cup champagne
- Salt and ground black pepper, as required

Preparation:

1. In a bowl, mix together all the ingredients.
2. Divide the salmon mixture over 2 pieces of foil evenly.
3. Seal the foil around the salmon mixture to form the packet.
4. Press "Power" button of Ninja Foodi XL Pro Air Oven and select "Air Fry" function.
5. Press TEMP/SHADE +/- buttons to set the temperature at 355 degrees F. Select 2 LEVEL.
6. Now press TIME/SLICES +/- buttons to set the cooking time to 13 minutes.
7. Press "Start/Stop" button to start.
8. When the unit beeps to show that it is pre-heated, open the oven door.
9. Arrange the salmon parcels into the air fry basket on Level 4 and roast tray over wire rack on Level 2.
10. When cooking time is completed, open the oven door and serve hot.

Serving Suggestions: Serve with the garnishing of fresh herbs.
Variation Tip: Don't overcook the salmon.
Nutritional Information per Serving:
Calories: 243 | Fat: 12.7g|Sat Fat: 2.2g|Carbohydrates: 9.4g|Fiber: 1.8g|Sugar: 6g|Protein: 25g

Pesto Salmon

Prep Time: 15 minutes
Cook Time: 15 minutes
Serves: 4

Ingredients:

- 1¼ pound fresh salmon fillet, cut into 4 fillets
- 2 tablespoons white wine
- 1 tablespoon fresh lemon juice
- 2 tablespoons pesto

Preparation:

1. Arrange the salmon fillets onto a foil-lined baking pan, skin-side down.
2. Drizzle the salmon fillets with wine and lemon juice.
3. Set aside for about 15 minutes.
4. Spread pesto over each salmon fillet evenly.
5. Press "Power" button of Ninja Foodi XL Pro Air Oven and select the "Broil" function.
6. Press TIME/SLICES +/- buttons to set the cooking time to 15 minutes.
7. Press the TEMP/SLICES +/- buttons to select HI.
8. Press "START/STOP" button to start.
9. When the unit beeps to show that it is pre-heated, open the lid.
10. Insert the baking pan in oven.
11. When cooking time is completed, open the lid and serve hot.

Serving Suggestions: Serve with lemon slices.
Variation Tip: Feel free to add seasoning of your choice.
Nutritional Information per Serving:
Calories: 228 | Fat: 12g|Sat Fat: 1.9g|Carbohydrates: 0.8g|Fiber: 0.2g|Sugar: 0.6g|Protein: 28.3g

Crispy Flounder

Prep Time: 15 minutes
Cook Time: 12 minutes
Serves: 3

Ingredients:

- 1 egg
- 1 cup dry Italian breadcrumb
- ¼ cup olive oil
- 3 (6-ounce) flounder fillets

Preparation:

1. In a shallow bowl, beat the egg.
2. In another bowl, add the breadcrumbs and oil and mix until a crumbly mixture is formed.
3. Dip the flounder fillets into the beaten egg and then coat with the breadcrumb mixture.
4. Press "Power" button of Ninja Foodi XL Pro Air Oven and select "Air Fry" function.
5. Press TEMP/SHADE +/- buttons to set the temperature at 355 degrees F.
6. Now press TIME/SLICES +/- buttons to set the cooking time to 12 minutes.
7. Press "START/STOP" button to start.
8. When the unit beeps to show that it is preheated, open the lid and grease the air fry basket.
9. Place the flounder fillets into the prepared air fry basket and insert in the oven.
10. When cooking time is completed, open the lid and serve hot.

Serving Suggestions: Serve with potato chips.
Variation Tip: To avoid gluten, use crushed pork rinds instead of breadcrumbs.
Nutritional Information per Serving:
Calories: 508 | Fat: 22.8g|Sat Fat: 3.9g|Carbohydrates: 26.5g|Fiber: 1.8g|Sugar: 2.5g|Protein: 47.8g

Lobster Tail Casserole

Prep Time: 15 minutes.
Cook Time: 16 minutes.
Serves: 6

Ingredients:

- 1 pound salmon fillets, cut into 8 equal pieces
- 16 large sea scallops
- 16 large prawns, peeled and deveined
- 8 East Coast lobster tails split in half
- ⅓ cup butter
- ¼ cup white wine
- ¼ cup lemon juice
- 2 tablespoons chopped fresh tarragon
- 2 medium garlic cloves, minced
- ½ teaspoon paprika
- ¼ teaspoon ground cayenne pepper

Preparation:

1. Whisk butter with lemon juice, wine, garlic, tarragon, paprika, salt, and cayenne pepper in a small saucepan.
2. Stir cook this mixture over medium heat for 1 minute.
3. Toss scallop, salmon fillet, and prawns in the sheet pan and pour the butter mixture on top.
4. Transfer the pan to the 2nd rack position of Ninja Foodi XL Pro Air Oven and close the door.
5. Select the "Bake" Mode using FUNCTION +/- buttons and select Rack Level 2.
6. Set its cooking time to 15 minutes and temperature to 450 degrees F, then press "START/STOP" to initiate cooking.
7. Serve warm.

Serving Suggestion: Serve the casserole with fresh greens and chili sauce on the side.
Variation Tip: Add breadcrumbs on top for a crispy touch.
Nutritional Information Per Serving:
Calories 457 | Fat 19g |Sodium 557mg | Carbs 9g | Fiber 1.8g | Sugar 1.2g | Protein 32.5g

Fish in Yogurt Marinade

Prep Time: 15 minutes.
Cook Time: 10 minutes.
Serves: 2

Ingredients:

- 1 cup plain Greek yogurt
- Finely grated zest of 1 lemon
- 1 tablespoon lemon juice
- 1 tablespoon finely minced garlic
- 3 tablespoons fresh oregano leaves
- 1 teaspoon ground cumin
- ¼ teaspoon ground allspice
- ½ teaspoon salt
- ½ teaspoon freshly ground black pepper
- 1½ pounds perch filets

Preparation:

1. Mix lemon zest, yogurt, garlic, cumin, oregano, black pepper, salt, and allspices in a shallow pan.
2. Add fish to this marinade, mix well to coat then cover it with a plastic wrap.
3. Marinate for 15 minutes in the refrigerator, then uncover.
4. Transfer the fish pan to the 2nd rack position of Ninja Foodi XL Pro Air Oven and close the door.
5. Select the "Bake" Mode using FUNCTION +/- buttons and select Rack Level 2.
6. Set its cooking time to 10 minutes and temperature to 450 degrees F, then press "START/STOP" to initiate cooking.
7. Serve warm.

Serving Suggestion: Serve the fish with lemon slices and fried rice.

Variation Tip: Use white pepper for seasoning for a change of flavor.

Nutritional Information Per Serving:
Calories 438 | Fat 21g |Sodium 146mg | Carbs 7.1g | Fiber 0.1g | Sugar 0.4g | Protein 23g

Rum-Glazed Shrimp

Prep Time: 10 minutes.
Cook Time: 5 minutes.
Serves: 4

Ingredients:

- 1 ½ pounds shrimp, peeled and deveined
- 3 tablespoons olive oil
- ⅓ cup sweet chili sauce
- ¼ cup soy sauce
- ¼ Captain Morgan Spiced Rum
- 2 garlic cloves, minced
- Juice of 1 lime
- ½ teaspoon crushed red pepper flakes
- 1 green onion, thinly sliced

Preparation:

1. Mix shrimp with all the ingredients in a bowl.
2. Cover and marinate the shrimp for 30 minutes.
3. Spread the glazed shrimp in a sheet pan.
4. Transfer the pan to the 2nd rack position of Ninja Foodi XL Pro Air Oven and close the door.
5. Select the "Bake" Mode using FUNCTION +/- buttons and select Rack Level 2.
6. Set its cooking time to 5 minutes and temperature to 375 degrees F, then press "START/STOP" to initiate cooking.
7. Serve warm.

Serving Suggestion: Serve the shrimp with sautéed asparagus.

Variation Tip: Spread the shrimp on top of the lettuce leaves.

Nutritional Information Per Serving:
Calories 378 | Fat 7g |Sodium 316mg | Carbs 6.2g | Fiber 0.3g | Sugar 0.3g | Protein 26g

Beer-Battered Fish

Prep Time: 15 minutes.
Cook Time: 15 minutes.
Serves: 4

Ingredients:

- 1 ½ cups all-purpose flour
- Kosher salt, to taste
- ½ teaspoon Old Bay seasoning
- 1 (12-ounce) bottle lager
- 1 large egg, beaten
- 2 pounds cod, cut into 12 pieces
- Freshly ground black pepper
- Vegetable oil for frying
- Lemon wedges, for serving

Preparation:

1. Mix flour with old bay, salt, egg, and beer in a bowl.
2. Rub the cod with black pepper and salt.
3. Coat the codfish with the beer batter and place it in the air fry basket.
4. Transfer the basket to the 3rd rack position of Ninja Foodi XL Pro Air Oven and close the door.
5. Select the "Air Fry" Mode using FUNCTION +/- buttons and select Rack Level 3.
6. Set its cooking time to 15 minutes and temperature to 350 degrees F, then press "START/STOP" to initiate cooking.
7. Serve warm.

Serving Suggestion: Serve the fish with potato fries and tomato ketchup.

Variation Tip: Rub the fish with lemon juice before coating.

Nutritional Information Per Serving:
Calories 428 | Fat 17g |Sodium 723mg | Carbs 21g | Fiber 2.5g | Sugar 2g | Protein 43g

Crispy Cod

Prep Time: 15 minutes
Cook Time: 15 minutes
Serves: 4

Ingredients:

- 4 (4-ounce) (¾-inch thick) cod fillets, with fish scale removed
- Salt, as required
- 2 tablespoons all-purpose flour
- 2 eggs
- ½ cup panko breadcrumbs
- 1 teaspoon fresh dill, minced
- ½ teaspoon dry mustard
- ½ teaspoon lemon zest, grated
- ½ teaspoon onion powder
- ½ teaspoon paprika
- Olive oil cooking spray

Preparation

1. Season the cod fillets with salt generously.
2. In a shallow bowl, place the flour.
3. Crack the eggs in a second bowl and beat well.
4. In a third bowl, mix the panko, dill, lemon zest, mustard, and spices together.
5. Coat each cod fillet with the flour, then dip into beaten eggs and finally, coat with panko mixture.
6. Press "Power" button of Ninja Foodi XL Pro Air Oven and select "Air Fry" function.
7. Press TEMP/SHADE +/- buttons to set the temperature at 400 degrees F.
8. Now press TIME/SLICES +/- buttons to set the cooking time to 15 minutes.
9. Press "START/STOP" button to start.
10. When the unit beeps to show that it is preheated, open the lid and grease the air fry basket.
11. Place the cod fillets into the prepared air fry basket and insert in the oven.
12. Flip the cod fillets once halfway through.
13. When cooking time is completed, open the lid and serve hot.

Serving Suggestions: Serve with steamed green beans.

Variation Tip: Feel free to add seasoning of your choice.

Nutritional Information per Serving:
Calories: 190 | Fat: 4.3g|Sat Fat: 1.1g|Carbohydrates: 5.9g|Fiber: 0.4g|Sugar: 0.4g|Protein: 24g

Fish Newburg with Haddock

Prep Time: 15 minutes.
Cook Time: 29 minutes.
Serves: 4

Ingredients:

- 1 ½ pounds haddock fillets
- Salt and freshly ground black pepper
- 4 tablespoons butter
- 1 tablespoon 2 teaspoons flour
- ¼ teaspoon sweet paprika
- ¼ teaspoon ground nutmeg
- Dash cayenne pepper
- ¾ cup heavy cream
- ½ cup milk
- 3 tablespoons dry sherry
- 2 large egg yolks
- 4 pastry shells

Preparation:

1. Rub haddock with black pepper and salt, then place in a sheet pan.
2. Place the spiced haddock in the pastry shell and close it like a calzone.
3. Drizzle 1 tablespoon of melted butter on top.
4. Transfer the pan to the 2nd rack position of Ninja Foodi XL Pro Air Oven and close the door.
5. Select the "Bake" Mode using FUNCTION +/- buttons and select Rack Level 2.
6. Set its cooking time to 25 minutes and temperature to 350 degrees F, then press "START/STOP" to initiate cooking.
7. Meanwhile, melt 3 tablespoons of butter in a suitable saucepan over low heat.
8. Stir in nutmeg, cayenne, paprika, and salt, then mix well.
9. Add flour to the spice butter and whisk well to avoid lumps.
10. Cook for 2 minutes, then add milk and cream. Mix well and cook until thickens.
11. Beat egg yolks with sherry in a bowl and stir in a ladle of cream mixture.
12. Mix well and return the mixture to its saucepan.
13. Cook the mixture on low heat for 2 minutes.
14. Add the baked wrapped haddock to its sauce and cook until warm.
15. Serve warm.

Serving Suggestion: Serve the haddock with fried rice.
Variation Tip: Drizzle parmesan cheese on top before cooking.

Nutritional Information Per Serving:
Calories 421 | Fat 7.4g |Sodium 356mg | Carbs 9.3g | Fiber 2.4g | Sugar 5g | Protein 37.2g

Prawns in Butter Sauce

Prep Time: 15 minutes
Cook Time: 6 minutes
Serves: 2

Ingredients:

- ½ pound large prawns, peeled and deveined
- 1 large garlic clove, minced
- 1 tablespoon butter, melted
- 1 teaspoon fresh lemon zest, grated

Preparation:

1. In a bowl, add all the ingredients and toss to coat well.
2. Set aside at room temperature for about 30 minutes.
3. Arrange the prawn mixture into a baking pan.
4. Press "Power" button of Ninja Foodi XL Pro Air Oven and select "Bake" function.
5. Press TEMP/SHADE +/- buttons to set the temperature at 450 degrees F.
6. Now press TIME/SLICES +/- buttons to set the cooking time to 6 minutes.
7. Press "START/STOP" button to start.
8. When the unit beeps to show that it is preheated, open the lid.
9. Arrange the pan over the wire rack and insert in the oven.
10. When cooking time is completed, open the lid and serve immediately.

Serving Suggestions: Avoid shrimp from smelling like ammonia. Serve with fresh salad.
Variation Tip: Feel Free to add seasoning of your choice.
Nutritional Information per Serving:
Calories: 189 | Fat: 7.7g|Sat Fat: 4.2g|Carbohydrates: 2.4g|Fiber: 0.1g|Sugar: 0.1g|Protein: 26g

Salmon Burgers

Prep Time: 15 minutes
Cook Time: 22 minutes
Serves: 6

Ingredients:

- 3 large russet potatoes, peeled and cubed
- 1 (6-ounce) cooked salmon fillet
- 1 egg
- ¾ cup frozen vegetables (of your choice), parboiled and drained
- 2 tablespoons fresh parsley, chopped
- 1 teaspoon fresh dill, chopped
- Salt and ground black pepper, as required
- 1 cup breadcrumbs
- ¼ cup olive oil

Preparation:

1. In a pan of boiling water, cook the potatoes for about 10 minutes.
2. Drain the potatoes well.
3. Transfer the potatoes into a bowl and mash with a potato masher.
4. Set aside to cool completely.
5. In another bowl, add the salmon and flake with a fork.
6. Add the cooked potatoes, egg, parboiled vegetables, parsley, dill, salt and black pepper and mix until well combined.
7. Make 6 equal-sized patties from the mixture.
8. Coat patties with breadcrumb evenly and then drizzle with the oil evenly.
9. Press "Power" button of Ninja Foodi XL Pro Air Oven and select "Air Fry" function.
10. Press TEMP/SHADE +/- buttons to set the temperature at 355 degrees F.
11. Now press TIME/SLICES +/- buttons to set the cooking time to 12 minutes.
12. Press "START/STOP" button to start.
13. When the unit beeps to show that it is preheated, open the lid.
14. Arrange the patties in greased air fry basket and insert in the oven.
15. Flip the patties once halfway through.
16. When cooking time is completed, open the lid and serve hot.

Serving Suggestions: Serve your favorite dipping sauce.

Variation Tip: You can use herbs of your choice in this recipe.

Nutritional Information per Serving:
Calories: 334 | Fat: 12.1g|Sat Fat: 2g|Carbohydrates: 45.2g|Fiber: 6.3g|Sugar: 4g|Protein: 12.5g

Spicy Salmon

Prep Time: 10 minutes
Cook Time: 11 minutes
Serves: 2

Ingredients:

- 1 teaspoon smoked paprika
- 1 teaspoon cayenne pepper
- 1 teaspoon onion powder
- 1 teaspoon garlic powder
- Salt and ground black pepper, as required
- 2 (6-ounce) (1½-inch thick) salmon fillets
- 2 teaspoons olive oil

Preparation:

1. Add the spices in a bowl and mix well.
2. Drizzle the salmon fillets with oil and then rub with the spice mixture.
3. Press "Power" button of Ninja Foodi XL Pro Air Oven and select "Air Fry" function.
4. Press TEMP/SHADE +/- buttons to set the temperature at 390 degrees F.
5. Now press TIME/SLICES +/- buttons to set the cooking time to 11 minutes.
6. Press "Start/Stop" button to start.
7. When the unit beeps to show that it is preheated, open the oven door.
8. Arrange the salmon fillets into the greased air fry basket on Level 3.
9. When cooking time is completed, open the oven door and serve hot.

Serving Suggestions: Serve with your favorite salad.

Variation Tip: Adjust the ratio of spices according to your taste.

Nutritional Information per Serving:
Calories: 280 | Fat: 15.5g|Sat Fat: 2.2g|Carbohydrates: 3.1g|Fiber: 0.8g|Sugar: 1g|Protein: 33.6g

Salmon with Broccoli

Prep Time: 15 minutes
Cook Time: 12 minutes
Serves: 2

Ingredients:

- 1½ cups small broccoli florets
- 2 tablespoons vegetable oil, divided
- Salt and ground black pepper, as required
- 1 (½-inch) piece fresh ginger, grated
- 1 tablespoon soy sauce
- 1 teaspoon rice vinegar
- 1 teaspoon light brown sugar
- ¼ teaspoon cornstarch
- 2 (6-ounce) skin-on salmon fillets

Preparation:

1. In a bowl, mix together the broccoli, 1 tablespoon of oil, salt, and black pepper.
2. In another bowl, mix well the ginger, soy sauce, vinegar, sugar, and cornstarch.
3. Coat the salmon fillets with remaining oil and then with the ginger mixture.
4. Press "Power" button of Ninja Foodi XL Pro Air Oven and select "Air Fry" function. Select 2 LEVEL.
5. Press TEMP/SHADE +/- buttons to set the temperature at 375 degrees F.
6. Now press TIME/SLICES +/- buttons to set the cooking time to 12 minutes.
7. Press "Start/Stop" button to start.
8. When the unit beeps to show that it is preheated, open the oven door.
9. Arrange the broccoli florets evenly into the greased air fry basket and roast tray top with the salmon fillets.
10. Insert the basket Level 3 and roast tray over wire rack on Level 1.
11. When cooking time is completed, remove basket and wire rack from oven and cool for 5 minutes before serving.

Serving Suggestions: Serve with the garnishing of lemon zest.
Variation Tip: Use low-sodium soy sauce.
Nutritional Information per Serving:
Calories: 385 | Fat: 24.4g|Sat Fat: 4.2g|Carbohydrates: 7.8g|Fiber: 2.1g|Sugar: 3g|Protein: 35.6g

Baked Tilapia with Buttery Crumb Topping

Prep Time: 15 minutes.
Cook Time: 16 minutes.
Serves: 4

Ingredients:

- 4 tilapia fillets
- Salt and pepper to taste
- 1 cup bread crumbs
- 3 tablespoons butter, melted
- ½ teaspoon dried basil

Preparation:

1. Rub the tilapia fillets with black pepper and salt, then place them in the sheet pan.
2. Mix butter, breadcrumbs, and seasonings in a bowl.
3. Sprinkle the breadcrumbs mixture on top of the tilapia.
4. Transfer the fish to the 2nd rack position of Ninja Foodi XL Pro Air Oven and close the door.
5. Select the "Bake" Mode using FUNCTION +/- buttons and select Rack Level 2.
6. Set its cooking time to 15 minutes and temperature to 375 degrees F, then press "START/STOP" to initiate cooking.
7. Switch to Broil at HI and cook for 1 minute.
8. Serve warm.

Serving Suggestion: Serve the tilapia with vegetable rice.
Variation Tip: Add crushed corn flakes on top for more crispiness.
Nutritional Information Per Serving:
Calories 558 | Fat 9g |Sodium 994mg | Carbs 1g | Fiber 0.4g | Sugar 3g | Protein 16g

Tangy Sea Bass

Prep Time: 10 minutes
Cook Time: 12 minutes
Serves: 2

Ingredients:

- 2 (5-ounce) sea bass fillets
- 1 garlic clove, minced
- 1 teaspoon fresh dill, minced
- 1 tablespoon olive oil
- 1 tablespoon balsamic vinegar
- Salt and ground black pepper, as required

Preparation:

1. In a large resealable bag, add all the ingredients.
2. Seal the bag and shake well to mix.
3. Refrigerate to marinate for at least 30 minutes.
4. Remove the fish fillets from bag and shake off the excess marinade.
5. Arrange the fish fillets onto the greased sheet pan in a single layer.
6. Press "Power" button of Ninja Foodi XL Pro Air Oven and select "Bake" function.
7. Press TEMP/SHADE +/- buttons to set the temperature at 450 degrees F.
8. Now press TIME/SLICES +/- buttons to set the cooking time to 12 minutes.
9. Press "Start/Stop" button to start.
10. When the unit beeps to show that it is preheated, open the oven door and insert the sheet pan on Level 3.
11. Open the Flip the fish fillets once halfway through.
12. When cooking time is completed, open the oven door and serve hot.

Serving Suggestions: Serve with fresh salad.

Variation Tip: Rinse fish with cool, running water and pat it dry.

Nutritional Information per Serving:
Calories: 241 | Fat: 10.7g|Sat Fat: 1.9g|Carbohydrates: 0.9g|Fiber: 0.1g|Sugar: 0.1g|Protein: 33.7g

Salmon with Prawns

Prep Time: 15 minutes
Cook Time: 18 minutes
Serves: 4

Ingredients:

- 4 (4-ounce) salmon fillets
- 2 tablespoons olive oil
- ½ pound cherry tomatoes, chopped
- 8 large prawns, peeled and deveined
- 2 tablespoons fresh lemon juice
- 2 tablespoons fresh thyme, chopped

Preparation:

1. In the bottom of a greased sheet pan, place salmon fillets and tomatoes in a greased baking dish in a single layer and drizzle with the oil.
2. Arrange the prawns on top in a single layer.
3. Drizzle with lemon juice and sprinkle with thyme.
4. Press "Power" button of Ninja Foodi XL Pro Air Oven and select "Air Fry" function.
5. Press TEMP/SHADE +/- buttons to set the temperature at 390 degrees F.
6. Now press TIME/SLICES +/- buttons to set the cooking time to 8 minutes.
7. Press "Start/Stop" button to start.
8. When the unit beeps to show that it is preheated, open the oven door.
9. Arrange the baking pan over wire rake and insert into rails of Level 3.
10. When cooking time is completed, open the oven door and serve immediately.

Serving Suggestions: Serve with pasta of your choice.

Variation Tip: Make sure to use fresh salmon and prawns.

Nutritional Information per Serving:
Calories: 239 | Fat: 14.5g|Sat Fat: 2.2g|Carbohydrates: 3.4g|Fiber: 1.2g|Sugar: 1.7g|Protein: 25.2g

Cod Burgers

Prep Time: 15 minutes
Cook Time: 7 minutes
Serves: 4

Ingredients:

- ½ pound cod fillets
- ½ teaspoon fresh lime zest, grated finely
- ½ egg
- ½ teaspoon red chili paste
- Salt, to taste
- ½ tablespoon fresh lime juice
- 3 tablespoons coconut, grated and divided
- 1 small scallion, chopped finely
- 1 tablespoon fresh parsley, chopped

Preparation:

1. In a food processor, add cod filets, lime zest, egg, chili paste, salt and lime juice and pulse until smooth.
2. Transfer the cod mixture into a bowl.
3. Add 1½ tablespoons of coconut, scallion and parsley and mix until well combined.
4. Make 4 equal-sized patties from the mixture.
5. In a shallow dish, place the remaining coconut.
6. Coat the patties in coconut evenly.
7. Press "Power" button of Ninja Foodi XL Pro Air Oven and select "Air Fry" function.
8. Press TEMP/SHADE +/- buttons to set the temperature at 375 degrees F.
9. Now press TIME/SLICES +/- buttons to set the cooking time to 7 minutes.
10. Press "Start/Stop" button to start.
11. When the unit beeps to show that it is preheated, open the oven door.
12. Arrange the patties into the greased air fry basket on Level 3.
13. When cooking time is completed, open the oven door and serve hot.

Serving Suggestions: Serve alongside the dipping sauce.
Variation Tip: Use unsweetened coconut.
Nutritional Information per Serving:
Calories: 70 | Fat: 2.4g|Sat Fat: 1.3g|Carbohydrates: 1.1g|Fiber: 0.4g|Sugar: 0.5g|Protein: 11g

Parmesan Flounder

Prep Time: 15 minutes.
Cook Time: 20 minutes.
Serves: 4

Ingredients:

- ¼ cup olive oil
- 4 fillets flounder
- Kosher salt, to taste
- Freshly ground black pepper
- ½ cup Parmesan, grated
- ¼ cup bread crumbs
- 4 garlic cloves, minced
- Juice and zest of 1 lemon

Preparation:

1. Mix parmesan, breadcrumbs, and all the ingredients in a bowl and coat the flounder well.
2. Place the fish in a sheet pan.
3. Transfer the fish to the 2nd rack position of Ninja Foodi XL Pro Air Oven and close the door.
4. Select the "Bake" Mode using FUNCTION +/- buttons and select Rack Level 2.
5. Set its cooking time to 20 minutes and temperature to 425 degrees F, then press "START/STOP" to initiate cooking.
6. Serve warm.

Serving Suggestion: Serve the flounder with fresh greens and yogurt dip.
Variation Tip: Drizzle cheddar cheese on top for a rich taste.
Nutritional Information Per Serving:
Calories 351 | Fat 4g |Sodium 236mg | Carbs 9.1g | Fiber 0.3g | Sugar 0.1g | Protein 36g

Maple Bacon Salmon

Prep Time: 15 minutes.
Cook Time: 29 minutes.
Serves: 4

Ingredients:

Salmon

- 1 lemon, sliced
- 1 (2 ¼ pounds) skin-on salmon fillet
- 2 ½ teaspoons salt, black pepper, and garlic seasoning
- 1 tablespoon Dijon mustard
- ⅓ cup olive oil
- 2 tablespoons lemon juice
- 2 tablespoons maple syrup
- Chopped chives for garnish

Candied Bacon

- 3 tablespoons maple syrup
- 1 tablespoon packed brown sugar
- ¼ teaspoon salt, black pepper and garlic seasoning

Preparation:

1. Place lemon slices in a sheet pan and top them with salmon.
2. Drizzle salt, black pepper, and garlic seasoning on top.
3. Mix mustard, oil, maple syrup, lemon juice, salt, black pepper, and seasoning in a bowl.
4. Pour this sauce over the salmon.
5. Transfer the pan to the 2nd rack position of Ninja Foodi XL Pro Air Oven and close the door.
6. Select the "Air Fry" Mode using FUNCTION +/- buttons and select Rack Level 2.
7. Set its cooking time to 25 minutes and temperature to 350 degrees F, then press "START/STOP" to initiate cooking.
8. Meanwhile, mix brown sugar, salt, black pepper, and garlic seasoning in a bowl.
9. Sauté bacon in a skillet until crispy and pour the sugar syrup on top.
10. Cook for 4 minutes until the liquid is absorbed.
11. Allow the bacon to cool and then crumble it.
12. Garnish the salmon with crumbled bacon.
13. Serve warm.

Serving Suggestion: Serve the salmon with roasted broccoli florets.

Variation Tip: Drizzle lemon butter on top before cooking.

Nutritional Information Per Serving:
Calories 415 | Fat 15g |Sodium 634mg | Carbs 4.3g | Fiber 1.4g | Sugar 1g | Protein 23.3g

Spiced Shrimp

Prep Time: 15 minutes
Cook Time: 5 minutes
Serves: 3

Ingredients:

- 1 pound tiger shrimp
- 3 tablespoons olive oil
- 1 teaspoon old bay seasoning
- ½ teaspoon cayenne pepper
- ½ teaspoon smoked paprika
- Salt, as required

Preparation:

1. In a large bowl, add all the ingredients and stir to combine.
2. Press "Power" button of Ninja Foodi XL Pro Air Oven and select "Air Fry" function.
3. Press TEMP/SHADE +/- buttons to set the temperature at 390 degrees F.
4. Now press TIME/SLICES +/- buttons to set the cooking time to 5 minutes.
5. Press "Start/Stop" button to start.
6. When the unit beeps to show that it is preheated, open the oven door.
7. Arrange the shrimp into the greased air fry basket on Level 3.
8. When cooking time is completed, open the oven door and serve hot.

Serving Suggestions: Serve with fresh greens.

Variation Tip: You can use seasoning of your choice.

Nutritional Information per Serving:
Calories: 272 | Fat: 15.7g|Sat Fat: 2.5g|Carbohydrates: 0.4g|Fiber: 0.2g|Sugar: 0.1g|Protein: 31.7g

Crispy Catfish

Prep Time: 15 minutes
Cook Time: 15 minutes
Serves: 5

Ingredients:

- 5 (6-ounce) catfish fillets
- 1 cup milk
- 2 teaspoons fresh lemon juice
- ½ cup yellow mustard
- ½ cup cornmeal
- ¼ cup all-purpose flour
- 2 tablespoons dried parsley flakes
- ¼ teaspoon red chili powder
- ¼ teaspoon cayenne pepper
- ¼ teaspoon onion powder
- ¼ teaspoon garlic powder
- Salt and ground black pepper, as required
- Olive oil cooking spray

Preparation:

1. In a large bowl, place the catfish, milk, and lemon juice and refrigerate for about 15 minutes.
2. In a shallow bowl, add the mustard.
3. In another bowl, mix together the cornmeal, flour, parsley flakes and spices.
4. Remove the catfish fillets from milk mixture and with paper towels, pat them dry.
5. Coat each fish fillet with mustard and then roll into cornmeal mixture.
6. Then, spray each fillet with the cooking spray.
7. Arrange the 3 catfish fillets into the greased air fry basket and 2 into roast tray. Press "Power" button of Ninja Foodi XL Pro Air Oven and select "Air Fry" function. Select 2 LEVEL.
8. Press TEMP/SHADE +/- buttons to set the temperature at 400 degrees F.
9. Now press TIME/SLICES +/- buttons to set the cooking time to 15 minutes.
10. Press "Start/Stop" button to start.
11. When the unit beeps to show that it is preheated, open the oven door.
12. Slide the basket on Level 3 and roast tray over wire rack on Level 1.
13. After 10 minutes of cooking, flip the fillets and spray with the cooking spray.
14. When cooking time is completed, open the oven door and serve hot.

Serving Suggestions: Serve with cheese sauce.
Variation Tip: Use freshly squeezed lemon juice.
Nutritional Information per Serving:
Calories: 340 | Fat: 15.5g|Sat Fat: 3.1g|Carbohydrates: 18.3g|Fiber: 2g|Sugar: 2.7g|Protein: 30.9g

Baked Sardines with Garlic and Oregano

Prep Time: 15 minutes.
Cook Time: 45 minutes.
Serves: 4

Ingredients:

- 2 pounds fresh sardines
- Salt and black pepper to taste
- 2 tablespoons Greek oregano
- 6 cloves garlic, thinly sliced
- ½ cup olive oil
- ½ cup freshly squeezed lemon juice
- ½ cup water

Preparation:

1. Mix salt, black pepper, oregano, garlic, olive oil, lemon juice, and water in a sheet pan.
2. Spread the sardines in the marinade and rub well.
3. Leave the sardines for 10 minutes to marinate.
4. Transfer the pan to the 3rd rack position of Ninja Foodi XL Pro Air Oven and close the door.
5. Select the "Air Fry" Mode using FUNCTION +/- buttons and select Rack Level 3.
6. Set its cooking time to 45 minutes and temperature to 355 degrees F, then press "START/STOP" to initiate cooking.
7. Serve warm.

Serving Suggestion: Serve the sardines with crispy bread and sautéed veggies.
Variation Tip: Add chili flakes on top for more spice.
Nutritional Information Per Serving:
Calories 392 | Fat 16g |Sodium 466mg | Carbs 3.9g | Fiber 0.9g | Sugar 0.6g | Protein 48g

Cod with Sauce

Prep Time: 15 minutes
Cook Time: 15 minutes
Serves: 2

Ingredients:

- 2 (7-ounce) cod fillets
- Salt and ground black pepper, as required
- ¼ teaspoon sesame oil
- 1 cup water
- 5 little squares rock sugar
- 5 tablespoons light soy sauce
- 1 teaspoon dark soy sauce
- 2 scallions (green part), sliced
- ¼ cup fresh cilantro, chopped
- 3 tablespoons olive oil
- 5 ginger slices

Preparation:

1. Season each cod fillet evenly with salt, and black pepper and drizzle with sesame oil.
2. Set aside at room temperature for about 15-20 minutes.
3. Insert the wire rack on Level 1. Press "Power" button of Ninja Foodi XL Pro Air Oven and select "Air Fry" function. Select 2 LEVEL.
4. Press TEMP/SHADE +/- buttons to set the temperature at 355 degrees F.
5. Now press TIME/SLICES +/- buttons to set the cooking time to 12 minutes.
6. Press "Start/Stop" button to start.
7. When the unit beeps to show that it is preheated, open the oven door.
8. Arrange the cod fillets into the greased air fry basket on Level 3 and greased sheet pan over wire rack on Level 1.
9. Meanwhile, in a small pan, add the water and bring it to a boil.
10. Add the rock sugar and both soy sauces and cook until sugar is dissolved, stirring continuously.
11. Remove from the heat and set aside.
12. In a small frying pan, heat the olive oil over medium heat and sauté the ginger slices for about 2-3 minutes.
13. Remove the frying pan from heat and discard the ginger slices.
14. When cooking time is completed, open the oven door and transfer the cod fillets onto serving plates.
15. Top each fillet with scallion and cilantro.
16. Carefully pour the hot oil evenly over cod fillets.
17. Top with the sauce mixture and serve.

Serving Suggestions: Serve with boiled rice.

Variation Tip: For best result, use toasted sesame oil.

Nutritional Information per Serving:
Calories: 380 | Fat: 23.4g|Sat Fat: 3.1g|Carbohydrates: 5g|Fiber: 0.8g|Sugar: 1.1g|Protein: 38.3g

Garlic Shrimp with Lemon

Prep Time: 5 minutes
Cook Time: 12 minutes
Serves: 1

Ingredients:

- ½ pound raw shrimp
- ⅛ teaspoon garlic powder
- Salt and black pepper, to taste
- Vegetable oil, to coat shrimp
- Chili flakes
- Lemon wedges
- Parsley

Preparation:

1. Take a bowl and coat the shrimp with vegetable oil.
2. Add garlic powder, pepper and salt and toss to coat well.
3. Now, transfer shrimp to a plate or air fry basket.
4. Turn on your Ninja Foodi XL Pro Air Oven and select "Air Fry".
5. Select the timer for about 12 minutes and temperature for 400 degrees F.
6. When the unit beeps to signify it is preheated, open the oven and place the air fry basket on Level 3. Close the oven and let it cook.
7. Transfer shrimp to a bowl and add lemon wedges.
8. Sprinkle parsley and chili flakes evenly on top.
9. Serve and enjoy!

Serving Suggestions: Serve it with macaroni salad.

Variation Tip: Try not to cook for too long otherwise it can get dry.

Nutritional Information per Serving:
Calories: 398 | Fat: 17.9g|Sat Fat: 2.2g|Carbohydrates: 4.7g|Fiber: 0.4g|Sugar: 0.4g|Protein: 51.9g

Seafood Medley Mix

Prep Time: 5 minutes
Cook Time: 15 minutes
Serves: 1

Ingredients:

- ½ pound frozen seafood medley
- Oil or cooking spray
- Salt and black pepper, to taste

Preparation:

1. Take an air fry basket and evenly spray with a cooking spray.
2. Put frozen seafood medley in the air fry basket.
3. Turn on your Ninja Foodi XL Pro Air Oven and select "Air Fry".
4. Select the timer for 15 minutes and temperature for 400 degrees F.
5. When the unit beeps to signify it is preheated, open the oven and place the air fry basket into rail of Level 3.
6. Season the seafood medley with salt and pepper.
7. Serve and enjoy!

Serving Suggestions: Serve it with crispy garlic bread.

Variation Tip: Drizzle little bit of butter and lemon on top.

Nutritional Information per Serving:
Calories: 323 | Fat: 15.6g|Sat Fat: 3.8g|Carbohydrates: 5.1g|Fiber: 0g|Sugar: 0g|Protein: 32.4g

Garlic Butter Salmon Bites

Prep Time: 6 minutes
Cook Time: 10 minutes
Serves: 2

Ingredients:

- 1 tablespoon lemon juice
- 2 tablespoons butter
- ½ tablespoon garlic, minced
- ½ teaspoon pepper
- 4 ounces salmon
- ½ teaspoon salt
- ½ tablespoon apple cider or rice vinegar

Preparation:

1. Take a large bowl and add everything except salmon and whisk together until well combined.
2. Slice the salmon into small cubes and marinade them into the mixture.
3. Cover the bowl with plastic wrap and refrigerate it for about an hour.
4. Now, spread out the marinated salmon cubes into the air fry basket.
5. Turn on your Ninja Foodi XL Pro Air Oven and select "Air Fry".
6. Select the timer for 10 minutes and temperature for 350 degrees F.
7. When the unit beeps to signify it has preheated, open the oven and slide the air fry basket into rail of Level 3. Close the oven and let it cook.
8. Wait till the salmon is finely cooked.
9. Serve and enjoy!

Serving Suggestions: Serve with cheese on top.

Variation Tip: You can also coat salmon using bread crumbs for a fine taste.

Nutritional Information per Serving:
Calories: 159 | Fat: 12.2g|Sat Fat: 6g|Carbohydrates: 1.7g|Fiber: 0.2g|Sugar: 0.6g|Protein: 11.3g

Shrimp Fajitas

Prep Time: 5 minutes
Cook Time: 10 minutes
Serves: 2

Ingredients:

- ½ pound raw shrimp
- ½ small onion, sliced
- ½ tablespoon vegetable oil, divided
- ½ tablespoon fajita seasoning
- 1 red bell pepper, sliced
- 1 green bell pepper, sliced

Preparation:

1. Take a bowl and season the vegetables. Add half of the oil and fajita seasoning. Place the vegetable mixture into an air fry basket.
2. Turn on your Ninja Foodi XL Pro Air Oven and select "Air Fry".
3. Select the timer for 3 minutes and temperature for 375 degrees F.
4. When the unit beeps to signify it has preheated, open the oven and slide the air fry basket into rail of Level 3. Close the oven and let it cook.
5. Air fry the vegetables.
6. Now, meanwhile season the shrimp with rest of oil and fajita seasoning.
7. After 3 minutes add the seasoned shrimp to the side.
8. Now, air fry for another 6 minutes at the same temperature.
9. Serve and enjoy!

Serving Suggestions: Serve it with tortilla bread and fresh avocado slices.

Variation Tip: You can omit bell peppers if you like.

Nutritional Information per Serving:
Calories: 195 | Fat: 5.3g|Sat Fat: 1.3g|Carbohydrates: 9.4g|Fiber: 0.4g|Sugar: 5.2g|Protein: 26g

Air Fried Fish Sticks

Prep Time: 6 minutes
Cook Time: 15 minutes
Serves: 1

Ingredients:

- ½ pound fish fillets
- ¼ teaspoon ground black pepper, divided
- 1 egg
- ¼ cup flour
- ½ teaspoon salt, divided
- ½ cup breadcrumbs, dried

Preparation:

1. Take a bowl and add flour, salt and pepper.
2. In a second bowl, whisk the egg. In another bowl, add breadcrumbs.
3. Dredge the fish in flour, then dip in egg and lastly coat with breadcrumbs.
4. Once they are done, put them in an air fry basket.
5. Turn on your Ninja Foodi XL Pro Air Oven and select "Air Fry".
6. Select the timer for about 10 to 15 minutes and temperature for 400 degrees F.
7. When the unit beeps to signify it is preheated, open the oven and place the air fry basket into rail of Level 3. Close the oven and let it cook.
8. Serve and enjoy!

Serving Suggestions: Serve with fresh lemon juice.

Variation Tip: You can season fish with salt beforehand.

Nutritional Information per Serving:
Calories: 918 | Fat: 35.4g|Sat Fat: 8.5g|Carbohydrates: 101.9g|Fiber: 4.5g|Sugar: 3.8g|Protein: 49.3g

Tilapia with Herbs and Garlic

Prep Time: 4 minutes
Cook Time: 10 minutes
Serves: 1

Ingredients:

- 1 teaspoon olive oil
- 1 teaspoon fresh chives, chopped
- 1 fresh tilapia fillet
- ½ teaspoon garlic, minced
- 1 teaspoon fresh parsley, chopped
- Fresh ground pepper, to taste
- Salt, to taste

Preparation:

1. Take a small bowl and add everything except the tilapia fillets and stir together.
2. Dredge tilapia fillets in the prepared mixture.
3. Turn on your Ninja Foodi XL Pro Air Oven and select "Air Fry".
4. Select the timer for about 10 minutes and temperature for 400 degrees F.
5. When the unit beeps to signify it is preheated, open the oven and place the air fry basket into rail of Level 3.
6. Grease the air fry basket using little olive oil and place the seasoned fillets. Close the oven.
7. Let it cook and then serve.

Serving Suggestions: Serve with tomato salad.
Variation Tip: Try to pat tilapia fillets dry using a paper towel.
Nutritional Information per Serving:
Calories: 136 | Fat: 5.7g|Sat Fat: 1.1g|Carbohydrates: 0.6g|Fiber: 0.1g|Sugar: 0g|Protein: 21.2g

Breaded Shrimp

Prep Time: 8 minutes
Cook Time: 7 minutes
Serves: 2

Ingredients:

- ¼ teaspoon garlic powder
- ¼ teaspoon onion powder
- ¼ teaspoon salt
- ½ pound raw shrimp
- 1 egg
- 2 teaspoons flour
- ½ teaspoon corn starch
- 1 tablespoon water
- 6 tablespoons fine breadcrumbs
- 6 tablespoons panko breadcrumbs

Preparation:

1. Take a small bowl, add flour, corn starch, garlic powder, onion powder, and salt.
2. Add shrimp in the bowl and toss to coat well.
3. In a second bowl, whisk in the egg.
4. Mix the panko breadcrumbs and fine breadcrumbs together in another bowl.
5. Now, take seasoned shrimp, dip in the egg and place in the breadcrumbs mixture.
6. Lightly grease the air fry basket.
7. Turn on your Ninja Foodi XL Pro Air Oven and select "Air Fry".
8. Select the timer for about 7 minutes and temperature for 370 degrees F.
9. When the unit beeps to signify it is preheated, open the oven and place the air fry basket into rail of Level 3.
10. Place the coated shrimp to the air fry basket. Close the oven and let it cook.
11. Serve and enjoy!

Serving Suggestions: Serve it with tartar sauce or a dipping sauce of your choice.
Variation Tip: Try to rinse shrimp using cold water beforehand.
Nutritional Information per Serving:
Calories: 1351 | Fat: 26.6g|Sat Fat: 10.3g|Carbohydrates: 54.3g|Fiber: 1.3g|Sugar: 1g|Protein: 37.7g

Air Fried Fish Cakes

Prep Time: 5 minutes
Cook Time: 10 minutes
Serves: 1

Ingredients:

- ½ pound white fish, finely chopped
- ⅓ cup panko breadcrumbs
- 2 tablespoons cilantro, chopped
- 1 tablespoon chili sauce
- Cooking spray
- ½ egg
- 1 tablespoon mayonnaise
- ⅛ teaspoon ground pepper
- 1 pinch of salt

Preparation:

1. Take a bowl and add all ingredients together until well combined.
2. Shape the mixture into cakes.
3. Grease the air fry basket using cooking spray.
4. Turn on your Ninja Foodi XL Pro Air Oven and select "Air Fry".
5. Select the timer for about 10 minutes and temperature for 400 degrees F.
6. When the unit beeps to signify it is preheated, open the oven and place the air fry basket into rail of Level 3.
7. Let the fish cakes cook until they are golden brown.
8. Serve and enjoy!

Serving Suggestions: Serve with lemon wedges to enhance taste.

Variation Tip: Squeeze out any excess moisture before adding fish to the mixture.

Nutritional Information per Serving:
Calories: 517 | Fat: 17g|Sat Fat: 4.3g|Carbohydrates: 9.7g|Fiber: 0.3g|Sugar: 1.4g|Protein: 57.6g

Lemon Pepper Shrimp

Prep Time: 5 minutes
Cook Time: 8 minutes
Serves: 4

Ingredients:

- 2 lemons, juiced
- ½ tablespoon lemon pepper
- 2 tablespoons olive oil
- ½ teaspoon paprika
- ½ teaspoon garlic powder
- 1½ pounds shrimp

Preparation:

1. Take a bowl, add all the ingredients together and mix well.
2. Add shrimp and toss to coat well.
3. Turn on your Ninja Foodi XL Pro Air Oven and select "Air Fry".
4. Select the timer for about 6 to 8 minutes and temperature for 400 degrees F.
5. When the unit beeps to signify it is preheated, open the oven and place the air fry basket on Level 3.
6. Place shrimp in the air fry basket and cook until pink.
7. Serve and enjoy!

Serving Suggestions: Serve with lemon slices.

Variation Tip: You can also add a couple drops of tabasco with olive oil.

Nutritional Information per Serving:
Calories: 274 | Fat: 10g|Sat Fat: 1.9g|Carbohydrates: 6.2g|Fiber: 1.2g|Sugar: 0.9g|Protein: 39.3g

Lobster Tails with Lemon-Garlic Butter

Prep Time: 5 minutes
Cook Time: 10 minutes
Serves: 1

Ingredients:

- 2 tablespoons butter
- ½ teaspoon lemon zest
- 1 lobster tail
- ½ clove garlic, grated
- ½ teaspoon parsley, chopped
- Salt, to taste
- Fresh ground black pepper, to taste

Preparation:

1. Cut the lobster tail lengthwise through the center of the hard top shell.
2. Cut to the bottom of the shell and spread the tail halves apart.
3. Place the lobster tail in the roast tray.
4. Take a saucepan and melt butter on medium heat.
5. Add garlic and lemon zest and cook for 30 seconds.
6. Now, pour the butter mixture onto lobster tail.
7. Insert a wire rack on Level 3. Turn on your Ninja Foodi XL Pro Air Oven and select "Air Fry".
8. Select the timer for about 5 to 7 minutes and temperature for 380 degrees F.
9. When the unit beeps to signify it is preheated, open the oven and place the roast tray on sheet pan onto the wire rack. Close the oven.
10. Let it cook and serve with parsley as topping.

Serving Suggestions: Serve with lemon wedges on side.
Variation Tip: You can use small piece of foil to hold in the butter mixture.
Nutritional Information per Serving:
Calories: 337 | Fat: 24.3g|Sat Fat: 14.9g|Carbohydrates: 0.8g|Fiber: 0.1g|Sugar: 0.1g|Protein: 27.9g

Scallops with Chanterelles

Prep Time: 10 minutes
Cook Time: 15 minutes
Serves: 3

Ingredients:

- 1 tablespoon balsamic vinegar
- ½ pound scallops
- 3 tablespoons butter
- ½ tomato, peeled, seeded, and chopped
- 1 tablespoon butter
- ¼ pound chanterelle mushrooms

Preparation:

1. Take a pan and add half tablespoon butter over medium heat.
2. Stir in chanterelles and cook for 5 to 8 minutes.
3. Transfer to a bowl.
4. Add remaining butter in the same pan over low heat and cook for 5 minutes.
5. Stir in tomato and balsamic vinegar and cook for 2 minutes.
6. Stir the tomato mixture into mushrooms.
7. Place the mixture into a roast tray.
8. Turn on your Ninja Foodi XL Pro Air Oven and select "Broil".
9. Select the timer for about 2 minutes per side and temperature for HI.
10. Slide the roast tray on sheet pan on Level 3.
11. Serve warm and enjoy!

Serving Suggestions: Serve with mashed potatoes and green onions.
Variation Tip: Use extra chanterelles on top.
Nutritional Information per Serving:
Calories: 361 | Fat: 16.7g|Sat Fat: 9.1g|Carbohydrates: 22.2g|Fiber: 9.9g|Sugar: 0.8g|Protein: 23.7g

Fish Casserole

Prep Time: 10 minutes
Cook Time: 40 minutes
Serves: 3

Ingredients:

- ½ tablespoon unsalted butter, softened
- ¼ teaspoon salt
- 1 pound white fish fillet
- ¼ teaspoon pepper
- ½ sweet onion, thinly sliced
- 2 teaspoons extra-virgin olive oil, divided
- ¼ teaspoon dry thyme
- 1 pinch nutmeg
- 1 bread slice, crusts removed
- ¼ teaspoon paprika
- ⅛ teaspoon garlic powder
- ½ cup shredded Swiss cheese

Preparation:

1. Inset a wire rack on Level 3. Turn on your Ninja Foodi XL Pro Air Oven and select "Bake".
2. Preheat by selecting the timer for 3 minutes and temperature for 400 degrees F.
3. Arrange fish fillet on a dish and season with salt and pepper.
4. Take a pan and heat oil over medium-high heat. Add onion and cook until it starts to brown.
5. Stir in thyme and nutmeg.
6. Spread the onion mixture over fish.
7. In a food processor, add bread slice, paprika, garlic powder and a little oil.
8. Process until we have a moist mixture.
9. Sprinkle crumbs over the onion mixture.
10. Add cheese on top of casserole and place inside the Ninja Foodi XL Pro Air Oven.
11. Select the timer for about 18 to 22 minutes and temperature for 400 degrees F.
12. When the unit beeps to signify it is preheated, open the oven and place the dish on the wire rack.
13. Serve warm.

Serving Suggestions: Serve with rice or with potatoes.

Variation Tip: You can also add a tablespoon of lemon juice.

Nutritional Information per Serving:
Calories: 389 | Fat: 21.6g|Sat Fat: 6.7g|Carbohydrates: 4.6g|Fiber: 0.6g|Sugar: 1.2g|Protein: 42.4g

Broiled Scallops

Prep Time: 5 minutes
Cook Time: 8 minutes
Serves: 2

Ingredients:

- 1 pound bay scallops
- 1 tablespoon lemon juice
- 1 tablespoon butter, melted
- ½ tablespoon garlic salt

Preparation:

1. Turn on your Ninja Foodi XL Pro Air Oven and select "Broil".
2. Rinse scallop and place in a roast tray.
3. Season with garlic salt, butter and lemon juice.
4. Select the timer for about 8 minutes and temperature for HI.
5. Place the roast tray on a wire rack on Level 3.
6. Remove from oven and serve warm.

Serving Suggestions: Serve with margarine on side.

Variation Tip: You can use extra melted butter.

Nutritional Information per Serving:
Calories: 259 | Fat: 7.6g|Sat Fat: 3.9g|Carbohydrates: 7g|Fiber: 0.2g|Sugar: 0.7g|Protein: 38.5g

Fried Tortellini

Prep Time: 15 minutes.
Cook Time: 10 minutes.
Serves: 8

Ingredients:

- 1 (9-ounce) package cheese tortellini
- 1 cup Panko breadcrumbs
- ⅓ cup Parmesan, grated
- 1 teaspoon dried oregano
- ½ teaspoon garlic powder
- ½ teaspoon crushed red pepper flakes
- Kosher salt, to taste
- Freshly ground black pepper, to taste
- 1 cup all-purpose flour
- 2 large eggs

Preparation:

1. Boil tortellini according to salted boiling water according to package's instructions, then drain.
2. Mix panko with garlic powder, black pepper, salt, red pepper flakes, oregano, Parmesan in a small bowl.
3. Beat eggs in one bowl and spread flour on a plate.
4. Coat the tortellini with the flour, dip into the eggs and then coat with the panko mixture.
5. Spread the tortellini in the air fry basket and spray them with cooking oil.
6. Transfer the basket to the 3rd rack position of Ninja Foodi XL Pro Air Oven and close the door.
7. Select the "Air Fry" Mode using FUNCTION +/- buttons and select Rack Level 3.
8. Set its cooking time to 10 minutes and temperature to 400 degrees F, then press "START/STOP" to initiate cooking.
9. Serve warm.

Serving Suggestion: Serve the tortellini with tomato sauce on the side.
Variation Tip: Use crushed cornflakes to coat the tortellini.
Nutritional Information Per Serving:
Calories 151 | Fat 19g |Sodium 412mg | Carbs 23g | Fiber 0.3g | Sugar 1g | Protein 3g

Wine Braised Mushrooms

Prep Time: 10 minutes
Cook Time: 32 minutes
Serves: 6

Ingredients:

- 1 tablespoon butter
- 2 teaspoons Herbs de Provence
- ½ teaspoon garlic powder
- 2 pounds fresh mushrooms, quartered
- 2 tablespoons white wine

Preparation:

1. In a frying pan, mix together the butter, Herbs de Provence, and garlic powder over medium-low heat and stir fry for about 2 minutes.
2. Stir in the mushrooms and remove from the heat.
3. Transfer the mushroom mixture into a baking pan.
4. Press "Power" button of Ninja Foodi XL Pro Air Oven and select "Air Fry" function.
5. Press TEMP/SHADE +/- buttons to set the temperature at 320 degrees F.
6. Now press TIME/SLICES +/- buttons to set the cooking time to 30 minutes.
7. Press "START/STOP" button to start.
8. When the unit beeps to show that it is preheated, open the lid.
9. Arrange the pan over the wire rack and insert in the oven.
10. After 25 minutes of cooking, stir the wine into mushroom mixture.
11. When cooking time is completed, open the lid and serve hot.

Serving Suggestions: Serve with a garnishing of fresh herbs.
Variation Tip: White wine can be replaced with broth.
Nutritional Information per Serving:
Calories: 54 | Fat: 2.4g|Sat Fat: 1.2g|Carbohydrates: 5.3g|Fiber: 1.5g|Sugar: 2.7g|Protein: 4.8g

Stuffed Eggplants

Prep Time: 20 minutes
Cook Time: 11 minutes
Serves: 4

Ingredients:

- 4 small eggplants, halved lengthwise
- 1 teaspoon fresh lime juice
- 1 teaspoon vegetable oil
- 1 small onion, chopped
- ¼ teaspoon garlic, chopped
- ½ of small tomato, chopped
- Salt and ground black pepper, as required
- 1 tablespoon cottage cheese, chopped
- ¼ of green bell pepper, seeded and chopped
- 1 tablespoon tomato paste
- 1 tablespoon fresh cilantro, chopped

Preparation:

1. Carefully cut a slice from one side of each eggplant lengthwise.
2. With a small spoon, scoop out the flesh from each eggplant, leaving a thick shell.
3. Transfer the eggplant flesh into a bowl.
4. Drizzle the eggplants with lime juice evenly.
5. Press "Power" button of Ninja Foodi XL Pro Air Oven and select "Air Fry" function.
6. Press TEMP/SHADE +/- buttons to set the temperature at 320 degrees F.
7. Now press TIME/SLICES +/- buttons to set the cooking time to 3 minutes.
8. Press "Start/Stop" button to start.
9. When the unit beeps to show that it is preheated, open the oven door.
10. Arrange the hollowed eggplants into the greased air fry basket on Level 3.
11. Meanwhile, in a skillet, heat the oil over medium heat and sauté the onion and garlic for about 2 minutes.
12. Add the eggplant flesh, tomato, salt, and black pepper and sauté for about 2 minutes.
13. Stir in the cheese, bell pepper, tomato paste, and cilantro and cook for about 1 minute.
14. Remove the pan of the veggie mixture from heat.
15. When the cooking time is completed, open the oven door and arrange the cooked eggplants onto a plate.
16. Stuff each eggplant with the veggie mixture.
17. Close each with its cut part.
18. Again, arrange the eggplants shells into the greased air fry basket on Level 3.
19. Press "Power" button of Ninja Foodi XL Pro Air Oven and select "Air Fry" function.
20. Press TEMP/SHADE +/- buttons to set the temperature at 320 degrees F.
21. Now press TIME/SLICES +/- buttons to set the cooking time to 8 minutes.
22. Press "Start/Stop" button to start.
23. When cooking time is completed, open the oven door and transfer the eggplants onto serving plates.
24. Serve hot.

Serving Suggestions: Serve with the topping feta cheese.

Variation Tip: Clean the eggplant by running under cold running water.

Nutritional Information per Serving:
Calories: 131 | Fat: 2g|Sat Fat: 0.3g|Carbohydrates: 27.8g|Fiber: 5.3g|Sugar: 4.3g|Protein: 5.1g

Vegan Cakes

Prep Time: 15 minutes.
Cook Time: 15 minutes.
Serves:8

Ingredients:

- 4 potatoes, diced and boiled
- 1 bunch green onions
- 1 lime, zest, and juice
- 1½ inch knob of fresh ginger
- 1 tablespoon tamari

4 tablespoons red curry paste

- 4 sheets nori
- 1 (398 grams) can heart of palm, drained
- ¾ cup canned artichoke hearts, drained
- Black pepper, to taste
- Salt, to taste

Preparation:

1. Add potatoes, green onions, lime zest, juice, and the rest of the ingredients to a food processor.
2. Press the pulse button and blend until smooth.
3. Make 8 small patties out of this mixture.

4. Place the patties in the air fry basket.
5. Transfer the basket to the 3rd rack position of Ninja Foodi XL Pro Air Oven and close the door.
6. Select the "Air Fry" Mode using FUNCTION +/- buttons and select Rack Level 3.
7. Set its cooking time to 15 minutes and temperature to 400 degrees F, then press "START/STOP" to initiate cooking.
8. Serve warm.

Serving Suggestion: Serve the vegan cakes with roasted asparagus.

Variation Tip: Add boiled quinoa to the cake mixture.

Nutritional Information Per Serving:
Calories 324 | Fat 5g |Sodium 432mg | Carbs 13.1g | Fiber 0.3g | Sugar 1g | Protein 5.7g

Roast Cauliflower and Broccoli

Prep Time: 15 minutes.
Cook Time: 10 minutes.
Serves: 4

Ingredients:

- ½ pound broccoli, florets
- ½ pound cauliflower, florets
- 1 tablespoon olive oil
- Black pepper, to taste
- Salt, to taste
- ⅓ cup water

Preparation:

1. Toss all the veggies with seasoning in a large bowl.
2. Spread these vegetables in the air fry basket.
3. Transfer the basket to the 3rd rack position of Ninja Foodi XL Pro Air Oven and close the door.
4. Select the "Air Fry" Mode using FUNCTION +/- buttons and select Rack Level 3.
5. Set its cooking time to 10 minutes and temperature to 400 degrees F, then press "START/STOP" to initiate cooking.
6. Serve warm.

Serving Suggestion: Serve the roasted cauliflower with white rice.

Variation Tip: Add green beans to the mixture before baking.

Nutritional Information Per Serving:
Calories 318 | Fat 15.7g |Sodium 124mg | Carbs 7g | Fiber 0.1g | Sugar 0.3g | Protein 4.9g

Blue Cheese Soufflés

Prep Time: 15 minutes.
Cook Time: 17 minutes.
Serves: 4

Ingredients:

- 2 ounces unsalted butter
- 1-ounce breadcrumbs
- 1-ounce plain flour
- Pinch English mustard powder
- Pinch cayenne pepper
- 10 ounces semi-skimmed milk
- 3 ounces blue murder cheese
- 1 fresh thyme sprig, chopped
- 4 medium eggs, separated

Preparation:

1. Grease four ramekins with butter and sprinkle with breadcrumbs.
2. Melt butter in a suitable saucepan, stir in flour, cayenne, and mustard powder.
3. Then mix well and cook for 1 minute, then slowly pour in the milk.
4. Mix well until smooth, then boil its sauce. Cook for 2 minutes.
5. Stir in cheese, and mix well until melted.
6. Add black pepper, salt, and egg yolks.
7. Beat egg whites in a bowl with a mixer until they make stiff peaks.
8. Add egg whites to the cheese sauce, then mix well.
9. Divide the mixture into the ramekins and transfer to the Ninja Foodi XL Pro Air Oven, then close its door.
10. Select the "Air Fry" Mode using FUNCTION +/- buttons and select Rack Level 2.
11. Set its cooking time to 14 minutes and temperature to 350 degrees F, then press "START/STOP" to initiate cooking.
12. Serve warm.

Serving Suggestion: Serve the soufflé with sautéed asparagus and toasted bread slices.

Variation Tip: Add crumbled bacon to the soufflé.

Nutritional Information Per Serving:
Calories 236 | Fat 10g |Sodium 249mg | Carbs 8g | Fiber 2g | Sugar 3g | Protein 4g

Fajitas

Prep Time: 15 minutes.
Cook Time: 15 minutes.
Serves: 4

Ingredients:

- 3 bell peppers, sliced
- 1 large yellow onion, sliced
- 1 (15-ounce) can pinto beans, drained, rinsed
- 1 tablespoon olive oil
- ¼ teaspoon paprika
- ¼ teaspoon garlic powder
- ¼ teaspoon cumin
- ¼ teaspoon salt
- ¼ cup cheddar cheese, shredded
- Tortillas for serving

Preparation:

1. Spread the pinto beans in the Ninja Sheet pan, lined with parchment paper.
2. Top the beans with bell peppers, yellow onion, olive oil, paprika, garlic powder, cumin, salt, and cheese
3. Transfer the pan to the 2nd rack position of Ninja Foodi XL Pro Air Oven and close the door.
4. Select the "Bake" Mode using FUNCTION +/- buttons and select Rack Level 2.
5. Set its cooking time to 15 minutes and temperature to 350 degrees F, then press "START/STOP" to initiate cooking.
6. Serve in tortillas.

Serving Suggestion: Serve the fajitas in warmed tortillas, avocado slices, tomato sauce or guacamole.

Variation Tip: Add crushed tortillas on top before baking.

Nutritional Information Per Serving:
Calories 391 | Fat 2.2g |Sodium 276mg | Carbs 7.7g | Fiber 0.9g | Sugar 1.4g | Protein 8.8g

Tofu with Broccoli

Prep Time: 15 minutes
Cook Time: 15 minutes
Serves: 3

Ingredients:

- 8 ounces firm tofu, completely drained, pressed, and cubed
- 1 head broccoli, cut into florets
- 1 tablespoon butter, melted
- 1 teaspoon ground turmeric
- ¼ teaspoon paprika
- Salt and ground black pepper, as required

Preparation:

1. In a bowl, mix all ingredients together.
2. Place the tofu mixture in the greased cooking pan.
3. Press "Power" button of Ninja Foodi XL Pro Air Oven and select "Air Fry" function.
4. Press TEMP/SHADE +/- buttons to set the temperature at 390 degrees F.
5. Now press TIME/SLICES +/- buttons to set the cooking time to 15 minutes.
6. Press "START/STOP" button to start.
7. When the unit beeps to show that it is preheated, open the lid.
8. Insert the baking pan in oven.
9. Toss the tofu mixture once halfway through.
10. When cooking time is completed, open the lid and serve hot.

Serving Suggestions: Serve with cooked pasta.

Variation Tip: Add some seasoning as you like.

Nutritional Information per Serving:
Calories: 119 | Fat: 7.4g|Sat Fat: 3.1g|Carbohydrates: 7.5g|Fiber: 3.1g|Sugar: 1.9g|Protein: 8.7g

Quinoa Burgers

Prep Time: 10 minutes
Cook Time: 10 minutes
Serves: 4

Ingredients:

- ½ cup cooked and cooled quinoa
- 1 cup rolled oats
- 2 eggs, lightly beaten
- ¼ cup white onion, minced
- ¼ cup feta cheese, crumbled
- Salt and ground black pepper, as required
- Olive oil cooking spray

Preparation:

1. In a large bowl, add all ingredients and mix until well combined.
2. Make 4 equal-sized patties from the mixture.
3. Lightly spray the patties with cooking spray.
4. Press "Power" button of Ninja Foodi XL Pro Air Oven and select "Air Fry" function.
5. Press TEMP/SHADE +/- buttons to set the temperature at 400 degrees F.
6. Now press TIME/SLICES +/- buttons to set the cooking time to 10 minutes.
7. Press "Start/Stop" button to start.
8. When the unit beeps to show that it is preheated, open the oven door.
9. Arrange the patties into the greased air fry basket on Level 3.
10. Flip the patties once halfway through.
11. When cooking time is completed, open the oven door and transfer the patties onto a platter.
12. Serve warm.

Serving Suggestions: Serve with green sauce.
Variation Tip: For crispy texture, refrigerate the patties for at least 15 minutes before cooking.
Nutritional Information per Serving:
Calories: 215 | Fat: 6.6g|Sat Fat: 2.5g|Carbohydrates: 28.7g|Fiber: 3.7g|Sugar: 1.1g|Protein: 9.9g

Broccoli with Cauliflower

Prep Time: 15 minutes
Cook Time: 20 minutes
Serves: 4

Ingredients:

- 1½ cups broccoli, cut into 1-inch pieces
- 1½ cups cauliflower, cut into 1-inch pieces
- 1 tablespoon olive oil
- Salt, as required

Preparation:

1. In a bowl, add the vegetables, oil, and salt and toss to coat well.
2. Press "Power" button of Ninja Foodi XL Pro Air Oven and select "Air Fry" function.
3. Press TEMP/SHADE +/- buttons to set the temperature at 375 degrees F.
4. Now press TIME/SLICES +/- buttons to set the cooking time to 20 minutes.
5. Press "Start/Stop" button to start.
6. When the unit beeps to show that it is preheated, open the oven door.
7. Arrange the veggie mixture into the greased air fry basket and slide the basket on Level 3.
8. When cooking time is completed, open the oven door and serve hot.

Serving Suggestions: Serve with the drizzling of lemon juice.
Variation Tip: You can add spices according to your taste.
Nutritional Information per Serving:
Calories: 51 | Fat: 3.7g|Sat Fat: 0.5g|Carbohydrates: 4.3g|Fiber: 1.8g|Sugar: 1.5g|Protein: 1.7g

Sweet & Spicy Parsnips

Prep Time: 15 minutes
Cook Time: 44 minutes
Serves: 5

Ingredients:

- 1½ pounds parsnip, peeled and cut into 1-inch chunks
- 1 tablespoon butter, melted
- 2 tablespoons honey
- 1 tablespoon dried parsley flakes, crushed
- ¼ teaspoon red pepper flakes, crushed
- Salt and ground black pepper, as required

Preparation:

1. In a large bowl, mix together the parsnips and butter.
2. Press "Power" button of Ninja Foodi XL Pro Air Oven and select "Air Fry" function. Select 2 LEVEL.
3. Press TEMP/SHADE +/- buttons to set the temperature at 355 degrees F.
4. Now press TIME/SLICES +/- buttons to set the cooking time to 44 minutes.
5. Press "Start/Stop" button to start.
6. When the unit beeps to show that it is preheated, open the oven door.
7. Separate the parsnip chunks into the greased air fry basket on Level 3 and roast tray over sheet pan on Level 1.
8. Meanwhile, in another large bowl, mix together the remaining ingredients.
9. After 40 minutes of cooking, press "Start/Stop" button to pause the unit.
10. Transfer the parsnip chunks into the bowl of honey mixture and toss to coat well.
11. Again, arrange the parsnip chunks into the air fry basket on Level 3 and roast tray on Level 1.
12. When cooking time is completed, open the oven door and serve hot.

Serving Suggestions: Serve with garlic bread.
Variation Tip: Make sure to cut the parsnip into uniform-sized chunks.
Nutritional Information per Serving:
Calories: 149 | Fat: 2.7g|Sat Fat: 1.5g|Carbohydrates: 31.5g|Fiber: 6.7g|Sugar: 13.5g|Protein: 1.7g

Cauliflower in Buffalo Sauce

Prep Time: 10 minutes
Cook Time: 12 minutes
Serves: 4

Ingredients:

- 1 large head cauliflower, cut into bite-size florets
- 1 tablespoon olive oil
- 2 teaspoons garlic powder
- Salt and ground black pepper, as required
- ⅔ cup warm buffalo sauce

Preparation:

1. In a large bowl, add cauliflower florets, olive oil, garlic powder, salt and pepper and toss to coat.
2. Press "Power" button of Ninja Foodi XL Pro Air Oven and select "Air Fry" function. Select 2 LEVEL.
3. Press TEMP/SHADE +/- buttons to set the temperature at 375 degrees F.
4. Now press TIME/SLICES +/- buttons to set the cooking time to 12 minutes.
5. Press "Start/Stop" button to start.
6. When the unit beeps to show that it is preheated, open the oven door.
7. Arrange the cauliflower florets in the air fry basket on Level 1 and roast tray over wire rack on Level 3.
8. After 7 minutes of cooking, coat the cauliflower florets with buffalo sauce.
9. When cooking time is completed, open the oven door and serve hot.

Serving Suggestions: Serve with the garnishing of scallions.
Variation Tip: Use best quality buffalo sauce.
Nutritional Information per Serving:
Calories: 183 | Fat: 17.1g|Sat Fat: 4.3g|Carbohydrates: 5.9g|Fiber: 1.8g|Sugar: 1.0g|Protein: 1.6g

Vinegar Green Beans

Prep Time: 10 minutes
Cook Time: 20 minutes
Serves: 2

Ingredients:

- 1 (10-ounce) bag frozen cut green beans
- ¼ cup nutritional yeast
- 3 tablespoons balsamic vinegar
- Salt and ground black pepper, as required

Preparation:

1. In a bowl, add the green beans, nutritional yeast, vinegar, salt, and black pepper and toss to coat well.
2. Press "Power" button of Ninja Foodi XL Pro Air Oven and select "Air Fry" function. Select 2 LEVEL.
3. Press TEMP/SHADE +/- buttons to set the temperature at 400 degrees F.
4. Now press TIME/SLICES +/- buttons to set the cooking time to 20 minutes.
5. Press "Start/Stop" button to start.
6. When the unit beeps to show that it is preheated, open the oven door.
7. Separate the green beans into the greased air fry basket on Level 3 and roast tray over wire rack on Level 1.
8. When cooking time is completed, open the oven door and serve hot.

Serving Suggestions: Serve with the garnishing of sesame seeds.
Variation Tip: Balsamic vinegar can be replaced with lemon juice.
Nutritional Information per Serving:
Calories: 115 | Fat: 1.3g|Sat Fat: 0.2g|Carbohydrates: 18.5g|Fiber: 9.3g|Sugar: 1.8g|Protein: 11.3g

Herbed Bell Peppers

Prep Time: 10 minutes
Cook Time: 8 minutes
Serves: 4

Ingredients:

- 1½ pounds mixed bell peppers, seeded and sliced
- 1 small onion, sliced
- ½ teaspoon dried thyme, crushed
- ½ teaspoon dried savory, crushed
- Salt and ground black pepper, as required
- 2 tablespoon butter, melted

Preparation:

1. In a bowl, add the bell peppers, onion, herbs, salt and black pepper and toss to coat well.
2. Press "Power" button of Ninja Foodi XL Pro Air Oven and select "Air Fry" function.
3. Press TEMP/SHADE +/- buttons to set the temperature at 360 degrees F.
4. Now press TIME/SLICES +/- buttons to set the cooking time to 8 minutes.
5. Press "Start/Stop" button to start.
6. When the unit beeps to show that it is preheated, open the oven door.
7. Arrange the bell peppers into the air fry basket on Level 3.
8. When cooking time is completed, open the oven door and transfer the bell peppers into a bowl.
9. Drizzle with butter and serve immediately.

Serving Suggestions: Serve with boiled rice.
Variation Tip: Feel free to use herbs of your choice.
Nutritional Information per Serving:
Calories: 73 | Fat: 5.9g|Sat Fat: 3.7g|Carbohydrates: 5.2g|Fiber: 1.1g|Sugar: 3g|Protein: 0.7g

Roasted Vegetables

Prep Time: 15 minutes.
Cook Time: 15 minutes.
Serves: 6

Ingredients:

- 2 medium bell peppers cored, chopped
- 2 medium carrots, peeled and sliced
- 1 small zucchini, ends trimmed, sliced
- 1 medium broccoli, florets
- ½ red onion, peeled and diced
- 2 tablespoons olive oil
- 1 ½ teaspoons Italian seasoning
- 2 garlic cloves, minced
- Salt and freshly ground black pepper
- 1 cup grape tomatoes
- 1 tablespoon fresh lemon juice

Preparation:

1. Toss all the veggies with olive oil, Italian seasoning, salt, black pepper, and garlic in a large salad bowl.
2. Spread this broccoli-zucchini mixture in the sheet pan.
3. Transfer the pan to the 2nd rack position of Ninja Foodi XL Pro Air Oven and close the door.
4. Select the "Bake" Mode using FUNCTION +/- buttons and select Rack Level 2.
5. Set its cooking time to 15 minutes and temperature to 400 degrees F, then press "START/STOP" to initiate cooking.
6. Serve warm with lemon juice on top.
7. Enjoy.

Serving Suggestion: Serve the roasted vegetables with guacamole on the side.

Variation Tip: Add olives or sliced mushrooms to the vegetable mixture.

Nutritional Information Per Serving:
Calories 346 | Fat 15g |Sodium 220mg | Carbs 4.3g | Fiber 2.4g | Sugar 1.2g | Protein 12.4g

Sweet Potato Casserole

Prep Time: 15 minutes.
Cook Time: 35 minutes.
Serves: 6

Ingredients:

- 3 cups sweet potatoes, mashed and cooled
- 1 ½ cups brown sugar, packed
- 2 large eggs, beaten
- 1 teaspoon vanilla extract
- ½ cup milk
- ¾ cup butter, melted
- ⅓ cup flour
- 4 ounces pecans, chopped

Preparation:

1. Mix the sweet potato mash with vanilla extract, milk, eggs, 1 cup of brown sugar, and ½ cup of melted butter in a large bowl.
2. Spread this sweet potato mixture in a casserole dish.
3. Now whisk remaining sugar and butter with flour in a separate bowl.
4. Fold in pecan, then top the sweet potatoes mixed with this pecan mixture.
5. Transfer the dish to the 2nd rack position of Ninja Foodi XL Pro Air Oven and close the door.
6. Select the "Bake" Mode using FUNCTION +/- buttons and select Rack Level 2.
7. Set its cooking time to 35 minutes and temperature to 350 degrees F, then press "START/STOP" to initiate cooking.
8. Slice and serve!

Serving Suggestion: Serve the sweet potato casserole with roasted pecans.

Variation Tip: Add breadcrumbs on top before baking for a crispy texture.

Nutritional Information Per Serving:
Calories 353 | Fat 3g |Sodium 510mg | Carbs 32g | Fiber 3g | Sugar 4g | Protein 4g

Veggie Rice

Prep Time: 15 minutes
Cook Time: 18 minutes
Serves: 2

Ingredients:

- 2 cups cooked white rice
- 1 tablespoon vegetable oil
- 2 teaspoons sesame oil, toasted and divided
- 1 tablespoon water
- Salt and ground white pepper, as required
- 1 large egg, lightly beaten
- ½ cup frozen peas, thawed
- ½ cup frozen carrots, thawed
- 1 teaspoon soy sauce
- 1 teaspoon Sriracha sauce
- ½ teaspoon sesame seeds, toasted

Preparation:

1. In a large bowl, add the rice, vegetable oil, one teaspoon of sesame oil, water, salt, and white pepper and mix well.
2. Transfer rice mixture into a lightly greased baking pan.
3. Press "Power" button of Ninja Foodi XL Pro Air Oven and select "Air Fry" function.
4. Press TEMP/SHADE +/- buttons to set the temperature at 380 degrees F.
5. Now press TIME/SLICES +/- buttons to set the cooking time to 18 minutes.
6. Press "START/STOP" button to start.
7. When the unit beeps to show that it is preheated, open the lid.
8. Place the pan over the wire rack and insert in the oven.
9. While cooking, stir the mixture once after 12 minutes.
10. After 12 minutes of cooking, place the beaten egg over rice.
11. After 16 minutes of cooking, stir in the peas and carrots into rice mixture.
12. Meanwhile, in a bowl, mix the soy sauce, Sriracha sauce, sesame seeds and the remaining sesame oil together.
13. When cooking time is completed, open the lid and transfer the rice mixture into a serving bowl.
14. Drizzle with the sauce mixture and serve.

Serving Suggestions: Serve with yogurt sauce.
Variation Tip: Thaw the vegetables completely before cooking.
Nutritional Information per Serving:
Calories: 443 | Fat: 16.4g|Sat Fat: 3.2g|Carbohydrates: 62.3g|Fiber: 3.6g|Sugar: 3.6g|Protein: 10.1g

Soy Sauce Green Beans

Prep Time: 10 minutes
Cook Time: 10 minutes
Serves: 2

Ingredients:

- 8 ounces fresh green beans, trimmed and cut in half
- 1 tablespoon soy sauce
- 1 teaspoon sesame oil

Preparation:

1. In a bowl, mix the green beans, soy sauce and sesame oil together.
2. Press "Power" button of Ninja Foodi XL Pro Air Oven and select "Air Fry" function.
3. Press TEMP/SHADE +/- buttons to set the temperature at 390 degrees F.
4. Now press TIME/SLICES +/- buttons to set the cooking time to 10 minutes.
5. Press "START/STOP" button to start.
6. When the unit beeps to show that it is preheated, open the lid.
7. Arrange the green beans in air fry basket and insert in the oven.
8. When cooking time is completed, open the lid and serve hot.

Serving Suggestions: Serve with the garnishing of sesame seeds.
Variation Tip: You can add seasoning of your choice.
Nutritional Information per Serving:
Calories: 62 | Fat: 2.6g|Sat Fat: 0.4g|Carbohydrates: 8.8g|Fiber: 4g|Sugar: 1.7g|Protein: 2.6g

Broccoli Casserole

Prep Time: 15 minutes.
Cook Time: 45 minutes.
Serves: 6

Ingredients:

- 1 cup mayonnaise
- 10 ½ ounces cream of celery soup
- 2 large eggs, beaten
- 20 ounces chopped broccoli
- 2 tablespoons onion, minced
- 1 cup Cheddar cheese, grated
- 1 tablespoon Worcestershire sauce
- 1 teaspoon seasoned salt
- Black pepper, to taste
- 2 tablespoons butter

Preparation:

1. Whisk mayonnaise with eggs, condensed soup in a large bowl.
2. Stir in salt, black pepper, Worcestershire sauce, and cheddar cheese.
3. Spread broccoli and onion in a greased casserole dish.
4. Top the veggies with the mayonnaise mixture.
5. Transfer this broccoli casserole to the Ninja Foodi XL Pro Air Oven and Close its lid.
6. Select the "Bake" Mode using FUNCTION +/- buttons and select Rack Level 2.
7. Set its cooking time to 45 minutes and temperature to 350 degrees F, then press "START/STOP" to initiate cooking.
8. Slice and serve warm.

Serving Suggestion: Serve the broccoli casserole with spaghetti or any other pasta.
Variation Tip: Top the casserole with a pepperoni slice before cooking.
Nutritional Information Per Serving:
Calories 341 | Fat 24g |Sodium 547mg | Carbs 26.4g | Fiber 1.2g | Sugar 1g | Protein 10.3g

Parmesan Broccoli

Prep Time: 10 minutes
Cook Time: 15 minutes
Serves: 8

Ingredients:

- 2 pounds broccoli, cut into 1-inch florets
- 2 tablespoons butter
- Salt and ground black pepper, as required
- ¼ cup Parmesan cheese, grated

Preparation:

1. In a pan of boiling water, add the broccoli and cook for about 3-4 minutes.
2. Drain the broccoli well.
3. In a bowl, place the broccoli, cauliflower, oil, salt, and black pepper and toss to coat well.
4. Press "Power" button of Ninja Foodi XL Pro Air Oven and select "Air Fry" function.
5. Press TEMP/SHADE +/- buttons to set the temperature at 400 degrees F.
6. Now press TIME/SLICES +/- buttons to set the cooking time to 15 minutes.
7. Press "START/STOP" button to start.
8. When the unit beeps to show that it is preheated, open the lid.
9. Arrange the broccoli mixture in air fry basket and insert in the oven.
10. Toss the broccoli mixture once halfway through.
11. When cooking time is completed, open the lid and transfer the veggie mixture into a large bowl.
12. Immediately stir in the cheese and serve immediately.

Serving Suggestions: Serve with a drizzling of lemon juice.
Variation Tip: Choose broccoli heads with tight, green florets and firm stalks.
Nutritional Information per Serving:
Calories: 73 | Fat: 3.9g|Sat Fat: 2.1g|Carbohydrates: 7.5g|Fiber: 3g|Sugar: 1.9g|Protein: 4.2g

Vegetable Casserole

Prep Time: 15 minutes.

Cook Time: 42 minutes.

Serves: 6

Ingredients:

- 2 cups peas
- 8 ounces mushrooms, sliced
- 4 tablespoons all-purpose flour
- 1 ½ cups celery, sliced
- 1 ½ cups carrots, sliced
- ½ teaspoon mustard powder
- 2 cups of milk
- Salt and black pepper, to taste
- 7 tablespoons butter
- 1 cup breadcrumbs
- ½ cup Parmesan cheese, grated

Preparation:

1. Grease and rub a casserole dish with butter and keep it aside.
2. Add carrots, onion, and celery to a saucepan, then fill it with water.
3. Cover this pot and cook for 10 minutes, then stir in peas.
4. Cook for 4 minutes, then strain the vegetables.
5. Now melt 1 tablespoon of butter in the same saucepan and toss in mushrooms to sauté.
6. Once the mushrooms are soft, transfer them to the vegetables.
7. Prepare its sauce by melting 4 tablespoons of butter in a suitable saucepan.
8. Stir in mustard and flour, then stir cook for 2 minutes.
9. Gradually pour in the milk and stir cook until thickened, then add salt and black pepper.
10. Add vegetables and mushrooms to the flour milk mixture and mix well.
11. Spread this vegetable blend in the casserole dish evenly.
12. Toss the breadcrumbs with the remaining butter and spread it on top of vegetables.
13. Top this casserole dish with cheese.
14. Transfer the dish to the 2nd rack position of Ninja Foodi XL Pro Air Oven and close the door.
15. Select the "Air Fry" Mode using FUNCTION +/- buttons and select Rack Level 2.
16. Set its cooking time to 25 minutes and temperature to 350 degrees F, then press "START/STOP" to initiate cooking.
17. Serve warm.

Serving Suggestion: Serve the vegetable casserole with a tortilla.

Variation Tip: Add broccoli florets to the mixture and then cook.

Nutritional Information Per Serving:
Calories 338 | Fat 24g |Sodium 620mg | Carbs 18.3g | Fiber 2.4g | Sugar 1.2g | Protein 5.4g

Caramelized Baby Carrots

Prep Time: 10 minutes

Cook Time: 15 minutes

Serves: 4

Ingredients:

- ½ cup butter, melted
- ½ cup brown sugar
- 1 pound bag baby carrots

Preparation:

1. In a bowl, mix the butter, brown sugar and carrots together.
2. Press "Power" button of Ninja Foodi XL Pro Air Oven and select "Air Fry" function.
3. Press TEMP/SHADE +/- buttons to set the temperature at 400 degrees F.
4. Now press TIME/SLICES +/- buttons to set the cooking time to 15 minutes.
5. Press "START/STOP" button to start.
6. When the unit beeps to show that it is preheated, open the lid.
7. Arrange the carrots in a greased air fry basket and insert in the oven.
8. When cooking time is completed, open the lid and serve warm.

Serving Suggestions: Serve with favorite greens.

Variation Tip: Make sure to pat dry the carrots before cooking.

Nutritional Information per Serving:
Calories: 312 | Fat: 23.2g|Sat Fat: 14.5g|Carbohydrates: 27.1g|Fiber: 3.3g|Sugar: 23g|Protein: 1g

Brussels Sprouts Gratin

Prep Time: 15 minutes.
Cook Time: 35 minutes.
Serves: 6

Ingredients:

- 1 pound Brussels sprouts
- 1 garlic clove, cut in half
- 3 tablespoons butter, divided
- 2 tablespoons shallots, minced
- 2 tablespoons all-purpose flour
- Kosher salt, to taste
- Freshly ground black pepper
- 1 dash ground nutmeg
- 1 cup milk
- ½ cup fontina cheese, shredded
- 1 strip of bacon, cooked and crumbled
- ½ cup fine bread crumbs

Preparation:

1. Trim the Brussels sprouts and remove their outer leaves.
2. Slice the sprouts into quarters, then rinse them under cold water.
3. Grease a gratin dish with cooking spray and rub it with garlic halves.
4. Boil salted water in a suitable pan, then add Brussels sprouts.
5. Cook the sprouts for 3 minutes, then immediately drain.
6. Place a suitable saucepan over medium-low heat and melt 2 tablespoons of butter in it.
7. Toss in shallots and sauté until soft, then stir in flour, nutmeg, ½ teaspoon of salt, and black pepper.
8. Stir cook for 2 minutes, then gradually add milk and a half and half cream.
9. Mix well and add bacon along with shredded cheese.
10. Fold in Brussels sprouts and transfer this mixture to the casserole dish.
11. Toss breadcrumbs with 1 tablespoon of butter and spread over the casserole.
12. Transfer the gratin to the 2nd rack position of Ninja Foodi XL Pro Air Oven and close the door.
13. Select the "Bake" Mode using FUNCTION +/- buttons and select Rack Level 2.
14. Set its cooking time to 25 minutes and temperature to 350 degrees F, then press "START/STOP" to initiate cooking.
15. Enjoy!

Serving Suggestion: Serve the gratin with mashed potatoes.

Variation Tip: Add crushed crackers on top for a crunchy taste.

Nutritional Information Per Serving:
Calories 378 | Fat 3.8g |Sodium 620mg | Carbs 33.3g | Fiber 2.4g | Sugar 1.2g | Protein 14g

Cheesy Kale

Prep Time: 10 minutes
Cook Time: 15 minutes
Serves: 3

Ingredients:

- 1 pound fresh kale, tough ribs removed and chopped
- 3 tablespoons olive oil
- Salt and ground black pepper, as required
- 1 cup goat cheese, crumbled
- 1 teaspoon fresh lemon juice

Preparation:

1. In a bowl, add the kale, oil, salt and black pepper and mix well.
2. Press "Power" button of Ninja Foodi XL Pro Air Oven and select "Air Fry" function.
3. Press TEMP/SHADE +/- buttons to set the temperature at 340 degrees F.
4. Now press TIME/SLICES +/- buttons to set the cooking time to 15 minutes.
5. Press "START/STOP" button to start.
6. When the unit beeps to show that it is preheated, open the lid and grease the air fry basket.
7. Arrange the kale into air fry basket and insert in the oven.
8. When cooking time is completed, open the lid and immediately transfer the kale mixture into a bowl.
9. Stir in the cheese and lemon juice and serve hot.

Serving Suggestions: Serve with a garnishing of lemon zest.

Variation Tip: Goat cheese can be replaced with feta.

Nutritional Information per Serving:
Calories: 327 | Fat: 24.7g|Sat Fat: 9.5g|Carbohydrates: 17.9g|Fiber: 2.3g|Sugar: 2g|Protein: 11.6g

Cheesy Green Bean Casserole

Prep Time: 15 minutes.
Cook Time: 35 minutes.
Serves: 6

Ingredients:

- 4 cups green beans, cooked and chopped
- 3 tablespoons butter
- 8 ounces mushrooms, sliced
- ¼ cup onion, chopped
- 2 tablespoons flour
- 1 teaspoon salt
- ¼ teaspoon ground black pepper
- 1 ½ cups milk
- 2 cups cheddar cheese, shredded
- 2 tablespoons sour cream
- 1 cup soft breadcrumbs
- 2 tablespoons butter, melted
- ¼ cup Parmesan cheese, grated
- 1 cup French fried onions

Preparation:

1. Add butter to a suitable saucepan and melt it over medium-low heat.
2. Toss in onion and mushrooms, then sauté until soft.
3. Stir in flour, salt, and black pepper. Mix well, then slowly pour in the milk.
4. Stir in sour cream, green beans, and cheddar cheese, then cook until it thickens.
5. Transfer this green bean mixture to a casserole dish and spread it evenly.
6. Toss breadcrumbs with fried onion and butter.
7. Top the casserole with this bread crumbs mixture.
8. Transfer the dish to the 2nd rack position of Ninja Foodi XL Pro Air Oven and close the door.
9. Select the "Bake" Mode using FUNCTION +/- buttons and select Rack Level 2.
10. Set its cooking time to 25 minutes and temperature to 350 degrees F, then press "START/STOP" to initiate cooking.
11. Serve and enjoy!

Serving Suggestion: Serve the casserole with mashed cauliflower.
Variation Tip: Add crispy dried onion for better taste.

Nutritional Information Per Serving:
Calories 304 | Fat 31g |Sodium 834mg | Carbs 21.4g | Fiber 0.2g | Sugar 0.3g | Protein 4.6g

Beans & Veggie Burgers

Prep Time: 15 minutes
Cook Time: 22 minutes
Serves: 4

Ingredients:

- 1 cup cooked black beans
- 2 cups boiled potatoes, peeled and mashed
- 1 cup fresh spinach, chopped
- 1 cup fresh mushrooms, chopped
- 2 teaspoons Chile lime seasoning
- Olive oil cooking spray

Preparation:

1. In a large bowl, add the beans, potatoes, spinach, mushrooms, and seasoning and with your hands, mix until well combined.
2. Make 4 equal-sized patties from the mixture.
3. Spray the patties with cooking spray evenly.
4. Press "Power" button of Ninja Foodi XL Pro Air Oven and select "Air Fry" function.
5. Press TEMP/SHADE +/- buttons to set the temperature at 370 degrees F.
6. Now press TIME/SLICES +/- buttons to set the cooking time to 22 minutes.
7. Press "START/STOP" button to start.
8. When the unit beeps to show that it is preheated, open the lid.
9. Arrange the patties in the greased air fry basket and insert in the oven.
10. Flip the patties once after 12 minutes.
11. When cooking time is completed, open the lid and transfer the patties onto a serving platter.
12. Serve warm.

Serving Suggestions: Serve with avocado and tomato salad.
Variation Tip: Feel free to add seasoning of your choice.

Nutritional Information per Serving:
Calories: 113 | Fat: 0.4g|Sat Fat: 0g|Carbohydrates:23.1g|Fiber: 6.2g|Sugar: 1.7g|Protein: 6g

Tofu in Sweet & Sour Sauce

Prep Time: 20 minutes
Cook Time: 20 minutes
Serves: 4
Ingredients:
For Tofu:
- 1 (14-ounce) block firm tofu, pressed and cubed
- ½ cup arrowroot flour
- ½ teaspoon sesame oil

For Sauce:
- 4 tablespoons low-sodium soy sauce
- 1½ tablespoons rice vinegar
- 1½ tablespoons chili sauce
- 1 tablespoon agave nectar
- 2 large garlic cloves, minced
- 1 teaspoon fresh ginger, peeled and grated
- 2 scallions (green part), chopped

Preparation:
1. In a bowl, mix the tofu, arrowroot flour, and sesame oil together.
2. Press "Power" button of Ninja Foodi XL Pro Air Oven and select "Air Fry" function.
3. Press TEMP/SHADE +/- buttons to set the temperature at 360 degrees F.
4. Now press TIME/SLICES +/- buttons to set the cooking time to 20 minutes.
5. Press "START/STOP" button to start.
6. When the unit beeps to show that it is pre-heated, open the lid.
7. Arrange the tofu cubes in greased air fry basket and insert in the oven.
8. Flip the tofu cubes once halfway through.
9. Meanwhile, for the sauce: in a bowl, add all the ingredients except scallions and beat until well combined.
10. When cooking time is completed, open the lid and remove the tofu.
11. Transfer the tofu into a skillet with sauce over medium heat and cook for about 3 minutes, stirring occasionally.
12. Garnish with scallions and serve hot.

Serving Suggestions: Serve with plain boiled rice.
Variation Tip: Add pineapple for a savory choice.
Nutritional Information per Serving:
Calories: 115 | Fat: 4.8g|Sat Fat: 1g|Carbohydrates: 10.2g|Fiber: 1.7g|Sugar: 5.6g|Protein: 0.1g

Spicy Potato

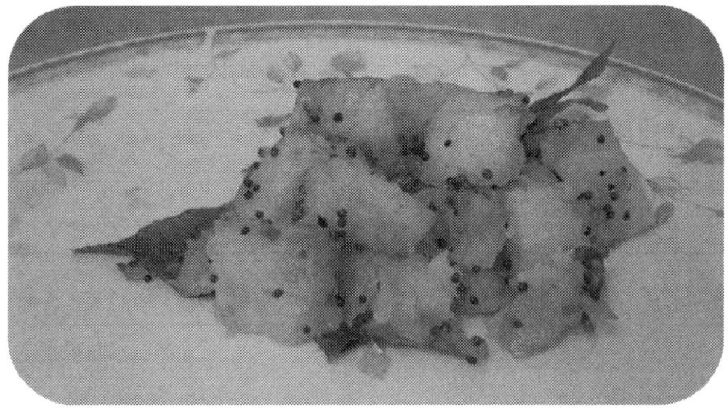

Prep Time: 15 minutes
Cook Time: 25 minutes
Serves: 4
Ingredients:
- 2 cups water
- 6 russet potatoes, peeled and cubed
- ½ tablespoon extra-virgin olive oil
- ½ of onion, chopped
- 1 tablespoon fresh rosemary, chopped
- 1 garlic clove, minced
- 1 jalapeño pepper, chopped
- ½ teaspoon garam masala powder
- ¼ teaspoon ground cumin
- ¼ teaspoon red chili powder
- Salt and ground black pepper, as required

Preparation:
1. In a large bowl, add the water and potatoes and set aside for about 30 minutes.
2. Drain well and pat dry with the paper towels.
3. In a bowl, add the potatoes and oil and toss to coat well.
4. Press "Power" button of Ninja Foodi XL Pro Air Oven and select "Air Fry" function.
5. Now press TIME/SLICES +/- buttons to set the cooking time to 5 minutes.
6. Press TEMP/SHADE +/- buttons to set the temperature at 330 degrees F.
7. Press "START/STOP" button to start.
8. When the unit beeps to show that it is pre-heated, open the lid.
9. Arrange the potato cubes in air fry basket and insert in the oven.
10. Remove from oven and transfer the potatoes into a bowl.
11. Add the remaining ingredients and toss to coat well.
12. Press "Power" button of Ninja Foodi XL Pro Air Oven and select "Air Fry" function.
13. Press TEMP/SHADE +/- buttons to set the temperature at 390 degrees F.
14. Now press TIME/SLICES +/- buttons to set the cooking time to 20 minutes.
15. Press "START/STOP" button to start.
16. When the unit beeps to show that it is pre-heated, open the lid.
17. Arrange the potato mixture in air fry basket and insert in the oven.
18. When cooking time is completed, open the lid and serve hot.

Serving Suggestions: Serve with plain bread.
Variation Tip: Adjust the ratio of spices.
Nutritional Information per Serving:
Calories: 274 | Fat: 2.3g|Sat Fat: 0.4g|Carbohydrates: 52.6g|Fiber: 8.5g|Sugar: 4.4g|Protein: 5.7g

Stuffed Zucchini

Prep Time: 20 minutes
Cook Time: 35 minutes
Serves: 4

Ingredients:

- 2 zucchinis, cut in half lengthwise
- ½ teaspoon garlic powder
- Salt, as required
- 1 teaspoon olive oil
- 4 ounces fresh mushrooms, chopped
- 4 ounces carrots, peeled and shredded
- 3 ounces onion, chopped
- 4 ounces goat cheese, crumbled
- 12 fresh basil leaves
- ½ teaspoon onion powder

Preparation:

1. Carefully, scoop the flesh from the middle of each zucchini half.
2. Season each zucchini half with a little garlic powder and salt.
3. Arrange the zucchini halves into the greased baking pan.
4. Place the oat mixture over salmon fillets and gently, press down.
5. Press "Power" button of Ninja Foodi XL Pro Air Oven and select the "Bake" function.
6. Now press TIME/SLICES +/- buttons to set the cooking time to 20 minutes.
7. Press TEMP/SHADE +/- buttons to set the temperature at 450 degrees F.
8. Press "START/STOP" button to start.
9. When the unit beeps to show that it is preheated, open the lid.
10. Insert the baking pan in oven.
11. Meanwhile, in a skillet, heat the oil over medium heat and cook the mushrooms, carrots, onions, onion powder and salt and cook for about 5-6 minutes.
12. Remove from the heat and set aside.
13. Remove the baking pan from oven and set aside.
14. Stuff each zucchini half with veggie mixture and top with basil leaves, followed by the cheese.
15. Press "Power" button of Ninja Foodi XL Pro Air Oven and select the "Bake" function.
16. Press TEMP/SHADE +/- buttons to set the temperature at 450 degrees F.
17. Now press TIME/SLICES +/- buttons to set the cooking time to 15 minutes.
18. Press "START/STOP" button to start.
19. When the unit beeps to show that it is preheated, open the lid.
20. Insert the baking pan in oven.
21. When cooking time is completed, open the lid and transfer the zucchini halves onto a platter.
22. Serve warm.

Serving Suggestions: Serve alongside fresh greens.
Variation Tip: Any kind of cheese can be used in this recipe.
Nutritional Information per Serving:
Calories: 181 | Fat: 11.6g|Sat Fat: 7.2g|Carbohydrates: 10.1g|Fiber: 2.6g|Sugar: 5.3g|Protein: 11.3g

Veggies Stuffed Bell Peppers

Prep Time: 20 minutes
Cook Time: 25 minutes
Serves: 6

Ingredients:

- 6 large bell peppers
- 1 bread roll, finely chopped
- 1 carrot, peeled and finely chopped
- 1 onion, finely chopped
- 1 potato, peeled and finely chopped
- ½ cup fresh peas, shelled
- 2 garlic cloves, minced
- 2 teaspoons fresh parsley, chopped
- Salt and ground black pepper, as required
- ⅓ cup cheddar cheese, grated

Preparation:

1. Remove the tops of each bell pepper and discard the seeds.
2. Chop the bell pepper tops finely.
3. In a bowl, place bell pepper tops, bread loaf, vegetables, garlic, parsley, salt and black pepper and mix well.
4. Stuff each bell pepper with the vegetable mixture.
5. Press "Power" button of Ninja Foodi XL Pro Air Oven and select "Air Fry" function. Select 2 LEVEL.
6. Press TEMP/SHADE +/- buttons to set the temperature at 330 degrees F.
7. Now press TIME/SLICES +/- buttons to set the cooking time to 25 minutes.
8. Press "Start/Stop" button to start.
9. When the unit beeps to show that it is preheated, open the oven door.

10. Separate the bell peppers into the greased air fry basket on Level 3 and sheet pan over wire rack on Level 1.
11. After 20 minutes, sprinkle each bell pepper with cheddar cheese.
12. When cooking time is completed, open the oven door and transfer the bell peppers onto serving plates.
13. Serve hot.

Serving Suggestions: Serve with fresh salad.
Variation Tip: For best result, remove the seeds from bell peppers completely.
Nutritional Information per Serving:
Calories: 123 | Fat: 2.7g|Sat Fat: 1.2g|Carbohydrates: 21.7g|Fiber: 3.7g|Sugar: 8g|Protein: 4.8g

Pita Bread Pizza

Prep Time: 10 minutes
Cook Time: 5 minutes
Serves: 1
Ingredients:

- 2 tablespoons marinara sauce
- 1 whole-wheat pita bread
- ½ cup fresh baby spinach leaves
- ½ of small plum tomato, cut into 4 slices
- ½ of garlic clove, sliced thinly
- ½ ounce part-skim mozzarella cheese, shredded
- ½ tablespoon Parmigiano-Reggiano cheese, shredded

Preparation:
1. Arrange the pita bread onto a plate.
2. Spread marinara sauce over 1 side of each pita bread evenly.
3. Top with the spinach leaves, followed by tomato slices, garlic and cheeses.
4. Press "Power" button of Ninja Foodi XL Pro Air Oven and select "Air Fry" function.
5. Press TEMP/SHADE +/- buttons to set the temperature at 350 degrees F.
6. Now press TIME/SLICES +/- buttons to set the cooking time to 5 minutes.
7. Press "Start/Stop" button to start.
8. When the unit beeps to show that it is preheated, open the oven door.
9. Arrange the pita bread into the greased air fry basket on Level 3.
10. When cooking time is completed, open the oven door and transfer the pizza onto a serving plate.
11. Set aside to cool slightly.
12. Serve warm.

Serving Suggestions: Serve alongside the greens.
Variation Tip: You can replace pizza sauce with marinara sauce.
Nutritional Information per Serving:
Calories: 266 | Fat: 6.2g|Sat Fat: 2.6g|Carbohydrates: 43.1g|Fiber: 6.5g|Sugar: 4.6g|Protein: 13g

Baked Potato

Prep Time: 5 minutes
Cook Time: 45 minutes
Serves: 4
Ingredients:

- 4 russet potatoes
- 1½ tablespoons olive oil
- 1½ tablespoons sea salt

Preparation:
1. Poke each potato, massage it all over with olive oil and sea salt.
2. Place the potato in the sheet pan.
3. Insert a wire rack on Level 3. Turn on Ninja Foodi XL Pro Air Oven and select "Bake".
4. Select the timer for 40 minutes and the temperature for 350 degrees F.
5. When the unit beeps to signify it has preheated, open the oven and place the sheet pan onto wire rack. Close the oven and let it cook.
6. Remove the baked potatoes from the Ninja Foodi, split them in half, and top them with chosen toppings!

Serving Suggestions: Top with chopped green onions.
Variation Tip: You can also add cheese on top.
Nutritional Information per Serving:
Calories: 213 | Fat: 5g|Sat Fat: 1g|Carbohydrates: 37g|Fiber: 4g|Sugar: 2g|Protein: 5g

Asparagus with Garlic and Parmesan

Prep Time: 5 minutes
Cook Time: 10 minutes
Serves: 4

Ingredients:

- 1 bundle asparagus
- 1 teaspoon olive oil
- ⅛ teaspoon garlic salt
- 1 tablespoon parmesan cheese
- Pepper to taste

Preparation:

1. Clean the asparagus and dry it. To remove the woody stalks, cut 1 inch off the bottom.
2. In a sheet pan, arrange asparagus in a single layer and spray with oil.
3. On top of the asparagus, evenly sprinkle garlic salt. Season with salt and pepper, then sprinkle with Parmesan cheese.
4. Turn on Ninja Foodi XL Pro Air Oven and select "Air Fry".
5. Select the timer for 10 minutes and the temperature for 350 degrees F.
6. When the unit beeps to signify it has preheated, open the oven and place the sheet pan onto Level 3 in oven. Close the oven and let it cook.
7. Enjoy right away.

Serving Suggestions: Sprinkle more parmesan cheese before serving.
Variation Tip: You can also sprinkle some paprika.
Nutritional Information per Serving:
Calories: 18 | Fat: 2g|Sat Fat: 1g|Carbohydrates: 1g|Fiber: 0g|Sugar: 0g|Protein: 1g

Green Tomatoes

Prep Time: 15 minutes
Cook Time: 7 minutes
Serves: 4

Ingredients:

- 3 green tomatoes
- ½ teaspoon salt
- ½ cup flour
- 2 eggs
- ⅓ cup cornmeal
- ⅓ cup breadcrumbs
- ⅛ teaspoon paprika

Preparation:

1. Slice the green tomatoes into 1/4-inch slices and generously coat with salt. Allow for at least 5 minutes of resting time.
2. Put the flour in one bowl, the egg (whisked) in the second, and the cornmeal, breadcrumbs, and paprika in the third bowl to make a breading station.
3. Using a paper towel, pat green tomato slices dry.
4. Dip each tomato slice into the flour, then the egg, and finally the cornmeal mixture, making sure the tomato slices are completely covered.
5. Place them in air fry basket in a single layer.
6. Turn on Ninja Foodi XL Pro Air Oven and select "Air Fry".
7. Select the timer for 9 minutes and the temperature for 380 degrees F.
8. When the unit beeps to signify it is preheated, open the oven and place the air fry basket into rail of Level 3.
9. Cook for 7-9 minutes, flipping and spritzing with oil halfway through.

Serving Suggestions: Sprinkle more parmesan cheese before serving.
Variation Tip: You can also add a pinch of cayenne pepper.
Nutritional Information per Serving:
Calories: 186 | Fat: 4g|Sat Fat: 1g|Carbohydrates: 31g|Fiber: 3g|Sugar: 4g|Protein: 8g

Parmesan Carrot

Prep Time: 10 minutes
Cook Time: 20 minutes
Serves: 2

Ingredients:

- 3 carrots
- 1 tablespoon olive oil
- 1 clove garlic, crushed
- 2 tablespoons parmesan cheese, grated
- ¼ teaspoon red pepper, crushed

Preparation:

1. Stir in the crushed garlic with olive oil.
2. Carrots should be washed and dried. Cut the tops in half and remove the tops. Then, to make flat surfaces, cut each half in half.
3. Toss the carrot fries with the garlic and olive oil mixture.
4. Combine the parmesan, red pepper, and black pepper in a mixing bowl. Half of the mixture should be sprinkled over the carrot fries that have been coated.
5. Toss in the remaining parmesan mixture and repeat.
6. Arrange evenly the carrot fries in an air fry basket and on a roast tray.
7. Turn on Ninja Foodi XL Pro Air Oven and select "Air Fry". Select 2 LEVEL.
8. Select the timer for 20 minutes and the temperature for 350 degrees F.
9. When the unit beeps to signify it is preheated, open the oven and place the air fry basket into the rail of Level 4 and the roast tray on a sheet pan on Level 2.
10. Remove from the Ninja Foodi XL Pro Air Oven to serve.

Serving Suggestions: Sprinkle more parmesan cheese before serving.
Variation Tip: You can also add a pinch of cayenne pepper.
Nutritional Information per Serving:
Calories: 106 | Fat: 7g|Sat Fat: 1.1g|Carbohydrates: 10g|Fiber: 3g|Sugar: 5g|Protein: 1.2g

Roasted Green Beans

Prep Time: 5 minutes
Cook Time: 15 minutes
Serves: 4

Ingredients:

- 2 tablespoons lard
- 290g whole green beans
- 1 tablespoon minced garlic
- 2 tablespoons pimentos, diced
- Garlic powder, to taste
- Onion powder, to taste
- Salt, to taste

Preparation:

1. In a stovetop pot, melt the lard.
2. Sauté until the green beans are bright green and glossy, then add the additional ingredients.
3. Using parchment paper, line the air fry basket.
4. Arrange the greens in a single layer on the air fry basket.
5. Turn on Ninja Foodi XL Pro Air Oven and select "Air Fry".
6. Select the timer for 15 minutes and the temperature at 390 degrees F.
7. When the unit beeps to signify it is preheated, open the oven and place the air fry basket into rail of Level 3 in oven. Close the oven and let it cook.
8. Remove from the Ninja Foodi XL Pro Air Oven to serve.

Serving Suggestions: Sprinkle some sesame seeds on top.
Variation Tip: You can also add pinch of black pepper.
Nutritional Information per Serving:
Calories: 91 | Fat: 7g|Sat Fat: 3g|Carbohydrates: 6g|Fiber: 2g|Sugar: 3g|Protein: 2g

Broiled Broccoli

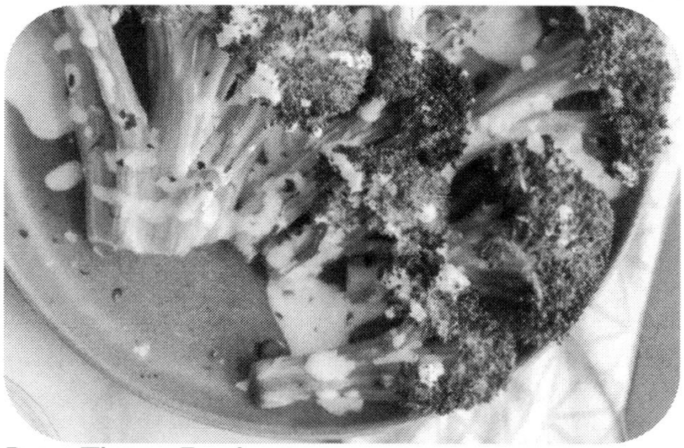

Prep Time: 5 minutes
Cook Time: 20 minutes
Serves: 4

Ingredients:

- 2 heads of broccoli, diced into large chunks
- 1½ teaspoons olive oil
- Salt and pepper, to taste

Preparation:

1. Slice your broccoli into large chunks. Left the stems long to make sure they would not break apart.
2. Sprinkle the broccoli with 1 tablespoon of olive oil in a large mixing bowl and season to taste with salt and pepper. Toss everything together to make sure the broccoli is well-coated.
3. Place the broccoli on the sheet pan in a single layer.
4. Insert a wire rack on Level 3. Turn on Ninja Foodi XL Pro Air Oven and select "Broil".
5. Select the timer for 15 minutes and temperature to LO.
6. When the unit beeps to signify it is preheated, open the oven and place the sheet pan onto wire rack. Close the oven and let it cook.
7. Serve and enjoy.

Serving Suggestions: Top with some garlic sauce.

Variation Tip: You can also serve with steam rice.

Nutritional Information per Serving:
Calories: 20 | Fat: 1g|Sat Fat: 0.3g|Carbohydrates: 0g|Fiber: 0g|Sugar: 0g|Protein: 0g

Stuffed Peppers

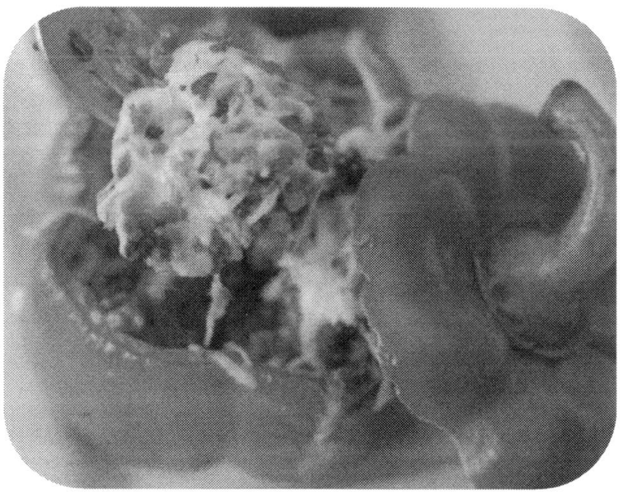

Prep Time: 15 minutes
Cook Time: 15 minutes
Serves: 6

Ingredients:

- 6 green bell peppers
- 1 pound lean ground beef
- 1 tablespoon olive oil
- ¼ cup green onion, diced
- ¼ cup fresh parsley
- ½ teaspoon ground sage
- ½ teaspoon garlic salt
- 1 cup rice, cooked
- 1 cup marinara sauce to taste
- ¼ cup mozzarella cheese, shredded

Preparation:

1. Cook the ground beef in a medium sized skillet until it is well done.
2. Return the beef to the pan after draining it.
3. Combine the olive oil, green onion, parsley, sage, and salt in a large mixing bowl and add to the skillet with beef.
4. Add the cooked rice and marinara sauce in the skillet and stir this rice-beef mixture thoroughly.
5. Remove the tops off each pepper and discard the seeds.
6. Scoop the mixture into each pepper and place it in the air fry basket.
7. Turn on Ninja Foodi XL Pro Air Oven and select "Air Fry".
8. Select the timer for 10 minutes and temperature for 355 degrees F.
9. When the unit beeps to signify it is preheated, open the oven and place the air fry basket into the rail of Level 3. Close the oven and let it cook.
10. Dish out to serve and enjoy.

Serving Suggestions: Top with some fresh parsley.

Variation Tip: You can use any cheese.

Nutritional Information per Serving:
Calories: 296 | Fat: 13g|Sat Fat: 4g|Carbohydrates: 19g|Fiber: 2g|Sugar: 6g|Protein: 25g

Eggplant Parmesan

Prep Time: 5 minutes
Cook Time: 20 minutes
Serves: 2

Ingredients:

- 1 medium eggplant
- 2 eggs, beaten
- ¼ cup panko breadcrumbs
- 1 cup mozzarella cheese
- 2 cups marinara sauce
- Olive oil spray
- 2 tablespoons parmesan cheese

Preparation:

1. Peel the eggplant and cut it into 1/4-inch slices.
2. In a shallow plate, place the breadcrumbs.
3. Whisk the eggs in a small bowl.
4. Dip the eggplant slices in the egg mixture gently. After that, cover both sides in breadcrumbs.
5. Fill your air fry basket with eggplant in a single layer. Using an olive oil spray, coat the tops of the slices.
6. Turn on Ninja Foodi XL Pro Air Oven and select "Air Roast".
7. Select the timer for 12 minutes and the temperature for 400 degrees F.
8. When the unit beeps to signify it has preheated, open the oven and slide the air fry basket into rail of Level 3. Open the oven and let it cook.
9. Flip your eggplant slices after 8 minutes and drizzle the tops with olive oil.
10. Cook for another 4 minutes after spraying the tops of your eggplant.
11. Spread marinara sauce evenly over the top of your eggplant rounds and sprinkle with mozzarella and parmesan cheese.
12. Select "Air Fry".
13. Set the time for 3 minutes and temperature for 350 degrees F.
14. Dish out to serve hot.

Serving Suggestions: Top with some fresh parsley.
Variation Tip: You can also put a slice of low-fat mozzarella cheese on top and broil for 3 minutes.
Nutritional Information per Serving:
Calories: 69 | Fat: 2g|Sat Fat: 0.1g|Carbohydrates: 6.3g|Fiber: 2g|Sugar: 2.6g|Protein: 5.9g

Vegetable Nachos

Prep Time: 10 minutes
Cook Time: 5 minutes
Serves: 3

Ingredients:
- 8 ounces tortilla chips
- ½ cup grilled chicken
- 1 can (15 ounces) black beans, drained, rinsed
- 1 cup white queso
- ½ cup grape tomatoes, halved
- ⅓ cup green onion, diced

Preparation:
1. Use foil to line the air fry basket.
2. Using a nonstick spray, coat the surface.
3. Assemble the nachos by layering the chips, chicken, and beans on top.
4. Place a layer of queso on top.
5. Add tomatoes and onions to the top.
6. Turn on Ninja Foodi XL Pro Air Oven and select "Air Fry".
7. Select the timer for 5 minutes and the temperature for 355 degrees F.
8. When the unit beeps to signify it is preheated, open the oven and place the air fry basket into rail of Level 3. Open the oven and let it cook.
9. Remove from the Ninja Foodi XL Pro Air Oven to serve.

Serving Suggestions: Top with some fresh parsley.
Variation Tip: You can add cheese.
Nutritional Information per Serving:
Calories: 43 | Fat: 1.3g|Sat Fat: 0.4g|Carbohydrates: 7.3g|Fiber: 1.2g|Sugar: 1.6g|Protein: 1.9g

Cauliflower Tots

Prep Time: 5 minutes
Cook Time: 10 minutes
Serves: 4

Ingredients:
- Cooking spray
- 450g cauliflower tots

Preparation:
1. Using nonstick cooking spray, coat the air fry basket.
2. Place cauliflower tots evenly in the air fry basket and roast tray, ensuring sure they do not touch, and air fry in batches if needed.
3. Turn on Ninja Foodi XL Pro Air Oven and select "Air Fry". Select 2 LEVEL.
4. Select the timer for 6 minutes and the temperature for 400 degrees F.
5. When the unit beeps to signify it is preheated, open the oven and place the air fry basket into rail of Level 4 and the roast tray on sheet pan on Level 2. Close the oven and let it cook.
6. Pull the basket out, flip the tots, and cook for another 3 minutes, or until browned and cooked through.
7. Remove from the Ninja Foodi XL Pro Air Oven to serve.

Serving Suggestions: Serve with garlic sauce.
Variation Tip: You can top with parmesan cheese.
Nutritional Information per Serving:
Calories: 147 | Fat: 6g|Sat Fat: 0.7g|Carbohydrates: 20g|Fiber: 6g|Sugar: 1.6g|Protein: 2g

Dessert Recipes

Air Fried Churros

Prep Time: 15 minutes.
Cook Time: 12 minutes.
Serves: 8

Ingredients:

- 1 cup of water
- ⅓ cup butter, cut into cubes
- 2 tablespoons granulated sugar
- ¼ teaspoons salt
- 1 cup all-purpose flour
- 2 large eggs
- 1 teaspoon vanilla extract
- oil spray

Cinnamon Coating:

- ½ cup granulated sugar
- ¾ teaspoons ground cinnamon

Preparation:

1. Grease the sheet pan with cooking spray.
2. Warm water with butter, salt, and sugar in a suitable saucepan until it boils.
3. Now reduce its heat, then slowly stir in flour and mix well until smooth.
4. Remove the mixture from the heat and leave it for 4 minutes to cool.
5. Add vanilla extract and eggs, then beat the mixture until it comes together as a batter.
6. Transfer this churro mixture to a piping bag with star-shaped tips and pipe the batter on the prepared pan to get 4-inch churros using this batter.
7. Refrigerate these churros for 1 hour, then transfer them to the air fry basket.
8. Transfer the basket to the 3rd rack position of Ninja Foodi XL Pro Air Oven and close the door.
9. Select the "Air Fry" Mode using FUNCTION +/- buttons and select Rack Level 3.
10. Set its cooking time to 12 minutes and temperature to 375 degrees F, then press "START/STOP" to initiate cooking.
11. Meanwhile, mix granulated sugar with cinnamon in a bowl.
12. Drizzle this mixture over the air fried churros.
13. Serve.

Serving Suggestion: Serve the churros with chocolate dip.
Variation Tip: Add powdered cinnamon to the churros batter.
Nutritional Information Per Serving:
Calories 278 | Fat 10g |Sodium 218mg | Carbs 26g | Fiber 10g | Sugar 30g | Protein 4g

Nutella Banana Pastries

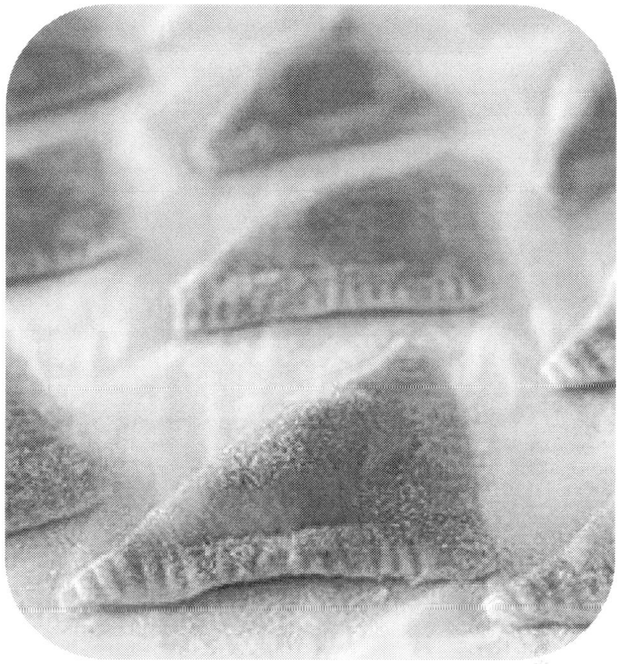

Prep Time: 15 minutes
Cook Time: 12 minutes
Serves: 4

Ingredients:

- 1 puff pastry sheet
- ½ cup Nutella
- 2 bananas, peeled and sliced

Preparation:

1. Cut the pastry sheet into 4 equal-sized squares.
2. Spread the Nutella on each square of pastry evenly.
3. Divide the banana slices over Nutella.
4. Fold each square into a triangle and with wet fingers, slightly press the edges.
5. Then with a fork, press the edges firmly.
6. Press "Power" button of Ninja Foodi XL Pro Air Oven and select "Air Fry" function.
7. Press TEMP/SHADE +/- buttons to set the temperature at 375 degrees F.
8. Now press TIME/SLICES +/- buttons to set the cooking time to 12 minutes.
9. Press "Start/Stop" button to start.
10. When the unit beeps to show that it is preheated, open the oven door.
11. Arrange the pastries into the greased air fry basket and insert into rail of Level 3.
12. When cooking time is completed, open the oven door and serve warm.

Serving Suggestions: Serve with the sprinkling of cinnamon.
Variation Tip: You can use the fruit of your choice.
Nutritional Information per Serving:
Calories: 221 | Fat: 10g|Sat Fat: 2.7g|Carbohydrates: 31.6g|Fiber: 2.6g|Sugar: 14.4g|Protein: 3.4g

Shortbread Fingers

Prep Time: 15 minutes
Cook Time: 12 minutes
Serves: 10

Ingredients:

- ⅓ cup caster sugar
- 1 ⅔ cups plain flour
- ¾ cup butter

Preparation:

1. In a large bowl, mix the sugar and flour together.
2. Add the butter and mix until a smooth dough forms.
3. Cut the dough into 10 equal-sized fingers.
4. With a fork, lightly prick the fingers.
5. Place the fingers into the lightly greased baking pan.
6. Press "Power" button of Ninja Foodi XL Pro Air Oven and select "Air Fry" function.
7. Press TEMP/SHADE +/- buttons to set the temperature at 355 degrees F.
8. Now press TIME/SLICES +/- buttons to set the cooking time to 12 minutes.
9. Press "START/STOP" button to start.
10. When the unit beeps to show that it is preheated, open the lid.
11. Arrange the pan in air fry basket and insert in the oven.
12. When cooking time is completed, open the lid and place the baking pan onto a wire rack to cool for about 5-10 minutes.
13. Now, invert the shortbread fingers onto the wire rack to completely cool before serving.

Serving Suggestions: For best result, chill the dough in the refrigerator for 30 minutes before cooking. Serve with a dusting of powdered sugar.

Variation Tip: Replace the plain flour with some other flour of your choice.

Nutritional Information per Serving:
Calories: 223 | Fat: 14g|Sat Fat: 8.8g|Carbohydrates: 22.6g|Fiber: 0.6g|Sugar: 0.7g|Protein: 2.3g

Apple Pastries

Prep Time: 15 minutes
Cook Time: 10minutes
Serves: 6

Ingredients:

- ½ of large apple, peeled, cored and chopped
- 1 teaspoon fresh orange zest, grated finely
- ½ tablespoon white sugar
- ½ teaspoon ground cinnamon
- 7.05 ounces prepared frozen puff pastry

Preparation:

1. In a bowl, mix all ingredients except puff pastry together.
2. Cut the pastry in 16 squares.
3. Place about a teaspoon of the apple mixture in the center of each square.
4. Fold each square into a triangle and press the edges slightly with wet fingers.
5. Then with a fork, press the edges firmly.
6. Press "Power" button of Ninja Foodi XL Pro Air Oven and select "Air Fry" function.
7. Press TEMP/SHADE +/- buttons to set the temperature at 390 degrees F.
8. Now press TIME/SLICES +/- buttons to set the cooking time to 10 minutes.
9. Press "START/STOP" button to start.
10. When the unit beeps to show that it is preheated, open the lid.
11. Arrange the pastries in the greased air fry basket and insert in the oven.
12. When cooking time is completed, open the lid and transfer the pastries onto a platter.
13. Serve warm.

Serving Suggestions: Serve with a dusting of powdered sugar.

Variation Tip: Use sweet apple.

Nutritional Information per Serving:
Calories: 198 | Fat: 12.7g|Sat Fat: 3.2g|Carbohydrates: 18.8g|Fiber: 1.1g|Sugar: 3.2g|Protein: 2.5g

Honeyed Banana

Prep Time: 10 minutes
Cook Time: 10 minutes
Serves: 2

Ingredients:

- 1 ripe banana, peeled and sliced lengthwise
- ½ teaspoon fresh lemon juice
- 2 teaspoons honey
- ⅛ teaspoon ground cinnamon

Preparation:

1. Coat each banana half with lemon juice.
2. Arrange the banana halves onto the greased sheet pan cut sides up.
3. Drizzle the banana halves with honey and sprinkle with cinnamon.
4. Press "Power" button of Ninja Foodi XL Pro Air Oven and select "Air Fry" function.
5. Press TEMP/SHADE +/- buttons to set the temperature at 350 degrees F.
6. Now press TIME/SLICES +/- buttons to set the cooking time to 10 minutes.
7. Press "START/STOP" button to start.
8. When the unit beeps to show that it is preheated, open the lid.
9. Insert the sheet pan in oven.
10. When cooking time is completed, open the lid and transfer the banana slices onto a platter.
11. Serve immediately.

Serving Suggestions: Serve with garnishing of almonds.

Variation Tip: Honey can be replaced with maple syrup.

Nutritional Information per Serving:
Calories: 74 | Fat: 0.2g|Sat Fat: 0.1g|Carbohydrates: 19.4g|Fiber: 1.6g|Sugar: 13g|Protein: 0.7g

Chocolate Chip Cookie

Prep Time: 15 minutes.
Cook Time: 12 minutes.
Serves: 6

Ingredients:

- ½ cup butter, softened
- ½ cup sugar
- ½ cup brown sugar
- 1 egg
- 1 teaspoon vanilla
- ½ teaspoons baking soda
- ¼ teaspoons salt
- 1 ½ cups all-purpose flour
- 1 cup of chocolate chips

Preparation:

1. Grease the sheet pan with cooking spray.
2. Beat butter with sugar and brown sugar in a mixing bowl.
3. Stir in vanilla, egg, salt, flour, and baking soda, then mix well.
4. Fold in chocolate chips, then knead this dough a bit.
5. Spread the prepared dough in the prepared sheet pan evenly.
6. Transfer the pan to the 2nd rack position of Ninja Foodi XL Pro Air Oven and close the door.
7. Select the "Bake" Mode using FUNCTION +/- buttons and select Rack Level 2.
8. Set its cooking time to 12 minutes and temperature to 400 degrees F, then press "START/STOP" to initiate cooking.
9. Serve oven fresh.

Serving Suggestion: Serve the cookies with warm milk.

Variation Tip: Dip the cookies in chocolate syrup to coat well.

Nutritional Information Per Serving:
Calories 173 | Fat 12g |Sodium 79mg | Carbs 24.8g | Fiber 1.1g | Sugar 18g | Protein 15g

Air Fried Doughnuts

Prep Time: 15 minutes.
Cook Time: 6 minutes.
Serves: 8

Ingredients:

- Cooking spray
- ½ cup milk
- ¼ cup & 1 teaspoon granulated sugar
- 2 ¼ teaspoons active dry yeast
- 2 cup all-purpose flour
- ½ teaspoons kosher salt
- 4 tablespoons melted butter
- 1 large egg
- 1 teaspoon pure vanilla extract

Preparation:

1. Warm up the milk in a suitable saucepan, then add yeast and 1 teaspoon of sugar.
2. Mix well and leave this milk for 8 minutes.
3. Add flour, salt, butter, egg, vanilla, and ¼ cup of sugar to the warm milk.
4. Mix well and knead over a floured surface until smooth.
5. Place this dough in a lightly greased bowl and brush it with cooking oil.
6. Cover the prepared dough and leave it in a warm place for 1 hour.
7. Punch the raised dough, then roll into ½-inch-thick rectangle.
8. Cut 3" circles out of this dough sheet using a biscuit cutter.
9. Now cut the rounds from the center to make a hole.
10. Place the doughnuts in the air fry basket.
11. Transfer the basket to the 2nd rack position of Ninja Foodi XL Pro Air Oven and close the door.
12. Select the "Air Fry" Mode using FUNCTION +/- buttons and select Rack Level 2.
13. Set its cooking time to 6 minutes and temperature to 375 degrees F, then press "START/STOP" to initiate cooking.
14. Cook the doughnuts in batches to avoid overcrowding.
15. Serve fresh.

Serving Suggestion: Serve the doughnuts with strawberry jam.
Variation Tip: Roll the doughnuts in the powder sugar to coat.
Nutritional Information Per Serving:
Calories 128 | Fat 20g |Sodium 192mg | Carbs 27g | Fiber 0.9g | Sugar 19g | Protein 5.2g-

Fudge Brownies

Prep Time: 15 minutes
Cook Time: 20 minutes
Serves: 8

Ingredients:

- 1 cup sugar
- ½ cup butter, melted
- ½ cup flour
- ⅓ cup cocoa powder
- 1 teaspoon baking powder
- 2 eggs
- 1 teaspoon vanilla extract

Preparation:

1. Grease a baking pan.
2. In a large bowl, add the sugar and butter and whisk until light and fluffy.
3. Add the remaining ingredients and mix until well combined.
4. Place mixture into the prepared pan and with the back of a spatula, smooth the top surface.
5. Press "Power" button of Ninja Foodi XL Pro Air Oven and select "Air Fry" function.
6. Press TEMP/SHADE +/- buttons to set the temperature at 350 degrees F.
7. Now press TIME/SLICES +/- buttons to set the cooking time to 20 minutes.
8. Press "START/STOP" button to start.
9. When the unit beeps to show that it is preheated, open the lid.
10. Arrange the pan in air fry basket and insert in the oven.
11. When cooking time is completed, open the lid and place the baking pan onto a wire rack to cool completely.
12. Cut into 8 equal-sized squares and serve.

Serving Suggestions: Serve with a drizzling of melted chocolate.
Variation Tip: Drizzle with some coconut flakes for a crispy taste.
Nutritional Information per Serving:
Calories: 250 | Fat: 13.2g|Sat Fat: 7.9g|Carbohydrates: 33.4g|Fiber: 1.3g|Sugar: 25.2g| Protein: 3g

Cannoli

Prep Time: 15 minutes.
Cook Time: 12 minutes.
Serves: 4

Ingredients:

Filling

- 1 (16-ounce) container ricotta
- ½ cup mascarpone cheese
- ½ cup powdered sugar, divided
- ¾ cup heavy cream
- 1 teaspoon vanilla extract
- 1 teaspoon orange zest
- ¼ teaspoon kosher salt
- ½ cup mini chocolate chips, for garnish

Shells:

- 2 cups all-purpose flour
- ¼ cup granulated sugar
- 1 teaspoon kosher salt
- ½ teaspoon cinnamon
- 4 tablespoons cold butter, cut into cubes
- 6 tablespoons white wine
- 1 large egg
- 1 egg white for brushing
- Vegetable oil for frying

Preparation:

1. For the filling, beat all the ingredients in a mixer and fold in whipped cream.
2. Cover and refrigerate this filling for 1 hour.
3. Mix all the shell ingredients in a bowl until smooth.
4. Cover this dough and refrigerate for 1 hour.
5. Roll the prepared dough into a ⅛-inch-thick sheet.
6. Cut 4 small circles out of the prepared dough and wrap it around the cannoli molds.
7. Brush the prepared dough with egg whites to seal the edges.
8. Place the shells in the air fry basket.
9. Transfer the basket to the 2nd rack position of Ninja Foodi XL Pro Air Oven and close the door.
10. Select the "Air Fry" Mode using FUNCTION +/- buttons and select Rack Level 2.
11. Set its cooking time to 12 minutes and temperature to 350 degrees F, then press "START/STOP" to initiate cooking.
12. Place filling in a pastry bag fitted with an open star tip. Pipe filling into shells, then dip ends in mini chocolate chips.
13. Transfer the prepared filling to a piping bag.
14. Pipe the filling into the cannoli shells.
15. Serve.

Serving Suggestion: Serve the cannoli with chocolate chips and chocolate syrup.
Variation Tip: Coat the cannoli shells with coconut shreds.
Nutritional Information Per Serving:
Calories 348 | Fat 16g |Sodium 95mg | Carbs 38.4g | Fiber 0.3g | Sugar 10g | Protein 14g

Cranberry-Apple Pie

Prep Time: 15 minutes.
Cook Time: 45 minutes.
Serves: 8

Ingredients:

- 2 ½ cups all-purpose flour
- 1 tablespoon sugar
- ¾ teaspoon salt
- ½ cup cold unsalted butter, cubed
- ⅓ cup cold shortening
- 7 tablespoons ice water

Filling

- ½ cup dried currants or raisins
- 2 tablespoons dark rum
- 1 cup fresh cranberries, divided
- ¾ cup sugar, divided
- 6 baking apples, peeled and cut into slices
- 2 tablespoons tapioca
- 1 tablespoon lemon juice
- 2 teaspoons grated lemon zest
- ½ teaspoon ground cinnamon

Egg Wash

- 2 teaspoons sugar
- Dash ground cinnamon
- 1 large egg
- 1 tablespoon milk

Preparation:

1. Mix flour with butter, salt, and sugar in a bowl.
2. Stir in water and mix well until smooth.
3. Divide the prepared dough into two halves and spread each into a ⅛-inch-thick round.
4. Blend cranberries with sugar in a food processor.
5. Transfer to a bowl and stir in remaining filling ingredients.
6. Spread one dough round on a 9-inch pie plate.
7. Spread the prepared filling in the crust.

8. Slice the other dough round into strips and make a criss-cross pattern on top.
9. Brush the pie with egg and milk mixture, then drizzle sugar and cinnamon top.
10. Transfer the pan to the 2nd rack position of Ninja Foodi XL Pro Air Oven and close the door.
11. Select the "Bake" Mode using FUNCTION +/- buttons and select Rack Level 2.
12. Set its cooking time to 45 minutes and temperature to 325 degrees F, then press "START/STOP" to initiate cooking.
13. Cool on a wire rack for 30 minutes.
14. Serve.

Serving Suggestion: Serve the pie with whipped cream on top.

Variation Tip: Add a tablespoon of apple sauce to the filling for sweeter taste.

Nutritional Information Per Serving:
Calories 145 | Fat 3g |Sodium 355mg | Carbs 20g | Fiber 1g | Sugar 25g | Protein 1g

Caramel Apple Pie

Prep Time: 15 minutes.
Cook Time: 48 minutes.
Serves: 6

Ingredients:

Topping

- ¼ cup all-purpose flour
- ⅓ cup packed brown sugar
- 2 tablespoons butter, softened
- ½ teaspoon ground cinnamon

Pie

- 6 cups sliced peeled tart apples
- 1 tablespoon lemon juice
- ½ cup sugar
- 3 tablespoons all-purpose flour
- ½ teaspoon ground cinnamon
- 1 unbaked pastry shell (9 inches)
- 28 caramels
- 1 can (5 ounces) evaporated milk

Preparation:

1. Mix flour with cinnamon, butter, and brown sugar.
2. Spread this mixture in an 8-inch baking pan.
3. Transfer the pan to the 2nd rack position of Ninja Foodi XL Pro Air Oven and close the door.
4. Select the "Bake" Mode using FUNCTION +/- buttons and select Rack Level 2.
5. Set its cooking time to 8 minutes and temperature to 350 degrees F, then press "START/STOP" to initiate cooking.
6. Meanwhile, mix apple with lemon juice, cinnamon, flour, and sugar.
7. Spread the filling in the baked crust and return to the oven.
8. Bake again for 35 minutes in the Ninja Foodi XL Pro Air oven.
9. Mix caramels with milk in a pan and cook until melted.
10. Spread the caramel on top of the pie and bake for 5 minutes.
11. Serve.

Serving Suggestion: Serve the pie with apple sauce on top.

Variation Tip: Crushed apple chips on top of the apple filling.

Nutritional Information Per Serving:
Calories 203 | Fat 8.9g |Sodium 340mg | Carbs 24.7g | Fiber 1.2g | Sugar 11.3g | Protein 5.3g

Brownie Muffins

Prep Time: 10 minutes
Cook Time: 10 minutes
Serves: 12

Ingredients:

- 1 package Betty Crocker fudge brownie mix
- ¼ cup walnuts, chopped
- 1 egg
- ⅓ cup vegetable oil
- 2 teaspoons water

Preparation:

1. Grease 12 muffin molds. Set aside.
2. In a bowl, mix together all the ingredients.
3. Place the mixture into the prepared muffin molds.
4. Press "Power" button of Ninja Foodi XL Pro Air Oven and select "Air Fry" function.
5. Press TEMP/SHADE +/- buttons to set the temperature at 300 degrees F.
6. Now press TIME/SLICES +/- buttons to set the cooking time to 10 minutes.
7. Press "Start/Stop" button to start.
8. When the unit beeps to show that it is preheated, open the oven door.
9. Arrange the muffin molds into the air fry basket and insert the basket into rail of Level 3.
10. When cooking time is completed, open the oven door and place the muffin molds onto a wire rack to cool for about 10 minutes.
11. Carefully invert the muffins onto the wire rack to completely cool before serving.

Serving Suggestions: Serve with the topping of coconut.
Variation Tip: You can use oil of your choice.
Nutritional Information per Serving:
Calories: 168 | Fat: 8.9g|Sat Fat: 1.4g|Carbohydrates: 20.8g|Fiber: 1.1g|Sugar: 14g|Protein: 2g

Peanut Brittle Bars

Prep Time: 15 minutes.
Cook Time: 28 minutes.
Serves: 6
Ingredients:
- 1 ½ cups all-purpose flour
- ½ cup whole wheat flour
- 1 cup packed brown sugar
- 1 teaspoon baking soda
- ¼ teaspoon salt
- 1 cup butter

Topping
- 1 cup milk chocolate chips
- 2 cups salted peanuts
- 12 ¼ ounces caramel ice cream topping
- 3 tablespoons all-purpose flour

Preparation:
1. Mix flours with salt, baking soda, and brown sugar in a large bowl.
2. Spread the batter in a greased sheet pan.
3. Transfer the pan to the 2nd rack position of Ninja Foodi XL Pro Air Oven and close the door.
4. Select the "Air Fry" Mode using FUNCTION +/- buttons and select Rack Level 2.
5. Set its cooking time to 12 minutes and temperature to 350 degrees F, then press "START/STOP" to initiate cooking.
6. Spread chocolate chips and peanuts on top.
7. Mix flour with caramels topping in a bowl and spread on top,
8. Bake again for 16 minutes.
9. Serve.

Serving Suggestion: Serve the bars with sweet cream cheese dip.
Variation Tip: Add crushed oats to bars for crumbly texture.
Nutritional Information Per Serving:
Calories 153 | Fat 1g |Sodium 8mg | Carbs 26g | Fiber 0.8g | Sugar 56g | Protein 11g

Brownie Bars

Prep Time: 15 minutes.
Cook Time: 28 minutes.
Serves: 8
Ingredients:
Brownie:
- ½ cup butter, cubed
- 1-ounce unsweetened chocolate
- 2 large eggs, beaten
- 1 teaspoon vanilla extract
- 1 cup of sugar
- 1 cup all-purpose flour
- 1 teaspoon baking powder
- 1 cup walnuts, chopped

Filling
- 6 ounces cream cheese softened
- ½ cup sugar
- ¼ cup butter, softened
- 2 tablespoons all-purpose flour
- 1 large egg, beaten
- ½ teaspoon vanilla extract

Topping
- 1 cup (6-ounce) chocolate chips
- 1 cup walnuts, chopped
- 2 cups mini marshmallows

Frosting
- ¼ cup butter
- ¼ cup milk
- 2 ounces cream cheese
- 1 ounce unsweetened chocolate
- 3 cups confectioners' sugar
- 1 teaspoon vanilla extract

Preparation:
1. In a small bowl, add and whisk all the ingredients for filling until smooth.
2. Melt butter with chocolate in a large saucepan over medium heat.
3. Mix well, then remove the melted chocolate from the heat.
4. Now stir in vanilla, eggs, baking powder, flour, sugar, and nuts then mix well.
5. Spread this chocolate batter in the sheet pan.
6. Drizzle nuts, marshmallows, and chocolate chips over the batter.
7. Transfer the pan to the 2nd rack position of Ninja Foodi XL Pro Air Oven and close the door.
8. Select the "Air Fry" Mode using FUNCTION +/- buttons and select Rack Level 2.
9. Set its cooking time to 28 minutes and temperature to 350 degrees F, then press "START/STOP" to initiate cooking.
10. Meanwhile, prepare the frosting by heating butter with cream cheese, chocolate and milk in a suitable saucepan over medium heat.
11. Mix well, then remove it from the heat.
12. Stir in vanilla and sugar, then mix well.

13. Pour this frosting over the brownie.
14. Allow the brownie to cool then slice into bars.
15. Serve.

Serving Suggestion: Serve the bars with whipped cream and chocolate syrup on top.

Variation Tip: Add crushed pecans or peanuts to the filling.

Nutritional Information Per Serving:
Calories 298 | Fat 14g |Sodium 272mg | Carbs 34g | Fiber 1g | Sugar 9.3g | Protein 13g

Cherry Jam tarts

Prep Time: 15 minutes.
Cook Time: 40 minutes.
Serves: 6

Ingredients:

- 2 sheets short crust pastry

For the frangipane

- 4 ounces butter softened
- 4 ounces golden caster sugar
- 1 egg
- 1 tablespoon plain flour
- 4 ounces ground almonds
- 3 ounces cherry jam

For the icing

- 1 cup icing sugar
- 12 glacé cherries

Preparation:

1. Grease the 12 cups of the muffin tray with butter.
2. Roll the puff pastry into a 10 cm sheet, then cut 12 rounds out of it.
3. Place these rounds into each muffin cup and press them into these cups.
4. Transfer the muffin tray to the refrigerator and leave it for 20 minutes.
5. Add dried beans or pulses into each tart crust to add weight.
6. Transfer the muffin tray to the 2nd rack position of Ninja Foodi XL Pro Air Oven and close the door.
7. Select the "Bake" Mode using FUNCTION +/- buttons and select Rack Level 2.
8. Set its cooking time to 10 minutes and temperature to 350 degrees F, then press "START/STOP" to initiate cooking.
9. Meanwhile, prepare the filling beat, beat butter with sugar and egg until fluffy.
10. Stir in flour and almonds ground, then mix well.
11. Divide this filling in the baked crusts and top them with a tablespoon of cherry jam.
12. Now again, place the muffin tray in the Ninja Foodi XL Pro Air Oven.
13. Continue cooking on the "Bake" mode for 20 minutes at 350 degrees F.
14. Whisk the icing sugar with 2 tablespoons of water and top the baked tarts with sugar mixture.
15. Serve.

Serving Suggestion: Serve the tarts with cherries on top.

Variation Tip: Add rum-soaked raisins to the tart filling.

Nutritional Information Per Serving:
Calories 193 | Fat 3g |Sodium 277mg | Carbs 21g | Fiber 1g | Sugar 9g | Protein 2g

Blueberry Hand Pies

Prep Time: 15 minutes.
Cook Time: 25 minutes.
Serves: 6

Ingredients:

- 1 cup blueberries
- 2 ½ tablespoons caster sugar
- 1 teaspoon lemon juice
- 1 pinch salt
- 14 ounces refrigerated pie crust
- water
- vanilla sugar to sprinkle on top

Preparation:

1. Toss the blueberries with salt, lemon juice, and sugar in a medium bowl.
2. Spread the pie crust into a round sheet and cut 6-4-inch circles out of it.
3. Add a tablespoon of blueberry filling at the center of each circle.
4. Moisten the edges of these circles and fold them in half, then pinch their edges together.

5. Press the edges using a fork to crimp its edges.
6. Place the hand pieces in the air fry basket and spray them with cooking oil.
7. Drizzle the vanilla sugar over the hand pies.
8. Transfer the sandwich to the 2nd rack position of Ninja Foodi XL Pro Air Oven and close the door.
9. Select the "Air Fry" Mode using FUNCTION +/- buttons and select Rack Level 2.
10. Set its cooking time to 25 minutes and temperature to 400 degrees F, then press "START/STOP" to initiate cooking.
11. Serve fresh.

Serving Suggestion: Serve the pies with cream frosting and blueberry sauce on top.
Variation Tip: Add vanilla extract to the blueberry filling.
Nutritional Information Per Serving:
Calories 253 | Fat 14g |Sodium 122mg | Carbs 36g | Fiber 1.2g | Sugar 12g | Protein 12g

Chocolate Bites

Prep Time: 15 minutes
Cook Time: 13 minutes
Serves: 8
Ingredients:
- 2 cups plain flour
- 2 tablespoons cocoa powder
- ½ cup icing sugar
- Pinch of ground cinnamon
- 1 teaspoon vanilla extract
- ¾ cup chilled butter
- ¼ cup chocolate, chopped into 8 chunks

Preparation:
1. In a bowl, mix the flour, icing sugar, cocoa powder, cinnamon and vanilla extract together.
2. With a pastry cutter, cut the butter and mix till a smooth dough forms.
3. Divide the dough into 8 equal-sized balls.
4. Press 1 chocolate chunk in the center of each ball and cover with the dough completely.
5. Place the balls into the baking pan.
6. Press "Power" button of Ninja Foodi XL Pro Air Oven and select the "Air Fry" function.
7. Press TEMP/SHADE +/- buttons to set the temperature at 355 degrees F.
8. Now press TIME/SLICES +/- buttons to set the cooking time to 8 minutes.
9. Press "START/STOP" button to start.
10. When the unit beeps to show that it is preheated, open the lid.
11. Arrange the pan in air fry basket and insert in the oven.
12. After 8 minutes of cooking, set the temperature at 320 degrees F for 5 minutes.
13. When cooking time is completed, open the lid and place the baking pan onto the wire rack to cool completely before serving.

Serving Suggestions: Serve with a sprinkling of coconut shreds.
Variation Tip: Add some mix-ins as you like.
Nutritional Information per Serving:
Calories: 328 | Fat: 19.3g|Sat Fat: 12.2g|Carbohydrates: 35.3g|Fiber: 1.4g|Sugar: 10.2g|Protein: 4.1g

Cherry Clafoutis

Prep Time: 15 minutes
Cook Time: 25 minutes
Serves: 4
Ingredients:
- 1½ cups fresh cherries, pitted
- 3 tablespoons vodka
- ¼ cup flour
- 2 tablespoons sugar
- Pinch of salt
- ½ cup sour cream
- 1 egg
- 1 tablespoon butter
- ¼ cup powdered sugar

Preparation:
1. In a bowl, mix the cherries and vodka together.
2. In another bowl, mix the flour, sugar, and salt together.
3. Add the sour cream, and egg and mix until a smooth dough forms.
4. Grease a cake pan.
5. Place flour mixture evenly into the prepared cake pan.
6. Spread cherry mixture over the dough.
7. Place butter on top in the form of dots.
8. Press "Power" button of Ninja Foodi XL Pro Air Oven and select "Air Fry" function.
9. Press TEMP/SHADE +/- buttons to set the temperature at 355 degrees F.
10. Now press TIME/SLICES +/- buttons to set the cooking time to 25 minutes.
11. Press "START/STOP" button to start.
12. When the unit beeps to show that it is preheated, open the lid.

13. Arrange the pan in air fry basket and insert in the oven.
14. When cooking time is completed, open the lid and place the pan onto a wire rack to cool for about 10-15 minutes before serving.
15. Now, invert the Clafoutis onto a platter and sprinkle with powdered sugar.
16. Cut the Clafoutis into desired sized slices and serve warm.

Serving Suggestions: Serve with a topping of whipped cream.

Variation Tip: Replace vodka with kirsch.

Nutritional Information per Serving:
Calories: 241 | Fat: 10.1g|Sat Fat: 5.9g|Carbohydrates: 29g|Fiber: 1.3g|Sugar: 20.6g|Protein: 3.9g

Vanilla Soufflé

Prep Time: 15 minutes
Cook Time: 23 minutes
Serves: 6

Ingredients:

- ¼ cup butter, softened
- ¼ cup all-purpose flour
- ½ cup plus 2 tablespoons sugar, divided
- 1 cup milk
- 3 teaspoons vanilla extract, divided
- 4 egg yolks
- 5 egg whites
- 1 teaspoon cream of tartar
- 2 tablespoons powdered sugar plus extra for dusting

Preparation:

1. In a bowl, add the butter, and flour and mix until a smooth paste forms.
2. In a medium pan, mix ½ cup of sugar and milk over medium-low heat and cook for about 3 minutes or until the sugar is dissolved, stirring continuously together.
3. Add the flour mixture, whisking continuously and simmer for about 3-4 minutes or until mixture becomes thick.
4. Remove from the heat and stir in 1 teaspoon of vanilla extract.
5. Set aside for about 10 minutes to cool.
6. In a bowl, add the egg yolks and 1 teaspoon of vanilla extract and mix well.
7. Add the egg yolk mixture into milk mixture and mix until well combined.
8. In another bowl, add the egg whites, cream of tartar, remaining sugar, and vanilla extract and with a wire whisk, beat until stiff peaks form.
9. Fold the egg whites mixture into milk mixture.
10. Grease 6 ramekins and sprinkle each with a pinch of sugar.
11. Place mixture into the prepared ramekins and with the back of a spoon, smooth the top surface.
12. Press "Power" button of Ninja Foodi XL Pro Air Oven and select "Air Fry" function.
13. Press TEMP/SHADE +/- buttons to set the temperature at 330 degrees F.
14. Now press TIME/SLICES +/- buttons to set the cooking time to 16 minutes.
15. Press "START/STOP" button to start.
16. When the unit beeps to show that it is preheated, open the lid.
17. Arrange the ramekins in air fry basket and insert in the oven.
18. When cooking time is completed, open the lid and place the ramekins onto a wire rack to cool slightly.
19. Sprinkle with the powdered sugar and serve warm.

Serving Suggestions: Room temperature eggs will get the best results. Serve with caramel sauce.

Variation Tip: Add some berries as you like.

Nutritional Information per Serving:
Calories: 250 | Fat: 11.6g|Sat Fat: 6.5g|Carbohydrates: 29.8g|Fiber: o.1g|Sugar: 25g|Protein: 6.8g

Nutella Banana Muffins

Prep Time: 15 minutes
Cook Time: 25 minutes
Serves: 12

Ingredients:

- 1 ⅔ cups plain flour
- 1 teaspoon baking soda
- 1 teaspoon baking powder
- 1 teaspoon ground cinnamon
- ¼ teaspoon salt
- 4 ripe bananas, peeled and mashed
- 2 eggs
- ½ cup brown sugar
- 1 teaspoon vanilla essence
- 3 tablespoons milk
- 1 tablespoon Nutella
- ¼ cup walnuts

Preparation:

1. Grease 12 muffin molds. Set aside.
2. In a large bowl, sift together the flour, baking soda, baking powder, cinnamon, and salt.
3. In another bowl, mix the remaining ingredients except walnuts together.

4. Add the banana mixture into flour mixture and mix until just combined.
5. Fold in the walnuts.
6. Place the mixture into the prepared muffin molds.
7. Press "Power" button of Ninja Foodi XL Pro Air Oven and select "Air Fry" function.
8. Press TEMP/SHADE +/- buttons to set the temperature at 250 degrees F.
9. Now press TIME/SLICES +/- buttons to set the cooking time to 25 minutes.
10. Press "START/STOP" button to start.
11. When the unit beeps to show that it is preheated, open the lid.
12. Arrange the muffin molds in air fry basket and insert in the oven.
13. When cooking time is completed, open the lid and place the muffin molds onto a wire rack to cool for about 10 minutes.
14. Carefully, invert the muffins onto the wire rack to completely cool before serving.

Serving Suggestions: Have all ingredients at room temperature before you start making the batter. Enjoy with a glass of milk.

Variation Tip: Add some nuts for a crispy choice.

Nutritional Information per Serving:
Calories: 227 | Fat: 6.6g|Sat Fat: 1.5g|Carbohydrates: 38.1g|Fiber: 2.4g|Sugar: 15.8g|Protein: 5.2g

Blueberry Muffins

Prep Time: 15 minutes
Cook Time: 20 minutes
Serves: 6

Ingredients:

- 1 egg, beaten
- 1 ripe banana, peeled and mashed
- 1¼ cups almond flour
- 2 tablespoons granulated sugar
- ½ teaspoon baking powder
- 1 tablespoon coconut oil, melted
- ⅛ cup maple syrup
- 1 teaspoon apple cider vinegar
- 1 teaspoon vanilla extract
- 1 teaspoon lemon zest, grated
- Pinch of ground cinnamon
- ½ cup fresh blueberries, ripened

Preparation:

1. In a large bowl, add all the ingredients except for blueberries and mix until well combined.
2. Gently fold in the blueberries.
3. Grease a 6 cups muffin pan.
4. Place the mixture into prepared muffin cups about ¾ full.
5. Press "Power" button of Ninja Foodi XL Pro Air Oven and select "Bake" function.
6. Press TEMP/SHADE +/- buttons to set the temperature at 375 degrees F.
7. Now press TIME/SLICES +/- buttons to set the cooking time to 12 minutes.
8. Press "START/STOP" button to start.
9. When the unit beeps to show that it is preheated, open the lid.
10. Arrange the muffin pan over the wire rack and insert in the oven.
11. When cooking time is completed, open the lid and place the muffin molds onto a wire rack to cool for about 10 minutes.
12. Carefully invert the muffins onto the wire rack to completely cool before serving.

Serving Suggestions: Serve with a hot cup of coffee.

Variation Tip: Replace the blueberries with raspberries as you like.

Nutritional Information per Serving:
Calories: 223 | Fat: 14.8g|Sat Fat: 3g|Carbohydrates: 20.1g|Fiber: 3.4g|Sugar: 12.5g|Protein: 6.2g

Walnut Brownies

Prep Time: 15 minutes
Cook Time: 22 minutes
Serves: 4

Ingredients:

- ½ cup chocolate, roughly chopped
- ⅓ cup butter
- 5 tablespoons sugar
- 1 egg, beaten
- 1 teaspoon vanilla extract
- Pinch of salt
- 5 tablespoons self-rising flour
- ¼ cup walnuts, chopped

Preparation:

1. In a microwave-safe bowl, add the chocolate and butter. Microwave on high heat for about 2 minutes, stirring after every 30 seconds.
2. Remove from microwave and set aside to cool.
3. In another bowl, add the sugar, egg, vanilla extract, and salt and whisk until creamy and light.
4. Add the chocolate mixture and whisk until well combined.
5. Add the flour, and walnuts and mix until well combined.
6. Line a sheet pan with a greased parchment paper.
7. Place mixture into the prepared pan and with the back of spatula, smooth the top surface.
8. Press "Power" button of Ninja Foodi XL Pro Air Oven and select "Air Fry" function.
9. Press TEMP/SHADE +/- buttons to set the temperature at 355 degrees F.
10. Now press TIME/SLICES +/- buttons to set the cooking time to 20 minutes.
11. Press "Start/Stop" button to start.
12. When the unit beeps to show that it is preheated, open the oven door.
13. Arrange the pan over wire rack and insert into rail of Level 3.
14. When cooking time is completed, open the oven door and place the sheet pan onto a wire rack to cool completely.
15. Cut into 4 equal-sized squares and serve.

Serving Suggestions: Serve with the dusting of powdered sugar.
Variation Tip: You can also use almond extract in the recipe.
Nutritional Information per Serving:
Calories: 407 | Fat: 27.4g|Sat Fat: 14.7g|Carbohydrates: 35.9g|Fiber: 1.5g|Sugar: 26.2g|Protein: 6g

Chocolate Soufflé

Prep Time: 15 minutes
Cook Time: 16 minutes
Serves: 2
Ingredients:

- 3 ounces semi-sweet chocolate, chopped
- ¼ cup butter
- 2 eggs, yolks and whites separated
- 3 tablespoons sugar
- ½ teaspoon pure vanilla extract
- 2 tablespoons all-purpose flour
- 1 teaspoon powdered sugar plus extra for dusting

Preparation:
1. In a microwave-safe bowl, place the butter and chocolate. Microwave on high heat for about 2 minutes or until melted completely, stirring after every 30 seconds.
2. Remove from the microwave and stir the mixture until smooth.
3. In another bowl, add the egg yolks and whisk well.
4. Add the sugar and vanilla extract and whisk well.
5. Add the chocolate mixture and mix until well combined.
6. Add the flour and mix well.
7. In a clean glass bowl, add the egg whites and whisk until soft peaks form.
8. Fold the whipped egg whites in 3 portions into the chocolate mixture.
9. Grease 2 ramekins and sprinkle each with a pinch of sugar.
10. Place mixture into the prepared ramekins and with the back of a spoon, smooth the top surface.
11. Insert wire rack on Level 3. Press "Power" button of Ninja Foodi XL Pro Air Oven and select "Air Fry" function.
12. Press TEMP/SHADE +/- buttons to set the temperature at 330 degrees F.
13. Now press TIME/SLICES +/- buttons to set the cooking time to 14 minutes.
14. Press "Start/Stop" button to start.
15. When the unit beeps to show that it is preheated, open the oven door.
16. Arrange the ramekins over wire rack on Level 3.
17. When cooking time is completed, open the oven door and place the ramekins onto a wire rack to cool slightly.
18. Sprinkle with the powdered sugar and serve warm.

Serving Suggestions: Serve with the garnishing of berries.
Variation Tip: Use high-quality chocolate.
Nutritional Information per Serving:
Calories: 591 | Fat: 87.3g|Sat Fat: 23g|Carbohydrates: 52.6g|Fiber: 0.2g|Sugar: 41.1g|Protein: 9.4g

Strawberry Cupcakes

Prep Time: 20 minutes
Cook Time: 8 minutes
Serves: 10

Ingredients:

For Cupcakes:

- ½ cup caster sugar
- 7 tablespoons butter
- 2 eggs
- ½ teaspoon vanilla essence
- ⅞ cup self-rising flour

For Frosting:

- 1 cup icing sugar
- 3½ tablespoons butter
- 1 tablespoon whipped cream
- ¼ cup fresh strawberries, pureed
- ½ teaspoon pink food color

Preparation:

1. In a bowl, add the butter and sugar and beat until fluffy and light.
2. Add the eggs, one at a time and beat until well combined.
3. Stir in the vanilla extract.
4. Gradually, add the flour, beating continuously until well combined.
5. Place the mixture into 10 silicone cups.
6. Press "Power" button of Ninja Foodi XL Pro Air Oven and select "Air Fry" function.
7. Press TEMP/SHADE +/- buttons to set the temperature at 340 degrees F.
8. Now press TIME/SLICES +/- buttons to set the cooking time to 8 minutes.
9. Press "Start/Stop" button to start.
10. When the unit beeps to show that it is preheated, open the oven door.
11. Arrange the silicone cups into the air fry basket and insert into rail of Level 3.
12. When cooking time is completed, open the oven door and place the silicon cups onto a wire rack to cool for about 10 minutes.
13. Carefully invert the muffins onto the wire rack to completely cool before frosting.
14. For frosting: in a bowl, add the icing sugar and butter and whisk until fluffy and light.
15. Add the whipped cream, strawberry puree, and color. Mix until well combined.
16. Fill the pastry bag with frosting and decorate the cupcakes.

Serving Suggestions: Serve with the garnishing of fresh strawberries.
Variation Tip: Use room temperature eggs.
Nutritional Information per Serving:
Calories: 250 | Fat: 13.6g|Sat Fat: 8.2g|Carbohydrates: 30.7g|Fiber: 0.4g|Sugar: 22.1g|Protein: 2.4g

Carrot Mug Cake

Prep Time: 10 minutes
Cook Time: 20 minutes
Serves: 1

Ingredients:

- ¼ cup whole-wheat pastry flour
- 1 tablespoon coconut sugar
- ¼ teaspoon baking powder
- ⅛ teaspoon ground cinnamon
- ⅛ teaspoon ground ginger
- Pinch of ground cloves
- Pinch of ground allspice
- Pinch of salt
- 2 tablespoons plus 2 teaspoons unsweetened almond milk
- 2 tablespoons carrot, peeled and grated
- 2 tablespoons walnuts, chopped
- 1 tablespoon raisins
- 2 teaspoons applesauce

Preparation:

1. In a bowl, mix together the flour, sugar, baking powder, spices and salt.
2. Add the remaining ingredients and mix until well combined
3. Place the mixture into a lightly greased ramekin.
4. Press "Power" button of Ninja Foodi XL Pro Air Oven and select the "Bake" function.

5. Press TEMP/SHADE +/- buttons to set the temperature at 350 degrees F.
6. Now press TIME/SLICES +/- buttons to set the cooking time to 20 minutes.
7. Press "Start/Stop" button to start.
8. When the unit beeps to show that it is preheated, open the oven door.
9. Arrange the ramekin over the wire rack and insert into rail of Level 3.
10. When cooking time is completed, open the oven door and place the ramekin onto a wire rack to cool slightly before serving.

Serving Suggestions: Serve with the topping of whipped cream.

Variation Tip: Applesauce can be replaced with honey.

Nutritional Information per Serving:
Calories: 301 | Fat: 10.1g|Sat Fat: 0.7g|Carbohydrates: 48.6g|Fiber: 3.2g|Sugar: 19.4g|Protein: 7.6g

Blueberry Cobbler

Prep Time: 15 minutes
Cook Time: 20 minutes
Serves: 6

Ingredients:

For Filling:

- 2½ cups fresh blueberries
- 1 teaspoon vanilla extract
- 1 teaspoon fresh lemon juice
- 1 cup sugar
- 1 teaspoon flour
- 1 tablespoon butter, melted

For Topping:

- 1¾ cups all-purpose flour
- 6 tablespoons sugar
- 4 teaspoons baking powder
- 1 cup milk
- 5 tablespoons butter

For Sprinkling:

- 2 teaspoons sugar
- ¼ teaspoon ground cinnamon

Preparation:

1. For filling: in a bowl, add all the filling ingredients and mix until well combined.
2. For topping: in another large bowl, mix together the flour, baking powder, and sugar.
3. Add the milk and butter and mix until a crumply mixture forms.
4. For sprinkling: in a small bowl, mix together the sugar and cinnamon.
5. In the bottom of a greased pan, place the blueberries mixture and top with the flour mixture evenly.
6. Sprinkle the cinnamon sugar on top evenly.
7. Press "Power" button of Ninja Foodi XL Pro Air Oven and select "Air Fry" function.
8. Press TEMP/SHADE +/- buttons to set the temperature at 320 degrees F.
9. Now press TIME/SLICES +/- buttons to set the cooking time to 20 minutes.
10. Press "Start/Stop" button to start.
11. When the unit beeps to show that it is preheated, open the oven door.
12. Arrange the pan in air fry basket and insert into the rail of Level 3.
13. When cooking time is complete, open the oven door and place the pan onto a wire rack to cool for about 10 minutes before serving.

Serving Suggestions: Serve with the topping of vanilla ice cream.

Variation Tip: If You want to use frozen blueberries, then thaw them completely.

Nutritional Information per Serving:
Calories: 459 | Fat: 12.6g|Sat Fat: 7.8g|Carbohydrates: 84g|Fiber: 2.7g|Sugar: 53.6g|Protein: 5.5g

Butter Cake

Prep Time: 15 minutes
Cook Time: 15 minutes
Serves: 6

Ingredients:

- 3 ounces butter, softened
- ½ cup caster sugar
- 1 egg
- 1 ⅓ cups plain flour, sifted
- Pinch of salt
- ½ cup milk
- 1 tablespoon icing sugar

Preparation:

1. In a bowl, add the butter and sugar and whisk until light and creamy.
2. Add the egg and whisk until smooth and fluffy.
3. Add the flour and salt and mix well alternately with the milk.
4. Grease a small Bundt cake pan.
5. Place mixture evenly into the prepared cake pan.
6. Press "Power" button of Ninja Foodi XL Pro Air Oven and select "Air Fry" function.
7. Press TEMP/SHADE +/- buttons to set the temperature at 350 degrees F.
8. Now press TIME/SLICES +/- buttons to set the cooking time to 15 minutes.
9. Press "Start/Stop" button to start.
10. When the unit beeps to show that it is preheated, open the oven door.
11. Arrange the pan over wire rack and insert into rail of Level 3.
12. When cooking time is completed, open the oven door and place the cake pan onto a wire rack to cool for about 10 minutes.
13. Carefully invert the cake onto the wire rack to completely cool before slicing.
14. Dust the cake with icing sugar and cut into desired-size slices.

Serving Suggestions: Serve with the sprinkling of cocoa powder.
Variation Tip: Use unsalted butter.
Nutritional Information per Serving:
Calories: 291 | Fat: 12.9g|Sat Fat: 7.8g|Carbohydrates: 40.3g|Fiber: 0.8g|Sugar: 19g|Protein: 4.6g

Raisin Bread Pudding

Prep Time: 15 minutes
Cook Time: 12 minutes
Serves: 3

Ingredients:
- 1 cup milk
- 1 egg
- 1 tablespoon brown sugar
- ½ teaspoon ground cinnamon
- ¼ teaspoon vanilla extract
- 2 tablespoons raisins, soaked in hot water for 15 minutes
- 2 bread slices, cut into small cubes
- 1 tablespoon chocolate chips
- 1 tablespoon sugar

Preparation:
1. In a bowl, mix together the milk, egg, brown sugar, cinnamon, and vanilla extract.
2. Stir in the raisins.
3. In a sheet pan, spread the bread cubes and top evenly with the milk mixture.
4. Refrigerate for about 15-20 minutes.
5. Insert the wire rack on Level 3. Press "Power" button of Ninja Foodi XL Pro Air Oven and select "Air Fry" function.
6. Press TEMP/SHADE +/- buttons to set the temperature at 375 degrees F.
7. Now press TIME/SLICES +/- buttons to set the cooking time to 12 minutes.
8. Press "Start/Stop" button to start.
9. When the unit beeps to show that it is preheated, open the oven door.
10. Arrange the pan over the wire rack on Level 3.
11. When cooking time is completed, open the oven door and place the sheet pan aside to cool slightly.
12. Serve warm.

Serving Suggestions: Serve with the drizzling of vanilla syrup.
Variation Tip: Use ode day-old bread.
Nutritional Information per Serving:
Calories: 143 | Fat: 4.4g|Sat Fat: 2.2g|Carbohydrates: 21.3g|Fiber: 6.7g|Sugar: 16.4g|Protein: 5.5g

Cookie Cake

Prep Time: 10 minutes
Cook Time: 10 minutes
Serves: 2

Ingredients:
- 1 stick butter, softened
- ½ cup brown sugar, packed
- ¼ cup sugar
- 1 egg
- 1 teaspoon vanilla extract
- 1½ cups all-purpose flour
- ½ teaspoon baking soda
- 1 cup semi-sweet chocolate chips

Preparation:
1. Mix the cream, butter, brown sugar, and sugar in a large mixing bowl.
2. Mix in the vanilla and eggs until everything is well mixed.
3. Slowly stir in the flour, baking soda, and salt until combined, then stir in the chocolate chips.

4. Spray a 6-inch pan with oil, pour half of the batter into the pan, and press it down to evenly fill it. Refrigerate the other half for later use.
5. Place it on sheet pan on Level 3 inside the oven.
6. Turn on Ninja Foodi XL Pro Air Oven and select "Air Fry".
7. Select the timer for 5 minutes and the temperature for 370 degrees F.
8. Remove it from the oven and set it aside for 5 minutes to cool.

Serving Suggestions: Serve some vanilla ice cream.
Variation Tip: You can also use almond butter.
Nutritional Information per Serving:
Calories: 673 | Fat: 38g|Sat Fat: 23g|Carbohydrates: 82g|Fiber: 4g|Sugar: 2g|Protein: 8g

Fried Oreo

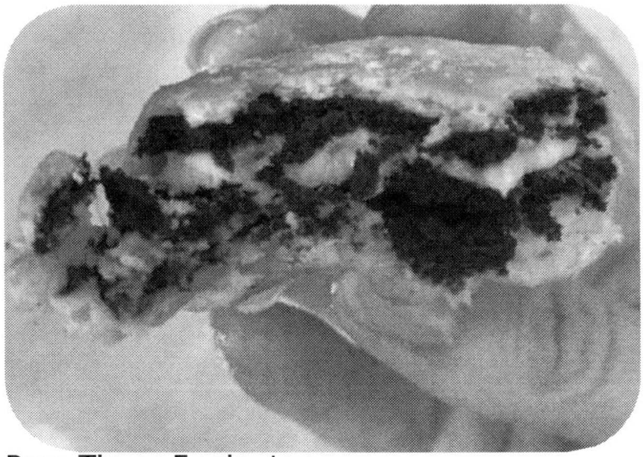

Prep Time: 5 minutes
Cook Time: 5 minutes
Serves: 8
Ingredients:

- 8 Oreo cookies
- 1 package of Pillsbury crescents rolls

Preparation:
1. On a cutting board or counter, spread out the crescent dough.
2. Press down into each perforated line with your finger to make one large sheet.
3. Cut the dough into eighths.
4. In the center of each crescent roll square, place one Oreo cookie and roll each corner up.
5. Bunch up the remaining crescent roll to completely cover the Oreo cookie.
6. Place the Oreos in an even row in the sheet pan.
7. Insert a wire rack on Level 3. Turn on Ninja Foodi XL Pro Air Oven and select "Bake".
8. Select the timer for 5 minutes and the temperature for 320 degrees F.
9. When the unit beeps to signify it has preheated, open the oven and place the sheet pan on the wire rack.
10. Close the oven and let it cook.
11. Allow cooling for two minutes before serving.

Serving Suggestions: Serve with chocolate sauce.
Variation Tip: Dust some powdered sugar on top.
Nutritional Information per Serving:
Calories: 172 | Fat: 4g|Sat Fat: 1g|Carbohydrates: 32g|Fiber: 1g|Sugar: 21g|Protein: 2g

Cinnamon Rolls

Prep Time: 5 minutes
Cook Time: 30 minutes
Serves: 6
Ingredients:

- 2 tablespoons butter, melted
- ⅓ cup packed brown sugar
- ½ teaspoon ground cinnamon
- Salt, to taste
- All-purpose flour for surface
- 1 tube refrigerated crescent rolls
- 56g cream cheese, softened
- ½ cup powdered sugar
- 1 tablespoon whole milk

Preparation:
1. Combine butter, brown sugar, cinnamon, and a large pinch of salt in a medium mixing bowl until smooth and fluffy.
2. Roll out crescent rolls in one piece on a lightly floured surface. Fold in half by pinching the seams together. Make a medium rectangle out of the dough.
3. Cover the dough with butter mixture, leaving a ¼-inch border. Roll the dough, starting at one edge and cutting crosswise into 6 pieces.
4. Line bottom of basket with parchment paper and brush with butter.
5. Place the pieces cut-side up in the prepared air fry basket, equally spaced.
6. Turn on Ninja Foodi XL Pro Air Oven and select "Broil".
7. Select the timer for 15 minutes and the temperature for LO.
8. When the unit beeps to signify it has preheated, open the oven and place the air fry basket on Level 3 in oven.
9. Close the oven and let it cook.
10. Allow cooling for two minutes before serving.

Serving Suggestions: Top with almond butter.
Variation Tip: You can also use almond milk.
Nutritional Information per Serving:
Calories: 183 | Fat: 8g|Sat Fat: 4g|Carbohydrates: 26g|Fiber: 0.4g|Sugar: 16g|Protein: 2.2g

Chocolate Chip Cookies

Prep Time: 10 minutes
Cook Time: 45 minutes
Serves: 4

Ingredients:

- ½ cup butter, melted
- ¼ cup packed brown sugar
- ¼ cup granulated sugar
- 1 large egg
- 1 teaspoon pure vanilla extract
- 1½ cups all-purpose flour
- ½ teaspoon baking soda
- ½ teaspoon kosher salt
- ½ teaspoon chocolate chips

Preparation:

1. Insert a wire rack on Level 3. Turn on Ninja Foodi XL Pro Air Oven and select "Air Fry".
2. Select the timer for 8 minutes and the temperature for 350 degrees F.
3. Meanwhile, whisk together melted butter and sugars in a medium mixing bowl. Whisk in the egg and vanilla extract until fully combined.
4. Combine the flour, baking soda, and salt.
5. Scoop dough onto the sheet pan with a large cookie scoop (approximately 3 tablespoons), leaving 2 inches between each cookie, and press to flatten slightly.
6. When the unit beeps to signify it has preheated, open the oven and place the sheet pan onto the wire rack.
7. Close the oven and let it cook.
8. Allow cooling for two minutes before serving.

Serving Suggestions: Top some more chocolate chips.

Variation Tip: You can also add chopped walnuts.

Nutritional Information per Serving:
Calories: 319 | Fat: 16.6g|Sat Fat: 10.1g|Carbohydrates: 38.4g|Fiber: 0.9g|Sugar: 14.6g|Protein: 4.5g

Banana Pancakes Dippers

Prep Time: 10 minutes
Cook Time: 15 minutes
Serves: 2

Ingredients:

- 1½ cups all-purpose flour
- 3 bananas, halved and sliced lengthwise
- 1 tablespoon baking powder
- 1 tablespoon packed brown sugar
- 1 teaspoon salt
- ¾ cup whole milk
- ½ cup sour cream
- 2 large eggs
- 1 teaspoon vanilla extract

Preparation:

1. Combine flour, baking powder, brown sugar, and salt in bowl.
2. Mix the milk and sour cream in a separate bowl, then add the eggs one at a time. Pour in the vanilla extract.
3. Combine the wet and dry ingredients until just mixed.
4. Grease the sheet pan with cooking spray and line it with parchment paper.
5. Place bananas in a single layer on parchment paper after dipping them in pancake batter.
6. Insert a wire rack on Level 3. Turn on Ninja Foodi XL Pro Air Oven and select "Air Roast".
7. Select the timer for 16 minutes and the temperature to 375 degrees F.
8. When the unit beeps to signify it has preheated, open the oven and place the sheet pan on the wire rack.
9. Allow cooling for two minutes before serving.

Serving Suggestions: Serve with melted chocolate for dipping.

Variation Tip: You can also use almond milk.

Nutritional Information per Serving:
Calories: 670 | Fat: 18.6g|Sat Fat: 10g|Carbohydrates: 66g|Fiber: 5g|Sugar: 23g|Protein: 22g

Roasted Bananas

Prep Time: 5 minutes
Cook Time: 7 minutes
Serves: 1

Ingredients:

- 1 banana, sliced
- Avocado oil cooking spray

Preparation:

1. Using parchment paper, line the air fry basket.
2. Place banana slices in the air fry basket, making sure they do not touch.
3. Mist banana slices with avocado oil.
4. Turn on Ninja Foodi XL Pro Air Oven and select "Air Roast".
5. Select the timer for 5 minutes and the temperature for 370 degrees F.
6. Remove the banana slices from the basket and carefully flip them.
7. When the unit beeps to signify it has preheated, open the oven and place the air fry basket on Level 3.
8. Close the oven and cook for another 3 minutes, or until the banana slices are browning and caramelized. Remove from the basket with care.
9. Allow cooling for two minutes before serving.

Serving Suggestions: Sprinkle vanilla sugar on top.

Variation Tip: You can also use brown sugar.

Nutritional Information per Serving:
Calories: 107 | Fat: 0.7g|Sat Fat: 0.1g|Carbohydrates: 27g|Fiber: 3.1g|Sugar: 14g|Protein: 1.3g

Broiled Bananas with Cream

Prep Time: 5 minutes
Cook Time: 10 minutes
Serves: 3

Ingredients:

- 3 large bananas, ripe
- 2 tablespoons dark brown sugar
- ⅔ cup heavy cream
- 1 pinch flaky salt

Preparation:

1. On a bias, slice the bananas thickly.
2. Arrange in a roast tray, gently overlapping.
3. Sprinkle the brown sugar evenly on top, followed by the cream and then the salt.
4. Insert a sheet pan on Level 3. Turn on Ninja Foodi XL Pro Air Oven and select "Broil".
5. Select the unit for 7 minutes at HI.
6. When the unit beeps to signify it has preheated, open the oven and place the roast tray on the sheet pan on Level 3.
7. Close the oven and let it cook until the cream has thickened, browned, and become spotty.
8. Allow cooling for two minutes before serving.

Serving Suggestions: Sprinkle vanilla sugar on top.

Variation Tip: You can also use brown sugar.

Nutritional Information per Serving:
Calories: 236 | Fat: 10|Sat Fat: 6g|Carbohydrates: 30g|Fiber: 3g|Sugar: 22g|Protein: 2g

Chocolate Oatmeal Cookies

Prep Time: 15 minutes
Cook Time: 10 minutes
Serves: 36

Ingredients:

- 3 cups quick-cooking oatmeal
- 1½ cups all-purpose flour
- ½ cup cream
- ¼ cup cocoa powder
- ¾ cup white sugar
- 1 package instant chocolate pudding mix
- 1 teaspoon baking soda
- 1 teaspoon salt
- 1 cup butter, softened
- ¾ cup brown sugar
- 2 eggs
- 1 teaspoon vanilla extract
- 2 cups chocolate chips
- Cooking spray

Preparation:

1. Using parchment paper, line the air fry basket.
2. Using nonstick cooking spray, coat the air fry basket.
3. Combine the oats, flour, cocoa powder, pudding mix, baking soda, and salt in a mixing dish. Set aside.
4. Mix cream, butter, brown sugar, and white sugar in a separate bowl using an electric mixer.
5. Combine the eggs and vanilla essence in a mixing bowl. Mix in the oatmeal mixture thoroughly. Mix the chocolate chips and walnuts in a bowl.
6. Using a large cookie scoop, drop dough into the air fry basket; level out and leave about 1 inch between each cookie.
7. Turn on Ninja Foodi XL Pro Air Oven and select "Air Fry".
8. Select the timer for 10 minutes and the temperature for 350 degrees F.
9. When the unit beeps to signify it has preheated, open the oven and place the air fry basket on Level 3.
10. Close the oven and let it cook.
11. Before serving, cool on a wire rack.

Serving Suggestions: Sprinkle vanilla sugar on top.

Variation Tip: You can also add chopped walnuts.

Nutritional Information per Serving:
Calories: 199 | Fat: 10.7g|Sat Fat: 5g|Carbohydrates: 24g|Fiber: 1.9g|Sugar: 14g|Protein: 2g

4-Week Meal Plan

Week 1

Day 1:
Breakfast: Mushrooms Frittata
Lunch: Seafood Casserole
Snack: Carrot Chips
Dinner: Baked Tilapia with Buttery Crumb Topping
Dessert: Air Fried Churros

Day 2:
Breakfast: Pumpkin Muffins
Lunch: Vegan Cakes
Snack: Pasta Chips
Dinner: Za'atar Chops
Dessert: Air Fried Doughnuts

Day 3:
Breakfast: Ham and Cheese Scones
Lunch: Blue Cheese Soufflés
Snack: Potato Chips
Dinner: Pork Chops with Cashew Sauce
Dessert: Cannoli

Day 4:
Breakfast: Raisin Bran Muffins
Lunch: Fried Tortellini
Snack: Avocado Fries
Dinner: Minced Lamb Casserole
Dessert: Chocolate Chip Cookie

Day 5:
Breakfast: Blueberry-Lemon Scones
Lunch: Sheet Pan Fajitas
Snack: Onion Rings
Dinner: Greek lamb Farfalle
Dessert: Cranberry-Apple Pie

Day 6:
Breakfast: Banana Bread
Lunch: Roast Cauliflower and Broccoli
Snack: Mini Hot Dogs
Dinner: Lamb Rack with Lemon Crust
Dessert: Caramel Apple Pie

Day 7:
Breakfast: Breakfast Bake
Lunch: Broccoli Casserole
Snack: Baked Potatoes
Dinner: Mint Lamb with Toasted Hazelnuts
Dessert: Brownie Bars

Week 2

Day 1:
Breakfast: Sweet & Spiced Toasts
Lunch: Stuffed Zucchini
Snack: Roasted Peanuts
Dinner: Herbed Cornish Game Hen
Dessert: Chocolate Bites

Day 2:
Breakfast: Parmesan Eggs in Avocado Cups
Lunch: Salmon Burgers
Snack: Glazed Chicken Wings
Dinner: Simple Beef Tenderloin
Dessert: Apple Pastries

Day 3:
Breakfast: Potato & Corned Beef Casserole
Lunch: Veggie Rice
Snack: Cod Nuggets
Dinner: Lemony Chicken Thighs
Dessert: Cherry Clafoutis

Day 4:
Breakfast: Cloud Eggs
Lunch: Tofu in Sweet & Sour Sauce
Snack: Cauliflower Poppers
Dinner: Nuts Crusted Salmon
Dessert: Fudge Brownies

Day 5:
Breakfast: Savory Parsley Soufflé
Lunch: Lamb Burgers
Snack: Spicy Spinach Chips
Dinner: Pork Stuffed Bell Peppers
Dessert: Honeyed Banana

Day 6:
Breakfast: Date Bread
Lunch: Scallops with Capers Sauce
Snack: Beef Taquitos
Dinner: Herbs Crumbed Rack of Lamb
Dessert: Vanilla Soufflé

Day 7:
Breakfast: Sweet & Spiced Toasts
Lunch: Tofu with Broccoli
Snack: Potato Croquettes
Dinner: Gingered Chicken Drumsticks
Dessert: Shortbread Fingers

Week 3

Day 1:
Breakfast: Banana & Walnut Bread
Lunch: Quinoa Burgers
Snack: Roasted Cashews
Dinner: Spicy Salmon
Dessert: Walnut Brownies

Day 2:
Breakfast: Savory French Toast
Lunch: Crab Cakes
Snack: Spicy Carrot Fries
Dinner: Buttermilk Whole Chicken
Dessert: Nutella Banana Pastries

Day 3:
Breakfast: Sweet Potato Rosti
Lunch: Stuffed Eggplants
Snack: Crispy Avocado Fries
Dinner: Spiced Pork Shoulder
Dessert: Chocolate ScufflÉ

Day 4:
Breakfast: Cheddar & Cream Omelet
Lunch: Tofu with Broccoli
Snack: Beet Chips
Dinner: Parmesan Crusted Chicken Breasts
Dessert: Brownie Muffins

Day 5:
Breakfast: Carrot & Raisin Bread
Lunch: Herbed Bell Peppers
Snack: Cheesy Broccoli Bites
Dinner: Herbed Leg of Lamb
Dessert: Strawberry Cupcakes

Day 6:
Breakfast: Zucchini Fritters
Lunch: Herbed Shrimp
Snack: Risotto Bites
Dinner: Buttered Turkey Breast
Dessert: Carrot Mug Cake

Day 7:
Breakfast: Ricotta Toasts with Salmon
Lunch: Feta Turkey Burgers
Snack: Buttermilk Biscuits
Dinner: Balsamic Beef Top Roast
Dessert: Blueberry Cobbler

Week 4

Day 1:
Breakfast: Savory Sausage & Beans Muffins
Lunch: Scallops with Capers Sauce
Snack: Zucchini Fries
Dinner: Simple Turkey Breast
Dessert: Nutella Banana Muffins

Day 2:
Breakfast: Puffed Egg Tarts
Lunch: Maple Bacon Salmon
Snack: Baked Potatoes
Dinner: Sauce Glazed Meatloaf
Dessert: Peanut Brittle Bars

Day 3:
Breakfast: Mushroom Frittata
Lunch: Salmon Burgers
Snack: Spicy Spinach Chips
Dinner: Steak with Bell Peppers
Dessert: Blueberry Muffins

Day 4:
Breakfast: Simple Bread
Lunch: Scallops with Spinach
Snack: Tortilla Chips
Dinner: Oat Crusted Chicken Breasts
Dessert: Honeyed Banana

Day 5:
Breakfast: Pancetta & Spinach Frittata
Lunch: Pita Bread Pizza
Snack: Crispy Prawns
Dinner: Lamb Chops with Carrots
Dessert: Butter Cake

Day 6:
Breakfast: Eggs, Tofu & Mushroom Omelet
Lunch: Quinoa Burgers
Snack: Chicken & Parmesan Nuggets
Dinner: Lemony Chicken Thighs
Dessert: Raisin Bread Pudding

Day 7:
Breakfast: Bacon, Spinach & Egg Cups
Lunch: Beans & Veggie Burgers
Snack: Beef Taquitos
Dinner: Chinese Chicken Drumsticks
Dessert: Cherry Clafoutis

Conclusion

The Ninja Foodi XL Pro Air Oven will help you cook everything you want to serve on the dining table. Whether serving a large family gathering or cooking food for your small family, this kitchen appliance is perfect for you. To buy different cooking appliances when you can replace them with a single appliance that is simple to use and has different useful functions. If you already have this appliance, this cookbook can be your perfect cooking partner. You can prepare all types of foods using this appliance. Thank you for your appreciation. All the best!

Appendix 1 Measurement Conversion Chart

VOLUME EQUIVALENTS(DRY)

US STANDARD	METRIC (APPROXIMATE)
1/8 teaspoon	0.5 mL
1/4 teaspoon	1 mL
1/2 teaspoon	2 mL
3/4 teaspoon	4 mL
1 teaspoon	5 mL
1 tablespoon	15 mL
1/4 cup	59 mL
1/2 cup	118 mL
3/4 cup	177 mL
1 cup	235 mL
2 cups	475 mL
3 cups	700 mL
4 cups	1 L

WEIGHT EQUIVALENTS

US STANDARD	METRIC (APPROXIMATE)
1 ounce	28 g
2 ounces	57 g
5 ounces	142 g
10 ounces	284 g
15 ounces	425 g
16 ounces (1 pound)	455 g
1.5 pounds	680 g
2 pounds	907 g

VOLUME EQUIVALENTS(LIQUID)

US STANDARD	US STANDARD (OUNCES)	METRIC (APPROXIMATE)
2 tablespoons	1 fl.oz.	30 mL
1/4 cup	2 fl.oz.	60 mL
1/2 cup	4 fl.oz.	120 mL
1 cup	8 fl.oz.	240 mL
1 1/2 cup	12 fl.oz.	355 mL
2 cups or 1 pint	16 fl.oz.	475 mL
4 cups or 1 quart	32 fl.oz.	1 L
1 gallon	128 fl.oz.	4 L

TEMPERATURES EQUIVALENTS

FAHRENHEIT(F)	CELSIUS(C) (APPROXIMATE)
225 °F	107 °C
250 °F	120 °C
275 °F	135 °C
300 °F	150 °C
325 °F	160 °C
350 °F	180 °C
375 °F	190 °C
400 °F	205 °C
425 °F	220 °C
450 °F	235 °C
475 °F	245 °C
500 °F	260 °C

Appendix 2 Recipes Index

D

E

F

G

H

L

M

N

O

P

Q

R

S

T

V

W

Z

Printed in Great Britain
by Amazon

13440067R00100